LAUNCH

How to Get Your Kids Through
COLLEGE DEBT-FREE
and Into Jobs They Love Afterward

JEANNIE BURLOWSKI

Falcon Heights Publishing

Minneapolis

Published by Falcon Heights Publishing in Minneapolis, Minnesota
FalconHeightsPublishing.com
For permissions, email permissions@falconheightspublishing.com.

In order to protect client privacy, some identifying details have been changed. Although the author and publisher have made every effort to ensure that the information in this book was correct at press time, the author and publisher do not assume and hereby disclaim any liability to any party for any loss, damage, or disruption caused by errors or omissions, whether such errors or omissions result from negligence, accident, or any other cause. This publication is designed to provide accurate and authoritative information with regard to the subject matter covered. It is not necessarily a complete summary of all materials on the subject. It is distributed with the understanding that the author and publisher are not engaged in rendering legal, accounting, financial planning, or other professional service. Access the services of a qualified legal, accounting, or financial planning professional to determine how the principles in this book apply to your individual financial situation.

Printed in the United States of America

First printing, 2017

Scripture taken from the Holy Bible, New International Version®, NIV®. Copyright ©1973, 1978, 1984, 2011 by Biblica, Inc.™ Used by permission of Zondervan. All rights reserved worldwide (www.zondervan.com). The "NIV" and "New International Version" are trademarks registered in the United States Patent and Trademark Office by Biblica, Inc.™

Edited by: Stacy Ennis and Kim Foster
Cover by: Angie Alaya
Designed by: Raphael Gideoni Albinati Batista

Author website: JeannieBurlowski.com

"The Spirit of the Sovereign Lord is on me, because the Lord has anointed me to proclaim good news to the poor. He has sent me to bind up the brokenhearted, to proclaim freedom for the captives and release from darkness for the prisoners."

Isaiah 61:1 NIV

Table of Contents

MY PLEA TO THE COLLEGE CONSULTING INDUSTRY

Please, let's stop selling college consulting services by telling parents, "We'll help your kid get into his or her dream school." Focusing on "dream schools" has shackled too many students and families to suffocating, devastating levels of student loan debt, while too often *not preparing kids for jobs in the real world.*

Together, let's change the focus of college consulting to, "We'll help you get your kids through college debt-free and into careers they love afterward." This book will help you do exactly that for the clients you serve.

Parents will deeply appreciate your individualized guidance, support, and mentoring as they walk through the steps in this book (especially when they get to chapter 13, where I tell them in no uncertain terms to go and find you).

Enough talk about dream schools. Together, let's focus on getting the kids we care about *dream lives.*

Section 1
Getting Started

I | *Invitation Into an Adventure*

Rachel was happy, but her parents were ecstatic. Rachel held the phone away from her ear as she and her college roommate, Abby, laughed out loud at the thin, tinny sound of her mom and dad hooting and shrieking from their home in Chicago.

Rachel shifted her weight on the dorm room bed and put the phone up to her ear again. "Yes, Mom, I'm sure. I went in for the meeting today. It's zero. Zero, zilch, nothing, nada." Rachel listened to her mom's response, smiling at her roommate and laughing even more at her parents. "Yes, Mom. It's a happy day. It sure is. I love you guys too. I'll see you when you get here tomorrow. OK—g'bye!"

Rachel set the phone down on her nightstand and turned to Abby, who was busy packing textbooks away into a deep cardboard box. "So, they were happy then?" Abby asked, flashing a smile. Rachel laughed again. This was a day her family had been

working toward off and on for years, and they were *all* happy.

They were happy because Rachel was about to graduate from an excellent private college in less than four years. She had an exciting job waiting for her, and at a meeting in the financial aid office that morning, she'd gotten the official notification: she would be graduating from college absolutely debt-free.

Rachel was graduating from a college her parents could *never* have afforded to pay cash for. She wasn't a straight-A student who'd had a massive amount of scholarship money just handed to her, yet she would be getting her degree without owing one penny of student loan money.

It truly was a day for hooting and shrieking with joy.

THE ADVENTURE BEGINS

Rachel was 12 when she and her parents set

a huge "stretch" goal for themselves. The three of them had decided as a team to do every clever thing they could think of to help Rachel graduate from college in four years or less, completely debt-free, ready to walk directly into work she'd excel at and love.

For Rachel and her parents, the whole idea had gotten its start at a family reunion the summer after Rachel had finished 7th grade. Rachel's older cousin, Gretchen—the redheaded three-sport athlete who'd been salutatorian of her high school class—had just graduated from an elite East Coast private university, and Gretchen's parents had arrived at the reunion looking tense and strained. In a quiet moment by the volleyball court, Rachel's dad had found out why.

Gretchen and her new husband, Nevil, the art history major, had just moved from their college apartment into Gretchen's parents' unfinished basement. Tiny high windows, cinderblocks, and all.

The reason?

In the five years it had taken Gretchen to graduate from college, she had run up $73,000 in student loan and credit card debt. And Nevil had racked up even more: a whopping $87,000. To make matters worse, when Gretchen finally put a résumé together and started looking for jobs after her college graduation, she found it a struggle to find employers who were excited about her comparative literature degree. Instead, interviewers kept asking her about her work experience.

"We understand you don't have a lot of permanent paid work in this field yet," the

human resources people said to her in job interviews. "Just tell us about all your interning and volunteering! We would love to hear about that."

Gretchen wailed to her parents about this afterward. "I didn't have time to do any interning or volunteering in college!" she cried. "All my time was taken up with schoolwork! The classes were hard!"

Things had gotten so bad that at one point, Gretchen's younger brother sarcastically suggested that they put Gretchen at a freeway exit with a cardboard sign reading: WILL COMPARE LITERATURE FOR FOOD. At that Gretchen burst into tears, ran down her parents' basement stairs, and threw herself, sobbing, onto the rollaway bed that she and Nevil had pushed up against a cinderblock wall.

> **GRETCHEN WAILED TO HER PARENTS ABOUT THIS AFTERWARD. "I DIDN'T HAVE TIME TO DO ANY INTERNING OR VOLUNTEERING IN COLLEGE!" SHE CRIED. "ALL MY TIME WAS TAKEN UP WITH SCHOOLWORK! THE CLASSES WERE HARD!"**

COLD FEAR

Standing at the side of the volleyball court on that family reunion day, Gretchen's dad confided the rest of the story to Rachel's dad. Gretchen had finally found a job she liked well enough, but it didn't pay much and it didn't even require a college degree. And Nevil? After emailing his résumé to a few local museums and hearing nothing back, Nevil had taken a part-time job as a cashier at a coffee shop. He was spending his off-hours, while Gretchen was at work, looking on the Internet for some other guys to form a band with.

When it finally hit Gretchen and Nevil just how much their monthly student loan payments would need to be if they were going to pay off $160,000 in student loans in the standard 10 years, Nevil made some passing, half-joking remarks about the two of them not even *trying* to make the payments.

"What can they do to us?" he said one night at Gretchen's parents' dinner table. "Throw us into some kind of debtor's prison? I don't think so. I don't think those things even exist anymore." Gretchen looked stricken at his words, but Nevil ignored her, plunging ahead, oblivious. "Lots of people default on student loans," he said. "Seriously. Guys. It's not that big a deal."

Hearing *that* put Gretchen's parents into a panic.

That night Gretchen's mother stayed up late at her computer, researching options for students with overwhelming and unmanageable student loan debt. Finally, reluctantly, Gretchen's parents convinced their daughter and her new husband to each apply for an Income-Based Repayment (IBR) Plan. It was a plan that would ease their monthly financial stress a little bit, but it would still cost them a hefty chunk of their income every month... for 25 years.

Hearing this at the side of the volleyball court that day, Rachel's dad's jaw dropped in shock.

"Yup," Gretchen's dad said, hands in his pockets, struggling to keep his voice steady. "And of course, anytime you stretch loan payments out over a long time like that, additional interest just keeps piling up and piling up. That $160,000 they owe between the two of them? It's gonna balloon over the next 25 years. Unless there are some big job changes and these two can somehow start paying a whole lot more money on their loan principal every month, they'll be out from under this sometime after Gretchen is 48 years old."

At this point, Rachel's dad started to panic.

Swallowing hard, Gretchen's dad continued. "Nevil talks vaguely about maybe applying to law school, but law school could add another $150,000 to their debt load. And besides, jobs for lawyers these days aren't guaranteed either."

Rachel's dad nodded.

"I'd like to believe there's gonna be some kind of miracle and this'll all be taken care of somehow," Gretchen's dad said. "But the truth is that a lot of setbacks can hit a married couple in the course of 25 years. All it would take is one season of high medical bills or skipped payments—one student loan default—and Gretchen and Nevil could be slammed with penalties that could double that debt."

A lot of pressure on a newly married couple just starting out, Rachel's dad thought. *A lot of pressure.*

"You know what really bites, Steve?" Gretchen's dad said. "Nevil probably could've qualified for a student loan forgiveness program where you start out on this terrible 25-year repayment plan, but you work 30 hours a week or more in some kind of public service like police, fire, EMT, military, any level of government employment, teaching in a public school, being a public librarian, working for a tax-exempt charity, or even being a congressional staffer, which can actually set you up for a lucrative law firm partnership someday. You just work at this kind of a public service job, make modest student loan payments on time for 10 years, and then after 10 years all the rest of your student loans are forgiven. Poof! Gone. No matter how high your debt load was, you get your life back. Fifteen whole years early!"

"So why doesn't Nevil qualify for that?" Rachel's dad asked.

Gretchen's dad sighed. "People can only qualify for public service loan forgiveness if they had the presence of mind as college students to take out only certain special kinds of loans called 'Federal Direct Loans.' Nevil was one of the hundreds of thousands of college students who didn't realize that the *one and only way* you can get these special loans is to fill out the FAFSA form every year."

Gretchen's dad wiped at the corner of his eye with one bent white knuckle, trying hard not to say anything negative about his new son-in-law. Finally, he spoke carefully and evenly. "Nevil never bothered to fill out any FAFSA forms, though. Even though it's the 'Free Application for Federal Student Aid' and wouldn't have cost him a dime, he never filled the FAFSA out, not even once."

Rachel's dad's eyes widened. He'd heard

of the FAFSA form. "Seriously?" he asked, incredulous. "In four years of college, Nevil never once filled out the FAFSA form?"

"Six years of college," Gretchen's dad corrected. "But yes, you're right. Without using any of those online calculators or anything, Nevil jumped to the conclusion that his normal, upper-middle-class parents probably made too much money for him to be able to get any financial aid help. So he decided that the FAFSA form would probably be a waste of time for him. He had no idea that families can make $200,000 a year or more and still get financial help paying for college. I can't tell you how many thousands of dollars this one bad decision cost him."

The two watched an especially long and energetic volley, and then Gretchen's dad spoke again.

"In Nevil's defense," he'd said, "I'm sure he had no idea about any of that. Honestly, most parents don't even know. High school guidance counselors mean well, but they don't have time to tell people this kind of stuff. Nobody told Nevil where to find the best loans. Nobody warned him to use his student loan money strictly for tuition, and not to buy cars or beer or go on sunny spring break beach vacations with it. His parents didn't help him figure this stuff out at all. His parents had this interesting philosophy. They told him that when he turned 18 he was legally an adult, so he should figure this all out by himself and live with the consequences. Unfortunately—"

At this, Gretchen's dad blew a long breath up into his hairline. When he spoke, his voice was tense.

"Unfortunately, it looks like it'll be my daughter who'll be living with the consequences."

DESPERATE REGRET

Rachel's dad stood beside Gretchen's dad quietly for several long minutes, the way a person stands beside someone they care about who's grieving at a funeral.

"Of course," Gretchen's dad said, "I can talk about Nevil all day long. But the fact is, it was *me* who stood by and allowed my daughter to run up $73,000 in student loan and credit card debt. The thought of how Gretchen's college was getting paid for was so sickening to me, I think I just tried not to think about it while it was happening. 'Everybody gets student loans!' I told myself. And of course, privacy laws make it so easy for parents to put on blinders like that. 'Well, she's 18! I can't legally look at any of her school grades or financial records!' That's what I kept telling myself. That whole privacy law thing made it so easy for me to completely ignore what was really going on."

Uncle Paul shook his head. "Here's what I should have done. Every single time she came to me for money, I should have said, 'Sure, Honey. Bring me your computer and log me in, and let's look at all your grades, your credit card statements, your bank statements, and your whole student loan situation, and let's strategize about whether we're on a good track. I like to do that kind of due diligence before I invest money in anything.'"

Gretchen's dad rolled his eyes.

"Instead she'd ask me for money and I'd feel all loving and tender, and I'd say something like, 'OK, Sweetie, but you be sure to spend it wisely!' and then I'd write her a check."

What happened next was something Rachel's dad would later tell Rachel and her mother about over and over.

Gretchen's dad wiped sweat from above his red eyebrows, staring at the volleyball players in a weary, shell-shocked daze. He shook his head in what was still stunned disbelief. "You know, Marjorie and I didn't think much about how we were going to pay for college until Gretchen was about halfway through 11th grade. Part of me, I guess, thought that free government financial aid was going to cover it—and then Gretchen's middle school and high school years were so insanely busy for us." He sighed wearily. "Driving her to all those activities. Debate. Soccer. Yearbook. Key Club. Games. Practices. We had her in a hundred different extracurricular activities so she'd 'look good on her college applications.' Honestly, it was exhausting for all of us. I think Marjorie and I had always planned to sit down and talk about how we were going to get Gretchen's college paid for, but we never really got around to it until Gretchen was almost done with the first semester of her junior year. By that time, we'd waited so long we'd pretty much screwed ourselves out of getting any financial aid to pay for anything."

> **HE SHOOK HIS HEAD IN WHAT WAS STILL STUNNED DISBELIEF. "YOU KNOW, MARJORIE AND I DIDN'T THINK MUCH ABOUT HOW WE WERE GOING TO PAY FOR COLLEGE UNTIL GRETCHEN WAS ABOUT HALFWAY THROUGH 11TH GRADE.**

"Really?" Rachel's dad said in disbelief. "If you wait to think about this until January of your kid's junior year, you can miss out on getting any financial help at all?"

Gretchen's dad nodded, biting at the corner of his lip. "Yep," he said. "That's right. There's this special one-year period where the financial aid people take a snapshot of all of your family income, and then they scrutinize that little snapshot to figure out how much your family can *probably* afford to pay for college. I had no idea this was happening, though," he continued, "so I didn't even have the presence of mind to think, 'Wow, Marjorie should not be taking this great second job right now! Wow, this is not the time for my dad to be giving me $30,000 so I can fix up his lake cabin! Wow, I'm getting a big sales commission at work; I should get that deal closed and all the paperwork in by December 31st instead of four days later on January 4th!' I didn't think of any of that stuff because I just didn't realize when that special year was starting."

"When does it start?" Rachel's dad asked.

"It starts January 1st of your kid's sophomore year of high school. By the time I started thinking about this when Gretchen was a junior, I was an entire year too late to do anything about it."

"So . . ." Rachel's dad said slowly.

"So," Gretchen's dad said, "when the financial aid people took that one-year snapshot of our finances, we looked about 10 times richer than we actually were. When the financial aid reports came back when Gretchen was a senior, they essentially said, 'Congratu-

lations! Your family's rich! Look at all this money you'll be able to pay for your daughter's college!' I just felt sick when I saw it. And all because we didn't think to plan just a little earlier than we did."

There was a long silence as both men stood thinking.

"You know," Gretchen's dad finally said, "we could've afforded to pay cash for Gretchen to go to the community college by our house and live at home for a couple of years. People do that, you know. Then she could have gone to a fancier college after that. She would've ended up with the fancy college name splashed across the top of her bachelor's degree just the same. But oh, no. Our family wasn't going to do anything like *that*. We were all off-the-charts excited when Gretchen opened up that acceptance letter from Millmore. Of course we were; we'd been preparing her for it her whole dang life. In about 10 minutes that acceptance letter was plastered all over Snapchat and Instagram, and Gretchen was on the phone excitedly telling all the grandparents where she was going in the fall. We didn't have any idea what the financial arrangements would be at that point, but that didn't matter to Gretchen. Or to her mom. The horse was out of the gate and around the first bend of the racetrack before I could even think to say, 'OK, let's all slow down a minute and think this through.'"

"So what did the financial stuff end up looking like?" Rachel's dad asked.

Gretchen's dad let out a short, humorless laugh. "So here's how it works. You get this acceptance letter, your kid gets all excited and tells everyone on the planet where she's going to college, and then days later you get to see the school's 'financial aid award letter.' Ours was a joke. When I saw for the first time what it was going to cost us to send our daughter to Millmore, seriously, Steve, it made me want to puke."

Gretchen's dad drew a deep, long breath and then said flatly, "That 'free' grant money we thought we were going to get from the government and from the college? There wasn't any. There in black and white was this astronomical number that our family would be expected to contribute—along with the expectation that we would take out loans to cover thousands of dollars over and above that. It was clear. There was absolutely no way I could send my daughter to Millmore without loans. Without a *ton* of loans. And some of the loans we had to get were these horrible 'Parent PLUS Loans' that have now put Marjorie and me on the hook for $1,200 every single month for 10 years. That is going to seriously mess with our retirement. And because Gretchen had only applied to colleges exactly like Millmore, we didn't have any other better four-year college options we could use as alternatives."

Rachel's dad shook his head.

"I just wanted to call up Millmore at that point and tell them to *forget it*. But Gretchen was so excited; she was bouncing in her chair. She'd seen that pretty brick clock tower they have there and she'd read those glossy brochures; she was raring to go. By the time I started trying to talk to her about costs, she and two friends had already picked out an expensive on-campus apartment with granite countertops. This was her

dream school! No other option would do. Well, there was no way Marjorie and I could say no to that! Gotta give your kids their dreams, right?"

Gretchen's dad rolled his eyes.

"Besides all that, you know that thing you always hear: you've gotta send your kid to a great college, or she might not be able to get a good job when she graduates! That's actually a huge lie, you know. Don't we all know people who went to so-called 'bad colleges' and they have great jobs?"

Gretchen's dad looked sideways at Rachel's dad, stifling a laugh.

> **BY THE TIME I STARTED TRYING TO TALK TO HER ABOUT COSTS, SHE AND TWO FRIENDS HAD ALREADY PICKED OUT AN EXPENSIVE ON-CAMPUS APARTMENT WITH GRANITE COUNTERTOPS. THIS WAS HER DREAM SCHOOL! NO OTHER OPTION WOULD DO.**

"Well," Gretchen's dad continued, "Of course, Gretchen had worked so hard to get that Millmore acceptance. She'd done everything we'd asked her to do. She'd driven herself practically insane trying to be the 'perfect' college applicant all the way through high school. She'd gotten the grades; she'd taken the SAT three times; she'd done all the hundreds of hours of frantic activity to prove she was 'well-rounded.' How could we say no? So we just gulped down the lumps in our throats, plunged ahead, signed all the student loan papers, and hoped for the best."

Uncle Paul wiped at the inside corner of one eye with a thumb, took off his baseball cap, ran his fingers through his auburn hair, and looked sideways at Rachel's dad.

"Honestly, Steve? What we wanted was to give Gretchen wings. But what I'm afraid of is that we may have tied a gigantic millstone around her neck."

Rachel's dad nodded slowly as Gretchen's dad looked up from the game, scanning the pretty houses with neat yards lining the park. Uncle Paul pressed his lips together in a tight line.

"I don't mean to go on and on about this, Steve, but geez—I see nice neighborhoods like this, and all I can think is, how many years before my daughter gets a house? At this point, Gretchen and Nevil can't even afford a dingy walk-up apartment in a bad part of town, let alone a house. Who knows if they'll ever be able to? And if a baby comes along? An unplanned baby at this point would be nothing less than a disaster. Seriously, how in the world can people like Gretchen and Nevil ever afford an extra $950 a month for diapers and day care and baby formula, when they can't even afford their own small apartment?"

SETTING THE GOAL

The drive home from the family reunion that night was a quiet one for 7th-grade Rachel and her parents. Rachel's dad, especially, spent most of the drive deep in thought. He'd been taking a class at his church that talked extensively about the trap of debt, how to avoid it, and practical steps for getting out of

it, and he knew one thing: he did not want a life of crippling student loan debt for Rachel. It was on that drive home that he made his proposal to Rachel and her mother.

"What if we set a huge, bold, audacious goal for ourselves," he said to his family. "What if we, as a team, spend the next eight years doing every creative thing we can think of to help Rachel graduate from college completely debt-free, ready to walk directly into a great job she'll excel at and love. Other people might say there's no way it can be done, but what do you say?"

He looked over at Rachel's mom and into the backseat at Rachel, beaming at them like he was inviting them into an adventure. "Are you in?"

Rachel and her mom agreed. They were in.

2 | *Tomorrow's Rich*

Over the past 15 years or so, there's been an increasing movement of people across the U.S. and around the world choosing to say no to compulsive acquisitiveness, greed, and the perilous quicksand of consumer debt. Bucking the culture around them, these people are quietly spending less than they earn, and they are saving, investing, and building real wealth while others around them are digging themselves deeper and deeper into dangerous sinkholes of debt.

A good number of these wise individuals, believe it or not, are college students.

Students who espouse this philosophy can be found on every college campus, wearing polo shirts they bought at consignment stores, sipping home-brewed coffee from reusable ceramic mugs, studying on scholarships they found and applied for themselves, and arranging hilarious, low-cost, group movie nights where movies are shown in parking lots on stretched-out bed sheets. These are clever, creative people who constantly strategize how to do more with less, and they are tomorrow's rich. And the college student in your life can be one of them.

This book is going to give you more ideas than you ever thought possible on how to pay for college without taking out student loans. Our discussion is going to go far beyond just saving up cash, getting financial aid, and applying for scholarships. If you follow the step-by-step instructions I provide in the coming chapters, you'll know exactly *when* and *how* to employ specific strategies that will allow your child to complete college faster, less expensively, and more effectively—and then jump directly into a fulfilling and rewarding job afterward.

Still—I cannot emphasize this enough—there's nothing like the power you have when you start early.

TELL EVERY PARENT YOU KNOW: START EARLY

Many of the parents you know are going to start thinking about how to pay for college when their oldest child is a junior or senior in high school. Urge them not to.

By the time a child reaches the junior year of high school, 75 percent of the best ideas for reducing college costs are gone. Unless you're rich, if you're going to capture the holy grail of college financing—the 100 percent debt-free college graduation—you'll need to take just a little time to plan during the *five years or more* before your child starts college.

> **BY THE TIME A CHILD REACHES THE JUNIOR YEAR OF HIGH SCHOOL, 75 PERCENT OF THE BEST IDEAS FOR REDUCING COLLEGE COSTS ARE GONE.**

And if you believe that your family cannot save one penny to pay for college? Then this applies doubly to you. You, more than anyone, will need to start early using all the creative non-saving strategies possible to get your child through college debt-free.

I must emphasize: you as a parent must take charge of this *yourself.*

We can't depend on school staff to train parents on this important topic. A four-page handout from financial aid night in the high school auditorium isn't enough to get your child through college debt-free and into a job he or she loves afterward. The guidance counselors at your child's school mean well, but years of budget and staffing cuts mean they simply don't have time to walk parents though applying to and financing college the way they might have 30 years ago. Every

parent must access outside resources on this subject—starting when their oldest child is in middle school.

HOW TO USE THIS BOOK

You can easily read this entire book in 10 hours, but I encourage you not to do that.

To keep this topic manageable and inspiring, I suggest you spread the reading of this book out over months and years.

Start by reading just the first two chapters. You've already read chapter 1, so this will take you only 20 more minutes. Do this as soon as you possibly can, because every day you wait is costing you money.

The first two chapters of this book are quick to read, engaging, and inspiring, and they will fill you in on accurate information related to college debt and paying for college—without asking you to do anything differently than what you're doing right now.

Once you've done this, get other key adults in your child's life on board: your child's mother, father, and helpful stepparents (if helpful stepparents are a part of the picture). Ask these people to also take less than an hour to read just the first two chapters of this book. Gift extra copies of this book if necessary. Once each key adult has read the first two chapters, schedule a special kid-free block of time to sit down together to discuss chapter 3, "7th Grade or Earlier." The suggestions in chapter 3 have the greatest power if you start applying them very, very early on—so I want you to start working on them first.

When you schedule the date and time to

discuss chapter 3, think of it as a book club meeting. Each parent reads chapter 3 in advance and then meets to discuss the chapter and plan some action steps. Don't worry if your family can't do everything I suggest. Pick out some items on the list that you know you *can* manage and, working as a team, make a plan for how you'll start doing them.

Then, before the meeting ends, get out your calendars and set up another similar meeting.

Make this a regular practice for the adults in your family. Set a meeting date, read and think about my instructions ahead of time, and then sit down together to discuss, strategize, and plan how you can apply them. Depending on your child's age, these parent meetings may end up happening quarterly (once every three months) or monthly.

If your child is on an Individualized Education Program (IEP) or has a diagnosis from a medical doctor, therapist, psychiatrist, psychologist, or other mental health professional, be sure to check with him or her before implementing any strategy I recommend.

Finally, be sure you're able to see all the current updates to the material in this book. Subscribe to my free weekly email newsletter at JeannieBurlowski.com, and then carefully whitelist it with your email provider as one you want to see in your primary inbox every week. For specific instructions from me on exactly how to whitelist an email, just type this shortcut into your web browser: Bit.ly/2gOJDqX.

This is important, because email is the only way I can keep in touch with you and alert you about updates to the strategies in this book in real time, as they happen.

WHEN YOUR CHILD IS IN MAY OF 8TH GRADE, KICK INTO HIGH GEAR

Once your child reaches May of 8th grade, meet regularly as parents to read, discuss, and implement only the chapter that applies to your child's current age. If you've just picked up this book and your child is already in 9th grade or even older, don't worry. Just start doing what I'm prescribing in the pages that follow as soon as you comfortably can.

The strategies for what you'll need to do to get your child through college debt-free are carefully laid out in this book in chronological, step-by-step order. The tasks in each chapter are clear and easy to follow. You won't have to use every strategy I suggest; just choose the ones you think will work for your family and either modify or discard the rest. At the end of each chapter, you'll find a simple, at-a-glance checklist you can use to keep track of the tasks you've completed.

Follow this pattern until your child has graduated from college debt-free, and your own (adult) family finances are also debt-free and stable. If you use this plan, you'll avoid being overwhelmed and stay firmly on track—from right now until your child graduates debt-free and moves into a job he or she loves.

WARNING: DON'T DEPEND ON YOUR CHILD TO TAKE CARE OF THIS

Parents, please—don't be tempted to hand off responsibility for figuring out college financing to your child, no matter how bright and capable she seems to be.

Before the age of 24, the prefrontal cortex of your child's brain is not sufficiently developed to be able to succeed at large-scale tasks that require high-level evaluation of risk and preparation for the future. College financing is an adult task, and doing it for your child will be one of the greatest gifts you can give her as she launches into adulthood.

Will planning for a debt-free college graduation take a little bit of time and some careful planning throughout your child's middle school and high school years? Yes. But the joy and satisfaction you'll feel when your child walks across the college graduation stage debt-free, ready for a career she excels at and loves, will be worth every bit of the time you took to plan it.

TIME TO RETIRE THAT COVERED WAGON, MRS. INGALLS

"Why the big emphasis on avoiding student debt? Everyone gets student loans, don't they? That's what my guidance counselor told me when I was in high school. Isn't that just the way it is?"

» "Our son needs a good education to get a good job, so we'll do everything we can to help him get into a good school, and then we'll apply for financial aid and cosign on lots of loans. I just need to accept that. Why make such a big deal out of avoiding student loans?"

This kind of thinking is sorely out of date.

Think about your hopes for your child's future. Is it your goal that your child will one day

» live independently from you?

» have the financial flexibility to do work she really loves?

» feel happy, fulfilled, confident, and highly motivated to work hard?

» have a marriage relatively free of money-related stress and anxiety?

» have the financial flexibility to manage the inevitable setbacks of life—without fear?

» have the financial flexibility to be able to go on to graduate school, seminary, or medical school, if that is her call?

» look at the possibility of a new baby as a happy, joyous blessing—rather than a devastating addition to an already impossible financial burden?

» have enough financial margin to be able to give generously to others?

I ask these questions because student loan

debt can very quickly undermine every one of these goals.

And if your child just throws up her hands and quits making her student loan payments? Borrowers who default on student loans will be hounded to the grave for the money they owe. Lenders can intercept their tax refunds and garnish their wages. A student loan default can result in your child not being able to get a cell-phone plan, rent an apartment, be approved for a home mortgage, get an auto loan, collect social security, or work for the government. It can even mean having a hard-won professional license revoked.

This is a nightmare scenario, but consider one that's not only worse, it's more likely. If student loan and credit card debt end up destroying your child's credit, she may not be able to get a job after college *at all*, since employers are increasingly scrutinizing credit reports as a part of the hiring process.

"But what about bankruptcy court? Can't student loans be wiped away simply by declaring bankruptcy?"

Student loans are *next to impossible* to discharge in bankruptcy court. Borrowers hoping to have their student loan debt wiped away by bankruptcy must enter into an "adversary proceeding" that demonstrates (proves) extraordinary, undue hardship. This is a very harsh standard, and typically fewer than 0.04 percent of those who attempt it win. Statistically, you're more likely to get colon cancer or die in a plane crash than to have your student loan debt discharged in bankruptcy court.

"But highly paid professionals don't struggle with student loan debt, do they?"

Many parents mistakenly believe that if their children will just become highly paid professionals, such as doctors or lawyers, they'll be able to easily pay back their student loans. Increasingly, though, even medical doctors are struggling to keep their heads above water when it comes to student debt.

At a conference I spoke at recently, a 55-year-old physician came to the edge of the stage when I was finished and said, "If I'd have heard you speak when I was 20 years old, I'd have been debt-free years and years ago. There are so many loans I'd have never taken out. Nobody told me I'd still be paying on these loans 28 years after med school, at the same time I'm trying to send my own kids to college, take care of my aging parents, and plan for my retirement."

> **IF STUDENT LOAN AND CREDIT CARD DEBT END UP DESTROYING YOUR CHILD'S CREDIT, SHE MAY NOT BE ABLE TO GET A JOB AFTER COLLEGE** *AT ALL,* **SINCE EMPLOYERS ARE INCREASINGLY SCRUTINIZING CREDIT REPORTS AS A PART OF THE HIRING PROCESS.**

And what are the consequences if a doctor just gives up on paying and defaults on a student loan? A student loan default for a doctor effectively eliminates more than 95 percent of his or her employment opportunities. Why is this? Because a doctor who's defaulted on a student loan is automatically ineligible for the Medicare program. And if you're a doctor who's ineligible for the Medicare program, no one else who takes Medicare can contract with you in any fashion. You can't even wash the floors at a hospital, or that hospital will lose its Medicare status.

If this doesn't scare you badly enough, consider this heart-wrenching story told to me by Cryn Johannsen, author of *Solving the Student Loan Crisis*.[1] Johannsen told me of interviewing despondent student loan debtors for an article entitled "The Ones We've Lost: The Student Loan Debt Suicides." One 47-year-old student loan debtor reported to her that he had borrowed what seemed like a very reasonable $69,000, using it mostly to pay for law school. It seemed like a financially sound decision at the time, but after his law school graduation, he was unable to find steady work as a lawyer. His student loans slid into default once, and then again and again. Multiple defaults and capitalized interest from years of not paying led to his being slammed with penalties in excess of $50,000, burying him under a total debt he was even less likely to be able to pay off. Since that time, his total student loan debt, including interest, fees, and penalties, has ballooned to over $320,000. That, though, is not the most upsetting part of his story.[2]

Since graduating from law school. this man has made his living primarily as a house-painter. Like many other former students hopelessly buried in suffocating student loan debt, he struggles with thoughts of suicide and admits to self-destructive behavior. And, last Johannsen heard from him, he was still living with his parents.[3]

"[A $320,000 student loan debt] sounds astounding, but it's not unusual," Johannsen told me. "Once a person defaults on a student loan, the balance grows exponentially, with interest compounding on interest, penalties, and fees. If this man can't start making payments soon, by the time he 're-tires' (at age 70), he'll owe somewhere in the neighborhood of $1.9 million."[4]

And woe to any family members who co-signed on those loans for him; they are just as much in debt as he is.

Does being in this situation have the potential to be depressing for former college students? Might it sap their motivation to work hard? Could it even make them less desirable as potential marriage partners? Once they are married, could their debt create anxiety over money that might stress a marriage? Could this financial situation make it difficult or even impossible to buy a car, rent an apartment, or save for retirement? Could it negatively affect future plans

1 Cryn Johannsen, *Solving the Student Loan Crisis: Dreams, Diplomas & a Lifetime Debt* (Los Angeles: New Insights Press, 2016). Used by permission.

2 Cryn Johannsen, "The Ones We've Lost: The Student Loan Debt Suicides," *Economic Hardship Reporting Project* and *Huffington Post* (September 1, 2012), http://www.huffingtonpost.com/c-cryn-johannsen/student-loan-debt-suicides_b_1638972.html. Used with the permission of EHRP. Any unauthorized duplication is strictly prohibited.

3 Ibid.

4 Cryn Johannsen, interview with the author, September 26, 2016.

for grad school, seminary, medical school, or having a baby?

Yes. But it doesn't have to be this way for *your* child.

"Going to a 'good' college is the easy solution to all of this . . . isn't it?"

"Well," I can hear some parents saying, "these adults struggling to pay back student loans probably didn't go to very good colleges. If my child goes to a top-notch private university, she's guaranteed to get a really good, really high-paying job when she graduates . . . isn't that right? Isn't that why people pay the big bucks for these great schools?

"In our family, we're really focused on top schools. We bought our daughter her first Harvard sweatshirt when she was in 3rd grade! We've stressed over and over again how important it is for her to get into an Ivy League school. And she's really motivated to do this too. We've gotten her to the point that she gets headaches and pains in her stomach when she gets a B on a test! Our plan is to get her into one of these top schools, and then she'll be able to easily get a job with a high-enough salary to pay these loans back. Won't she?"

Parents, here's the truth. A degree from an elite private university is no guarantee that your son or daughter will be able to get a high-paying job after college. Other things, like focused career goals early on and quality volunteering and interning, are far more likely to lead to the highest levels of career success after college. (I discuss this in depth in my book for students entitled *FLY: The 6*

Things You Absolutely Must Do to Be Brilliant in College and Get a Job You Love Afterward.)

If you're fixated on the idea that an expensive private education is the only one good enough for your designer offspring—and will be worth whatever it costs, even if that means a tremendously heavy debt burden after college—please reconsider that position.

In the more than 20 years I've been working with students applying to law, medical, business, and graduate schools at GetIntoMedSchool.com, I've seen thousands of students achieve truly awe-inspiring, extraordinary things without the benefit of an exorbitantly expensive private education.

Parents, if you can use the strategies in this book to pay mostly cash for an "elite" education, or if your child is awarded grants and scholarships sufficient to cover the cost of the top private college that just happens to be the exact right fit for your child, by all means, send your child there. But if the only way to get there is by taking on student loan debt, please seriously consider lower-cost but equally effective options. An honors program at a lower-cost college or university, for instance, can be an inexpensive route to a very high-quality education.

I can't emphasize this strongly enough: having your child be able to begin adult life debt-free is worth far, far more than any prestigious diploma.

A few years ago, a mother emailed me a Wikipedia list of 68 distinguished luminaries who'd graduated from NYU (which, at a whopping $179,380 for four years of tuition and required fees, was the priciest undergraduate institution in the country that year). The list of famous NYU grads this mother sent me (the majority of whom had graduate degrees) included authors, CEOs, television personalities, founders of law firms and big-box stores, one supermodel, the founder of Twitter, the designer of the modern snowboard, and Iceland's first billionaire. "Look at all these great people who've come out of NYU!" she chirped. "People who graduate from NYU get great jobs, so it's worth whatever we have to pay for it."

Whoa. Hold on a minute there, Mom.

While there's a lot of good to be said for the education at NYU, it's simply not logical to conclude that NYU *caused* these people to be successful, and therefore every student graduating from NYU is guaranteed to be equally as successful. Or even one percent as successful.

"What you're missing here," I replied to her, "is that most of the people on this list achieved greatness and notoriety not simply because of what NYU did for them, but because of what they did for themselves."

These successful NYU grads started out with raw talent, and then they practiced and rehearsed until that talent became skill. They birthed a creative idea. They pursued a dream. They honed a craft. They tried and failed and tried again. They sought out mentors and strategic partners. They sat their butts in their chairs and got the hard work done. Most of the people you see on that list achieved in this world because they worked hard at it, not because dear, blessed

NYU somehow magically programmed them for greatness. Focus, hard work, and strategy are the most pronounced precursors of every kind of success, and these things are available to your kid even if he or she doesn't attend NYU.

Parents, think hard about what ideas and beliefs you plant in your child concerning the "necessity" of an elite private education and college debt. Consider carefully before you cosign on a huge debt burden. Use all the power at your disposal to steer your teen *away* from the exorbitant student loans that could result in him or her living like a pauper after college, finding it financially impossible to do what he or she is actually called to do in life.

I am telling you the truth here: it will not be the expensive name on your daughter's bachelor's degree that will get her a job when she graduates from college; it will be the personal capital she's built into herself through focus and hard work, through real world professional experience, and by planning her career strategically.

These are the things that truly determine the brightness of a student's future.

Let me help you with that.

"But students who attend elite colleges end up happier as adults, don't they?"

When families push their teens toward top-ranked colleges and universities no matter the cost, there can be additional negative life consequences even beyond the financial ones described earlier. These parents—

parents who understandably just want the best for the children they believe in and love—may spend years setting up Ivy League admission as the "holy grail" of life accomplishment.

> **IT WILL NOT BE THE EXPENSIVE NAME ON YOUR DAUGHTER'S BACHELOR'S DEGREE THAT WILL GET HER A JOB WHEN SHE GRADUATES FROM COLLEGE; IT WILL BE THE PERSONAL CAPITAL SHE'S BUILT INTO HERSELF THROUGH FOCUS AND HARD WORK, THROUGH REAL WORLD PROFESSIONAL EXPERIENCE, AND BY PLANNING HER CAREER STRATEGICALLY.**

For the children of these parents, the ages of 14 through 18 can become a pressure cooker of prep school classes, frantic extracurricular activity, and expensive admissions coaching that can send teens this message: "You know what? You are so completely inadequate the way you are right now. The only way you'll ever be able to make anything of yourself is to go to one of these high-status, elite private colleges. If you're not good enough to get into one of these schools, you'll be shamed, our whole family will be shamed, and your life will essentially be over."

Students who live with this kind of pressure are at a significantly increased risk for anxiety, depression, eating disorders, and even thoughts of suicide, sometimes over something as minor as having received a B in a high school class.

> **BEFORE YOU TIE YOUR CHILD TO MAKING $950-PER-MONTH STUDENT LOAN PAYMENTS FOR 10 YEARS, ALL IN THE NAME OF "GIVING HER A HAPPIER, MORE FULFILLED LIFE," LET'S DIG DOWN INTO THE ASSUMPTIONS THAT UNDERLIE THESE STATEMENTS.**

One college girl I know of told of the day she overheard her grandmother telling her father that he shouldn't put her college decal in his car window, "because it was embarrassing that it wasn't the Harvard Crimson decal." No child needs to hear that.

"Oh, but the experience at an expensive private college is so enriching," some parents say. "Isn't it true that students who graduate from these top-ranked colleges live happier, more fulfilled lives? You can't put a price on that! We'll take on any amount of student loan debt if it will help our child to have a happy life."

Before you tie your child to making $950-per-month student loan payments for 10 years, all in the name of "giving her a happier, more fulfilled life," let's dig down into the assumptions that underlie these statements. Is it really true that elite private education is so enriching that it automatically leads to a better life? What does the research say?

In her May 2014 NPR article entitled "Poll: Prestigious Colleges Won't Make You Happier in Life or Work," Anya Kamenetz cites Gallup data demolishing the argument that graduates of top colleges lead more fulfilling lives later in life. "When you ask college graduates whether they're 'engaged' with their work or 'thriving' in all aspects of their lives," she writes, "their responses don't vary one bit whether they went to a prestigious college or not."

She goes on to say,

> The surprising findings come in a survey of 29,650 college graduates of all ages by Gallup pollsters working with researchers at Purdue University. The poll asked graduates a range of questions designed to measure how well they are doing in life across factors such as . . . sense of purpose, financial security, physical health, close relationships or community pride.

The kicker? Kamenetz says,

> [The results] did not vary based on whether the grads went to a fancy name-brand school or a regional state college, one of the top 100 in the U.S. News & World Report rankings or one of the bottom 100. A slight edge did go to those who attended campuses with more than 10,000 students, while for-profit college graduates saw worse outcomes.

But don't graduates of elite colleges earn more money throughout their lifetimes? Doesn't this lead to increased financial security, and doesn't that open the door to greater lifetime happiness? Kamenetz says no. "[This] isn't the first time studies have documented no edge for highly selective schools," she writes. "Previous studies have shown no link between expensive private colleges and later salary for graduates."

College debt, though, was shown to have near-devastating impact on happiness after college. As Kamenetz explains, the Gallup results showed that of those with $20,000 to $40,000 in undergraduate loans, only two percent said they were thriving. "That's pretty troubling," she adds, "since $29,400 is the national average for the 7 in 10 students who borrow."[5]

The take-home message for students is this: if you can go to Nowhere University debt-free versus Harvard or Yale for $260,000, go to Nowhere University. Just focus on doing some really interesting things while you're there.

"College kids should just work their way through school. That's what I did, by golly!"

Prior to about 1990, a hardworking college student could earn enough money in a summer of lifeguarding or burger flipping to pay for one year of college tuition. If she continued to work for wages for as many hours as possible during the school year, lived in a tiny apartment with multiple roommates,

---

and ate only macaroni and cheese, she had a chance of being able to pay for her own living expenses as well.

This is no longer possible.

Because of skyrocketing tuition costs and a flattening minimum wage, today's students would have to work full time for 25 straight weeks, all the way from Labor Day to March, to pay for just one year of state university college tuition. And if these students would like to cover their own room and board costs as well? Today, that would require working a minimum-wage job for more than 60 hours a week for 42 straight weeks.

But wait; these numbers don't tell the whole story. The sad reality is that vast numbers of college students simply can't graduate from state universities in four years, which means they'll have to tack another year or two of expenses onto these overwhelming totals.

Your child should *absolutely* work for wages during summers and during the academic years while in college. There is no question about this. But make no mistake; this work is not going to cover the cost of his college tuition and living expenses.

In sum, if you will (a) start planning earlier than most people do, (b) get others who love your child to join you on this journey, (c) recognize that out-of-control student loan debt can devastate and derail every one of your parenting goals, (d) challenge the assumptions about college that you're hearing from educational and financial institutions that stand to make money from your uninformed decisions, and (e) realize your kid can't get through this effectively alone, I will arm you with multiple strategies for getting your child through college debt-free and into a job he loves afterward.

Let's start that exciting journey together right now.

3 | *7th Grade or Earlier*

If you want your son or daughter to grad-uate college completely debt-free, there are a few things to start thinking about *as soon as possible.* The first seven tasks on the following list, especially, will have more power the earlier you start.

HOW TO USE THIS CHAPTER

Start by just reading through this chapter. As you read, don't worry about committing to any of it. Decision time will come at the end of the chapter, when I give you a clear, at-a-glance checklist of every task I'm suggesting you consider right now.

Remember, you won't have to use every strategy I suggest; just choose the ones you think will work for your family, and either modify or discard the rest.

[1] *Reevaluate your own values related to saving and spending, and model the joys of living a frugal life.*

Let's be honest here. Your son is not going to shop at a consignment store if he never sees you doing it. Your daughter is unlikely to see the financial logic behind making home-brewed coffee if she sees a $4 latte in your car's cup holder every morning.

Think intentionally about how your family could live more frugally, and then make doing so an adventurous game, starting when your children are very young. If you do this, your kids will naturally adopt the virtue of frugality as a normal part of everyday life. They'll go on to spend less on "living expenses" during the college years, and you'll be able to take the money you save over years of frugality and funnel it into an ever-growing college savings plan.

[2] *As early as possible, ask close relatives to reconsider gift giving.*

Think back to last Christmas or your child's last birthday. Who were the dear relatives who thoughtfully shopped for a gift for your child, wrapped it, and either brought it or mailed it to your house? Grandparents? Aunts? Uncles? Dear family friends? Godparents?

If you are close to these people, try this radical idea that other families have used with great success. Reach out to each of these loved ones. Thank them wholeheartedly for their generosity over the years, and then let them know about the bold, audacious, radical goal your family has set for itself.

Tell them that your family is rallying all possible forces to see to it that your child graduates from college completely debt-free in just four years, and that you're putting all the resources you can toward that goal. Then, invite these dear people to consider partnering with you in this exciting mission—by putting the money they *were* planning to spend on gifts into college savings instead.

Some parents hesitate to have this kind of frank and honest discussion with their child's gift-giving family members, close friends, and godparents. You may feel awkward approaching this subject—as though you're asking them to pay for something you should be paying for yourself.

If you find yourself thinking this way, please fix two things firmly in your mind: First, most people realize that in this day and age, most families are not just casually writing checks to cover their kids' $62,000-per-year college costs. Your family and friends will admire you for working hard to keep your child free of future student loan debt. Second, you're not asking them for money. All you're requesting is that they consider taking what they were giving anyway and setting it aside in a slightly more strategic way.

Besides that, you never know—Grandma and Uncle Joe may actually feel immensely happy and relieved at no longer having to shop for gifts for teenagers.

If you're thinking of trying this in your family, you may wonder what to do with the traditional gift-opening ceremony. Nobody wants Grandma and Grandpa to sit there empty-handed while everyone else in the room hands the birthday boy beautifully wrapped gift boxes.

What Grandma and Grandpa might try in this situation is wrapping up a *letter*.

Imagine this. The birthday boy opens his wrapped box from his grandparents, and inside he finds an envelope that says, "Bradley, read this later. Love, Grandma and Grandpa."

In this special birthday letter, Grandma and Grandpa can tell your child how much they love him, what admirable good character and potential they see in him, how proud they are of what he's accomplished the previous year, how excited they are to see him have a successful future, and that they have made a contribution to a fund where they're saving for his future education. If Grandma and Grandpa like to write, they may also include stories from their own lives, along with wise advice for your child's future.

NOBODY WANTS GRANDMA AND GRANDPA TO SIT THERE EMPTY-HANDED WHILE EVERYONE ELSE IN THE ROOM HANDS THE BIRTHDAY BOY BEAUTIFULLY WRAPPED GIFT BOXES.

Letters like these become precious to kids as the years go by—even if Grandma and Grandpa invest only $10 or $20 in the college savings account each year. *The amount saved is not what matters.* The loving gesture across the years is what matters.

Parents, I urge you: save these letters (along with photos of your child with this generous person), and later use an online service to create a scrapbook out of these letters and photos. When your child is an adult, this will mean more to him than a hundred sweaters or plastic toys.

As this fund gets larger, Grandma and Grandpa (or other generous friends and relatives) may decide to *invest* this money so it can grow and increase in value while they're sleeping. If any of these people *do* choose to invest this money, they should do so in such a way that it won't accidentally diminish the child's future financial aid eligibility. To help with this, I've created a free online resource that will gently explain to your loving, gift-giving friends and relatives exactly the idea I've just told you. In addition, this resource will coach these generous people on how they can set aside money in a college fund *without diminishing your child's future financial aid eligibility.* I strongly recommend that you as a parent read over this resource now and think through which

gift-giving friends and relatives you could share it with. It's free.

BONUS ONLINE CONTENT:
Download the article "Grandma Gave Me Something Awesome: How to Give College Savings as Birthday and Holiday Gifts" at JeannieBurlowski.com/LAUNCH.

The strategies in this online article will work whether your child is a newborn, a toddler, a teenager, or a college student.

Most adults, at some level, long to leave a legacy of some sort to those they love in the next generation. There are few greater gifts a person can give a child—few more powerful legacies a person can leave behind—than to help a loved one in the quest to graduate from college debt-free. I hope you feel good about helping your generous friends and relatives do that.

[3] *Open up a Upromise.com account, but be careful as you do so.*

You're going to buy necessities like groceries and drugstore items anyway, right? Sign up for a free account at Upromise.com and register your grocery store and drugstore loyalty cards there. Without doing another thing, a percentage of every dollar you spend at these stores will be funneled into a special account you'll be able to use for any student's college savings, current college-related expenses, or payment of certain student loans. Over 20,000 grocery stores and drugstores participate, and no credit card is required.

> **A PERCENTAGE OF EVERY DOLLAR YOU SPEND AT THESE STORES WILL BE FUNNELED INTO A SPECIAL ACCOUNT YOU'LL BE ABLE TO USE FOR ANY STUDENT'S COLLEGE SAVINGS, CURRENT COLLEGE-RELATED EXPENSES, OR PAYMENT OF CERTAIN STUDENT LOANS.**

Grandma and Uncle Joe can also sign up for Upromise accounts and give the college savings money they accumulate to anyone they like.

Sound great? It is. But *be careful.*

Upromise has a credit card that in some cases may add a small amount of additional cash to your Upromise account with each completed transaction. I don't recommend signing up for this credit card, since it's my mission to steer college students and their families *away* from credit card debt, not toward it.

[4] *Have a "parents only" family meeting once a month where you look frankly and honestly at what you could do to make your own financial situation more stable.*

Be strict about setting aside kid-free time in your family calendar for these meetings.

Plan the meetings for times when you know you'll be well fed and well rested.

If you struggle to find time in your schedule for these meetings, find another couple who also want to get their kids through college debt-free and ask them to trade childcare with you. ("Amanda, what would you think about taking our kids from five to nine o'clock on the evening of the 7th, and then we'll take yours on the 21st?")

In these meetings, brainstorm ways you might take small steps toward building up a $1,000 cash emergency fund for unforeseen medical bills or unexpected car repairs. Sell unused items from your garage or basement if necessary.

When you've achieved that $1,000 savings milestone, strategize about how you could take aggressive steps to pay off your own debts one by one, starting with paying off your smallest debt first. This may seem counterintuitive, but I urge you to do it. By starting with your smallest debt, even if it has a low interest rate, you'll experience success quickly and feel a sense of growing excitement as you watch your efforts snowball. Take the advice of syndicated talk radio host Dave Ramsey (DaveRamsey.com), author of the *New York Times* best-selling book *The Total Money Makeover*, who's helped millions of people get control of their money:

> The math seems to lean more toward paying the highest interest debts first, but what I have learned is that personal finance is 20% head knowledge and 80% behavior. You need some quick wins in order to stay pumped enough

to get out of debt completely. When you start knocking off the easier debts, you will start to see results and you will start to win in debt reduction. . . . The principle is to stop everything except minimum payments and focus on one thing at a time. Otherwise, nothing gets accomplished because all your effort is diluted.[6]

This is critically important for you, the parent of a future college student. On a day coming soon, when your child is a senior in high school, the financial aid calculation process is going to take one look at all your parental income and assets, and name a dollar amount that it believes your family can afford to pay out-of-pocket for college. If you have at least some of that money handy, available, and ready to pay for college, that will be great. But if that money has already been committed years ago to debt payments, you may find yourself looking at this dollar amount with your jaw dropped and your stomach tied in sickened knots.

"HOW ARE WE EVER GOING TO PAY THAT?" YOU'LL THINK, PANICKING. "DON'T THESE PEOPLE REALIZE THAT WE PAY THOUSANDS OF DOLLARS A MONTH ON CREDIT CARDS AND OTHER DEBTS THAT WE RACKED UP YEARS AGO, AND WE JUST DON'T HAVE THE MONEY TO PAY WHAT THEY'RE REQUIRING?" *NO, THEY DON'T.*

"How are we ever going to pay that?" you'll think, panicking. "Don't these people realize that we pay thousands of dollars a month on credit cards and other debts that we racked up years ago, and we just don't have the money to pay what they're requiring?"

No, Mom. No, Dad.

The financial aid calculations don't account for how far in debt you are and how little margin you have, because they don't take debt into consideration whatsoever when coming up with the dollar amount your family is expected to pay for college.

If you want to give your child a bright, debt-free future, one of the smartest things you can do is this: start early on taking intentional small steps to get yourself completely out of debt first. Start toward this goal as early as you can.

Once your own debt-reduction strategy is in place, create a plan where you start saving some money each month until you have three to six months of expenses saved for unforeseen family emergencies. I realize this idea can seem daunting, but millions of families have done it, and you can too if you take regular small steps in that direction.

If you need help with this, seek out quality professional help with the process. When I have clients grappling with these

---

6   Dave Ramsey, "Get Out of Debt with the Debt Snowball Plan," *Foundations U*, accessed November 19, 2016, http://www.foundationsu.com/articles/article/contentname/foundationsu-get-out-of-debt-with-the-debt-snowball-plan/. Used by permission.

issues, I refer them to the truly outstanding books, DVDs, local classes, and other tools available inexpensively at DaveRamsey.com. Whatever help you find for yourself, though, after you build your short-term emergency fund, pay off your own debts, and put away three months' worth of expenses, take this next important step.

[5] *Be certain you are providing for your own retirement every single month.*

Financial planners are adamant on this point. Parents must fund their own retirement first and then save for their children's college educations with the money that's left over. Parents must never sacrifice their retirement funds to pay for college. Why? Because if worse comes to absolutely worst, you can borrow money to pay for college. You cannot borrow money to pay for retirement.

Parent, it's a near certainty that you will slowly age, one day become elderly, and eventually require care in years you cannot work. You must provide for this period in your life ahead of time—in your young and working years. If you neglect to provide for yourself in this way, it will likely be your children who will have to sacrifice to care for you—right at a time in their lives when they are struggling to raise families and put their own children through college.

It is no gift to your children to pour all of your resources into their lives and neglect to provide for your own future. This is non-negotiable. Always provide for your own retirement first, and then save for college with what's left over.

[6] *Start a college savings plan the minute you have achieved the previous goals. Then add to it every single month.*

Once your own parental finances are in a good strong place, I suggest that you have some amount of money transferred automatically out of every paycheck you receive, directly into a college savings plan. If money is terribly tight for your family, consider dropping your child's tae kwon do lessons, sports camps, or expensive traveling cheerleading competitions in favor of putting funds into college savings. Take it from a professional academic consultant: saving for college is far more important than any of these other things.

Some families just getting their feet wet with college savings will start very small (perhaps $25 per month). Then make a note on the family calendar to increase the contribution amount bit by bit every six months. If you are convinced you cannot accommodate even that, then commit to taking the amount of your next raise and funneling it directly into college savings. Afterward, commit to increasing the amount you contribute to college savings, to a large or small degree, every six months.

THE KINDERGARTEN WINDFALL

If you happen to have a child under the age of five, you have a rare, golden opportunity to take a giant leap into college savings.

Think for a moment of that day when your

youngest child goes off to kindergarten. You will have written out your last check for full-time day care, or perhaps if you've been a stay-at-home parent, you'll go back to work. The financial turnaround at this time of life can feel like a joyous windfall. Suddenly your family has more disposable income than you've had in five whole years or more. Right at this point, I urge you: take this windfall income and use it strategically to pay off your consumer debt, fatten your retirement savings, and take a giant leap forward on college savings. Doing so at this point may feel nearly painless, and when you see the potential this money has for growth over the next 13 years, you might just feel giddy about what a good start you're off to in providing for your child's future.

IF YOU HAPPEN TO HAVE A CHILD UNDER THE AGE OF FIVE, YOU HAVE A RARE, GOLDEN OPPORTUNITY TO TAKE A GIANT LEAP INTO COLLEGE SAVINGS.

Who do you know who has a child under age five? Share this great idea with them as soon as you can.

Could saving for college keep you from getting financial aid later?

Do you find yourself worrying that if you save money for college, the government will one day find you too wealthy to qualify for federal financial aid? Don't worry.

As of this writing, for every $100 you save for college in your growing, interest-bearing college savings plan, your federal financial aid (if you end up qualifying for it) will be reduced by only $5.64. If your son or daughter has to take out a loan to pay that $100, though, the costs will far exceed that.

What kind of college savings plan should you consider? I am not a certified financial planner (CFP) or certified public accountant (CPA) myself, but here is the college savings plan that CFPs and CPAs tend to recommend most highly.

STATE-SPONSORED 529 COLLEGE SAVINGS PLANS

Most state-sponsored 529 college savings plans allow you to contribute after-tax dollars, watch them grow, and then withdraw them tax-free for qualified educational expenses (including living expenses if your student is in college at least half time). If your child decides not to go to college, you can usually transfer the funds to certain other select relatives. Or, if you decide you want to use the money to make a down payment on a house, go on a cruise, or start up a business, you can pay taxes on the earnings (plus an additional penalty of 10 percent) and do whatever you want with the money.

One important consideration in choosing a 529 plan is to choose one that is "flexible." A flexible 529 plan will allow you to choose and control the types of funds you invest in, determine the amount you invest in each type of fund, and decide when you want to move money from one fund type to another. I never recommend 529 plans that freeze your options or automatically change your investments based on the age of your child.

When it's time for *you* to set up a 529 plan, I suggest that you contact a certified public accountant or certified financial planner and have him or her help you set it up.

Some families have asked me if they should save money for college in a Roth IRA. I don't recommend it. Why? Because you'll pay taxes on the profits you take out of a Roth IRA for college expenses if you're under the age of 59 and a half and haven't waited five years since contributing. Besides, what you take out of a Roth IRA always counts as income for financial aid purposes, and that can disadvantage your student in future financial aid calculations. I also don't recommend saving for college using prepaid tuition plans, savings bonds, or insurance policies (such as the Gerber Grow-Up Plan). Insurance-based methods of paying for college, in particular, are mainly just very expensive whole-life insurances, and they hardly ever perform as well as you hope they will.

I cannot emphasize enough the value of starting at the level you can with college savings and then increasing the amount you save every six months. Think of it this way. Every $100 you can save is $100 you won't have to borrow. If you are able to sock away $200 a month at 6.8 percent interest for 10 years, you'll end up with about $34,433. But if instead of saving this money, you were to borrow it at 6.8 percent interest, you would end up paying $396 a month for 10 years, which would end up being *almost twice as much.*

Start early, save monthly, and increase as you're able. Do this, and you'll give your child the best chance at a debt-free college graduation.

[7] *Plan and save as though your child will be going to a very expensive college or university—but at the same time be completely OK with a far less expensive one.*

This is the diametric opposite of what many parents do.

Many parents continually—for years on end—harp at their kids with the erroneous message that the expensive education is the only one worth having, while neglecting to plan and strategize sufficiently to cover the costs of that education. The result can be highly pressured, anxious teens taking on massive, destructive debt to pay for expensive educations they may not even need.

For your family, let's choose a better path.

Parent, I want you to plan and strategize so effectively that your child will be well able to afford an expensive Ivy League university, a wonderful private Christian or other religious college, or some other excellent fit private university—without taking out one single student loan.

> **I'VE PERSONALLY SEEN THOUSANDS OF STUDENTS ACHIEVE AWE-INSPIRING, EXTRAORDINARY THINGS WITHOUT THE BENEFIT OF AN EXORBITANTLY EXPENSIVE PRIVATE EDUCATION.**

At the same time, though, I suggest that you gently—well ahead of time—start planting the idea in your child's head that a lower-priced college may very well end up being the most excellent option in her particular situation.

I promise: you will not destroy your son's or daughter's future by doing this.

Remember these words, which I said emphatically earlier: in the more than 20 years I've been working with students applying to law, medical, business, and graduate school, I've seen thousands of students achieve truly awe-inspiring, extraordinary things without the benefit of exorbitantly expensive private education.

Avoid student loans at all costs, even if it means

» attending community college for the first two years, working feverishly and saving during those two years, and then enrolling in the expensive private university as a college junior;

» enrolling in a lower-ranked private college that does an outstanding job with exactly the major the student wants to study. A college like this may give your son far more "merit aid" (no-strings-attached free money not connected to financial need) to pay for college than will a top-ranked university with thousands of highly qualified applicants to choose from;

» living at home with parents under their rules, working as many hours as possi-

ble, and commuting to the college campus every day; or

» giving up the Ivy League in favor of the honors department at a large state university.

That said, I still suggest that every student use the strategies I provide in this book to apply to *at least two or three* very expensive private schools that look like good fits—even if the sticker prices of those schools seem to be completely unaffordable at first glance. Why? Because expensive private schools may have huge amounts of free money at their disposal for giving out to students they've accepted. Because this is true, some students have been stunned and thrilled to find out that the expensive-looking private school actually ended up costing them less than the local community college would have!

If it turns out that attending the expensive school requires taking on suffocating student loan debt, though, I suggest you choose a less expensive option. Start early getting ready for that less expensive option, and be positive and hopeful as you look toward it.

[8] *Begin early valuing service to others, and thus help your child to become an outstanding candidate for eventual college scholarships.*

Without question, one of the most powerful strategies for graduating from college debt-free is to win multiple college scholarships.

Do you think that scholarships are reserved for high-achieving academic superstars who come from disadvantaged minority backgrounds, have poverty-level family incomes, and struggle with staggering financial need? It's not true.

Just so we are clear, free money private scholarships go to students at all different academic achievement levels, from all different backgrounds and income brackets who, though they may not be perfect students, show they're serious about learning by maintaining a respectable level of academic proficiency.

Many big money college scholarships simply ask that a student have a 2.75 grade point average (GPA) or better. For these scholarships, it doesn't matter whether a student has a 2.78 GPA or a 4.0 GPA. As long as your daughter exceeds the minimum bar, she can apply and be officially in the running, competing with other applicants based on nonacademic factors that the student herself can control. That's good news!

> **MANY BIG MONEY COLLEGE SCHOLARSHIPS SIMPLY ASK THAT A STUDENT HAVE A 2.75 GRADE POINT AVERAGE (GPA) OR BETTER. FOR THESE SCHOLARSHIPS, IT DOESN'T MATTER WHETHER A STUDENT HAS A 2.78 GPA OR A 4.0 GPA.**

While respectable academic proficiency is helpful, students can *also* greatly increase the possibility that they'll be awarded scholarships by

» applying for scholarships early and often;

» taking initiative to better the world through committed service to others (and, when possible, leading others into that community service as well); and

» keeping careful records on the acts of service performed, so the information is ready and accessible when it comes time to fill out scholarship applications.

The best time to start doing these things? When students are in *middle school.*

Parent, let me give you an eye into the future. When your daughter begins to apply for college scholarships, she's going to be asked how she has served others. She's going to be asked how she has used her time and her talents and her energy and her enthusiasm to make the world a better place, starting in her local area.

If her answer is that she has not had time for that, that all of her energies have been spent heaping the resources of the world on herself, that is not going to be impressive in the least to a college scholarship committee. Even if she has a 4.3 GPA on a 4.0 scale, the scholarships will go to others.

However, if she can write convincingly, and if she has a strong record of committed service over time to people or causes she genuinely cares about—even if her grades are lower— she will likely rise quickly to the top of any group of scholarship applicants.

For this reason, I urge parents and students

to start thinking about committed service to others from the very first days of middle school.

At first, Mom and Dad, you'll help your son to come up with ideas for service that make use of his natural talents and interests. You'll help your daughter to find committed, long-term service opportunities outside of the occasional ones provided by the Girl Scouts or the service club at school. You'll help your son find places to serve a world in need outside of the four comfortable walls of his local church or synagogue. You'll go with him as he serves others. You'll provide supplies and ideas, you'll drive him to his service locations, you'll keep good records about each time he volunteers, and you'll encourage him to commit in depth to one or two causes, rather than volunteering sporadically here and there with no sense of commitment to anything.

The kind of service I'm recommending doesn't need to take many hours per week or per month. The secret to high-quality service is *committed consistency*. Contributing on a regular, consistent basis over a lengthy period of time.

It's my hope that the kind of service I'm recommending won't be viewed as a burdensome, wearying imposition on a busy family's already hectic schedule. Serving others can give meaning, purpose, and significance to a child's life. It brings out important "emotional intelligence" qualities in kids, such as empathy and compassion. It breeds gratitude and contentment, it helps kids to develop meaningful work skills they'll need later, and it makes for strong, attention-getting college applications. Many families are deciding

to get off the runaway train of after-school busyness so they can set aside more time for service to others. You can too.

You may have purchased this book in a set along with my book for students entitled *FLY: The 6 Things You Absolutely Must Do to Be Brilliant in College and Get a Job You Love Afterward.* You'll find an entire section in that book devoted to service to others—every bit of it written to convince your child that service is both important and fulfilling. Read that section, and commit that your family will start a pattern of service to others from the first months after your child enters middle school. If you do so, your son or daughter will be a top candidate for multiple, free money college scholarships when the time comes to apply for them. (Hint: the time is coming soon.)

> **THE SECRET TO HIGH-QUALITY SERVICE IS** *COMMITTED CONSISTENCY.* **CONTRIBUTING ON A REGULAR, CONSISTENT BASIS OVER A LENGTHY PERIOD OF TIME.**

[9] *Read the book* Parenting Teens With Love and Logic *when your child is 12 years old.*

If your schedule makes it hard for you to find time to read, listen to the audiobook in your car.

The principles you'll learn in *Parenting Teens With Love and Logic* will make parenting your teen less stressful and more fun, and will increase the probability that you'll raise a child who will do his or her part when it comes to succeeding at college and career. You'll learn concrete, practical strategies for raising responsible teens who thoughtfully think through their options, make responsible decisions, and access resources to solve their own problems. You as a parent will be freed from the fruitless task of trying to control your child with demands, orders, lectures, threats, and angry ultimatums. You'll learn how to use empathy, understanding, and respect to help your child become a superstar at thinking for himself. Your home will be happier, you'll enjoy your teens more, and best of all—you'll build the solid psychological foundation that will allow your child to make excellent choices about money and about every other topic throughout middle school, high school, and college.

I wouldn't recommend this resource if I hadn't used it and loved it myself. My advice is do not even *try* to parent teens without this book. You can purchase it in print or audio form from the Love and Logic Institute in Golden, Colorado, at Loveandlogic. com, or you can order it by phone by calling 1-800-LUV-LOGIC. Please tell them that their biggest fan, Jeannie Burlowski, sent you.

[10] *Allow your children to learn to manage all of their own household chores and schoolwork, starting when they are in early middle school.*

Don't hover or helicopter. Middle school students need to learn to organize and manage their own household chores and schoolwork independently, without constant prodding and cajoling from Mom and Dad.

When it comes to developing academic

independence in children, I suggest that parents do two things at the beginning of each new middle school trimester: First, be sure that your son or daughter has a calendar, planner, or special notebook for recording assignments and due dates. Second, keeping your particular student's personality in mind, provide some individualized teaching on the subject of workflow process management. One excellent way to do this is to ask interested questions about how your child plans to manage the schoolwork process.

Ask your child these questions.

"So, Sarah, when the teacher gives you a printed sheet with math problems on it and tells you it's due Friday, where's the one place you always automatically put that sheet?"

"Then what's your plan for remembering to get it done by Friday?"

"What method are you going to use to remember to get it out during homework time at home without anyone asking you about it?"

"Where do you think is the safest place for you to put that sheet when you're finished with it?"

"What are you planning to do to be sure it gets back to school and back to this particular teacher on the right day without anyone reminding you?"

"Would you like to hear some ideas that other kids have tried for this?"

Help your child design a workflow process that is likely to work well for her as an individual. Whatever the plan, though, it should boil down to these steps:

» Listen carefully to everything the teacher says.

» Write down all assignments and due dates in an assignment notebook or calendar.

» Put worksheets and other not-yet-done paper assignments in one safe place where you know right where they are and (whether at home or at school) can always find them in under 10 seconds.

» Look at your assignment notebook or calendar every day after school and make a plan for how you will get your upcoming assignments done on time.

» Do the work neatly in a quality manner, always trying to give the teacher more than he or she expects.

» Immediately put finished assignments back in the one certain safe place where they are sure to make it back to the teacher on the right day without you thinking about it.

As you have this discussion with your middle school student at the beginning of each new school semester or trimester, think of yourself as a business consultant. Help your child think through what worked during the past two months and what processes might be tweaked or changed for the future. Every time you do so, emphasize that success in school and in life really has little to do with brains or luck and everything to do with organization, process management, and continuing to try hard every day.

During the trimester, let him or her manage the process of listening in class, recording due dates in a calendar, storing assignments in one certain spot, planning when to do homework, handing assignments in on time, and remembering to study for tests. Do, however, quietly keep a careful eye on your child's progress by using the online assignment tracking that the school provides and by checking in with teachers. You'll want to intervene (maybe with reduced amounts of TV and video games) if your child's effort in school takes a downward turn.

Even when intervening, however, resist the urge to micromanage, helicopter, or control. Consider this strategy used by one wise father when his son suddenly stopped putting forth effort in grade school. The dad kindly and empathetically suggested to the boy that it must be because he didn't have enough *time at home* to do homework. "We all know you're capable of doing well," the dad said to his son in a thoughtful voice, "so this has got to be a not-enough-time issue." The dad then told the son that he'd arranged the family schedule so the boy could simply sit at a table with his schoolwork, books, and pencils for an hour each evening, and either "do homework or think about it." Completely the boy's choice. It worked a miracle for this family, and it's a strategy I strongly recommend.

> **SUCCESS IN SCHOOL AND IN LIFE REALLY HAS LITTLE TO DO WITH BRAINS OR LUCK AND EVERYTHING TO DO WITH ORGANIZATION, PROCESS MANAGEMENT, AND CONTINUING TO TRY HARD EVERY DAY.**

Remember, it's important for middle school students to learn to successfully manage their own schoolwork well before they enter high school. If they don't, they're going to be academically ineligible for some of the greatest strategies there are for lowering future college costs during the high school years.

If you find yourself parenting a perennial underachiever, I highly recommend this award-winning book by Dr. Charles Fay of Loveandlogic.com: *From Bad Grades to a Great Life! Unlocking the Mystery of Achievement for Your Child*. This book will help you put a decisive end to fretting and nagging about homework, and build into your child the *character* that will lead to a lifetime of achievement, whether he or she ever goes to college or not.

[11] *Help your child apply for his or her first college scholarship (or scholarships) when he or she is in middle school.*

Are you stunned that there are college scholarships awarded to 7th graders? Brace yourself; there are even scholarships awarded to students younger than that.

The money younger students win is simply held for them until they start having to pay for college classes out of their own pockets.

Just for fun, try googling "scholarships for 7th graders." Then google "scholarships for 8th graders." Read down toward the bottom of the Google results so you can find the scholarships that most other people aren't seeing. What will really stun you will be how many different scholarships there are for students at all these different ages.

When you hear the word "scholarship," do you immediately worry that your family might have too high an income to qualify for one? Worry no more.

Remember, scholarships are granted to students based on *who they are as human beings.* The vast majority of scholarship applications don't ask about family financial need at all. (The college money that's handed out based on financial need is applied for differently. We'll cover that in later chapters.) You can have $10 million in the bank and your daughter can still win free money college scholarships based on her own accomplishments.

For middle school and younger students, parents will need to provide some help with scholarship applications. Later, students who've been filling out scholarship applications since 8th grade will feel practiced at the process and will be able to do it alone, especially because after they fill out the first one, it's (to some degree) just a cut-and-paste exercise.

THE VAST MAJORITY OF SCHOLARSHIP APPLICATIONS DON'T ASK ABOUT FAMILY FINANCIAL NEED AT ALL.

One mother of an 8th grader volunteered to start and lead a "Scholarship and Service Club" on her son's middle school campus. Students who joined the club brainstormed and planned service activities suitable for middle school students and then formally invited their classmates to participate. Club members were taught to keep careful records on every act of service they participated in, and then the mother leading the group helped them all choose a scholarship to apply for, using their service experience on the application. This mom also taught the students to keep a "scholarship notebook," a thick spiral notebook where the student dedicated one page to each scholarship he or she had applied for. Students were taught to record in this notebook the name of each scholarship they had applied for, the contact information for the organization sponsoring the scholarship, how the student heard about the scholarship, the date the student applied for it, when it would be possible to reapply for it, and (in big red letters) the result when money was won.

The point of this exercise is not necessarily to win a lot of money right away. It's to establish this pattern in students' minds: (a) we intentionally find ways to serve and lead, (b) we keep records on everything we do, (c) we find a scholarship that is a fit, (d) we write about our service experiences on our scholarship applications, and (e) we keep records on which scholarships we've applied for and let those inspire us to apply for more.

It's especially important to keep these records because, as I'll cover in chapter 14, your child may one day need to contact these donors and ask whether the scholarship money can keep flowing under certain special educational circumstances.

We want this process solidified in middle school students' minds, so when they are in 9th grade, they'll be ready to (with Mom or Dad's help at first) apply for 10 scholarships every single year throughout both high school and college. A total of 80 scholarship applications or more. Perhaps 20 to 40 *more* scholarship applications if the student goes on to graduate or professional school following college.

The great news is that for a student who fills out 10 scholarship applications every year, the scholarship awards will likely snowball. Every scholarship application includes a section where applicants enter in awards. The applying student should include in that spot the name of every scholarship award he or she has ever received. As this list grows, the student will look more and more like a substantial candidate for future scholarships.

THE GREAT NEWS IS THAT FOR A STUDENT WHO FILLS OUT 10 SCHOLARSHIP APPLICATIONS EVERY YEAR, THE SCHOLARSHIP AWARDS WILL LIKELY SNOWBALL.

Applying for scholarships is well worth your time.

I love to travel and speak to parents and students about how to create stunning, convincing scholarship application essays. Every time I speak on this subject, I hear amazing stories from students afterward. One student used the principles he learned from me to apply for 20 scholarships he thought he'd never get. He won eight of them and walked away with $20,000 extra to help pay his college bills. A mother came up to me and told me that her daughter had used the principles I taught her to apply for a $6,000 scholarship. When she won it, she was stunned to realize that it was renewable for four years! It was actually a $24,000 scholarship! This substantial award motivated this girl to apply for still more scholarships, so she could get the rest of her college paid for through her own effort.

Another high school student told me that he took 20 minutes one Saturday morning to fill out an application for a $3,000 scholarship. (The process was easy and fast for him, because he was able to just copy and paste much of the information from other scholarship applications he'd already filled out.) He won the $3,000 scholarship and is now joking that "I'm only 15, but I once had a job that made me an average of $9,000 an hour!"

Is it possible to apply for too many scholarships?

Maybe you worry that if your son applies for 80 scholarships over eight years, it'll seem like he's greedy. "Geez kid. Leave a few scholarships for some other people!" you imagine people saying. Let me respond to this in four ways.

First, if you're thinking this, you're severely underestimating how many private scholarships are out there and how few students are applying for them. If your son or daughter applies for 80 scholarships, there are still plenty—and I mean plenty—of scholarships left for other people.

Second, you're vastly underestimating how crestfallen scholarship committee members feel when they're handed a thin file contain-

ing only three applications for an important private scholarship. They feel even worse when they open the file and realize that two of the applicants didn't even bother to follow the instructions correctly. Most of the men and women who sit on scholarship committees wish fervently that more students would apply for their scholarships.

Third, you have to remember that there is no national database keeping track of how many scholarships any one student is applying for. If your daughter applies for 80 scholarships, no one will ever know unless she tells them. (She might want to make a point of mentioning this in job interviews, though. Future employers will be thrilled to hear about what a strategic and persistent hard worker she is.)

The final reason that students needn't worry about looking greedy when applying for many scholarships is this: when the average person looks at a list of scholarship awards a student has received, it doesn't usually occur to him or her that the student spent hours filling out applications in order to be considered for those scholarships. Most people imagine that scholarships just magically find their way to high-quality students somehow.

IF YOUR DAUGHTER APPLIES FOR 80 SCHOLARSHIPS, NO ONE WILL EVER KNOW UNLESS SHE TELLS THEM.

I cannot emphasize this enough: people *will not* jump to the conclusion that if you receive a lot of scholarships, something's wrong with you.

Look out for scholarship scams.

One caution for parents as you think about helping your child apply for college scholarships: beware of scholarship *scams.* The College Board reports that every year over 300,000 people are cheated by scholarship scams despite the Federal Trade Commission's best efforts to shut these scams down. If you are considering getting help searching for scholarships, locate the city and state of the headquarters of the organization offering to help you, and then call the Better Business Bureau in that city to see whether the firm has multiple complaints on file.

Be especially suspicious of any verbal or written claims trying to convince your daughter that (a) she's been selected for some vague honor she never applied for, (b) money has been somehow "reserved" for her, or (c) this organization has special, proprietary access to information "you can't get anywhere else." Do not, under any circumstances, *ever* give out your bank account number, credit card information, or Social Security Number so that an organization can "hold scholarship money for you." Reputable scholarship-granting organizations will never ask for your personal financial information.

If you think you may have come in contact with a scholarship scam, I urge you to report it to the U.S. Federal Trade Commission. You can get directly to the web page where the FTC accepts these reports by typing this shortcut into your web browser: Bit.ly/2gz8Hy4.

Remember, if you need help finding scholarships to apply for, I've written a blog post that will help you find 1.5 million of them. This post is free and available to everyone. You can get directly to this post by typing this shortcut into your web browser: Bit.ly/2gbSotu.

[12] *Require that your middle school son or daughter take a college study skills class as early in middle school as possible.*

I know this sounds odd. You're probably thinking, "Why in the world would we have *middle school students* take college study skills classes five to seven years before they're ever going to need them?"

I can understand your skepticism. On the surface, it would seem to make sense to offer college study skills classes to students just before they're going to need them—maybe the summer after they graduate from high school.

My experience tells me, though, that the best time to offer a college study skills class for the first time is when a student is in *middle school.*

Here's why.

First, middle school students tend to feel immensely flattered that someone (it could be a parent, a teacher, or a middle school youth pastor) sees them as so intellectually capable that the topic of college is already coming up. Oh, every student will object initially when an adult first brings up the idea of a class like this, but once the student knows that attending is a nonnegotiable, even a low- to average-achieving middle school student will secretly start to feel an internal glow of pride about it. These students will begin to feel a subtle but distinct shift in how they view themselves and their future. They'll start to see this line item being written into the overarching plan for their lives: "I'm going to college!"

Second, middle school students eagerly devour this kind of material. When they arrive at one of my half-day college study skills classes, it takes only about five minutes until they're sitting up straight on the edges of their chairs, ears and eyes wide open. The minute I finish explaining the importance of taking notes with pen and paper and not with computers, these students are drawing vertical lines down the margins of their papers and taking page after page of detailed notes. When I ask to see the notes they've taken at the end of the class and I marvel and exclaim over them, they swell up with pride. When I explain exactly how to review those notes later to lock in the concepts in as little time as possible, they write down every word I say. I find that middle school students are eager to listen, eager to take notes, eager to review, and eager to implement the strategies later. This presents an opportunity that is just too valuable for us to overlook.

Third, middle school is the best time for us as adults to lock in the skills we most want these students to have in the future. Middle school students' brains are growing at an explosive rate, faster than at any time since infancy.

MIDDLE SCHOOL STUDENTS' BRAINS ARE GROWING AT AN EXPLOSIVE RATE, FASTER THAN AT ANY TIME SINCE INFANCY.

Neural pathways are being pruned and strengthened, and so any experience they have during these years is likely to stick with them for years and years afterward. Often for a lifetime. I want it to be during these years that they are first reached with the message of what it takes to succeed in college.

Fourth, as these middle school students move through the high school years, they'll naturally use these college success principles to succeed in their *high school* classes. They'll be more proficient at passing CLEP and DSST tests, at succeeding in dual enrollment courses in 10th, 11th, and 12th grade, and at winning college scholarships. And when these students eventually hear their college dorm friends talking about ridiculously ineffective study strategies, such as keeping track of due dates in their heads or waiting until the last minute and cramming for exams, they'll look at those friends like they're completely out of their minds. Why? Because students trained and equipped for college success starting in middle school already have a seven-year history of knowing what it *really* takes to succeed in college.

Don't get me wrong; high school and college students should be taking college study skills classes too. No question about it. When they take them, though, I'd like what they hear to be a review and a deepening of concepts they've known and used since 7th grade.

It's unfortunate, but if you give students a college-level study skills class for the first time when they're in high school or in college, they may slouch in their chairs and refuse to take notes because they are just "too cool" to be interested. They "already know" everything. Take it from me: if you really want to lock concepts related to diligence and organization into students' minds, the best time to do it is when they're in middle school. I've spoken to thousands of students over the years, and I'm convinced of it.

COLLEGE READINESS PROGRAMS

Middle school students can get an additional leg up on eventual college confidence and success if they'll plan to attend a high school that has a specifically designed "college readiness program." Many of these programs last an entire academic year or more and have strong, proven track records of equipping students to do well in college. As an added benefit, many colleges offer financial aid packages padded with additional generous, free grant money to students who've successfully completed a college readiness program.

Some of these programs are reserved for students with high levels of need, or for students who are the first in their families to attend college, but it's still worth your while to ask your local high school guidance counselor if your child might be a candidate for one.

HERE'S WHAT TO DO NEXT

Coming up next you'll find a checklist of all 12 of the strategies I've recommended in this chapter. The earlier you start implementing these strategies, the easier this journey will be for you, but remember—*you don't have to use them all.* Work as a team with your child's other parent(s) to select the strategies that seem most useful to your individual family situation right now, and start working on those.

If you're having regularly scheduled parent meetings to talk about implementing

these strategies, come back to this checklist frequently to congratulate yourself on your progress and get more inspiration for additional steps you may be ready to take.

Finally, as we close this chapter, let me encourage you. No matter your current family situation or income level, you are doing something truly great for your children (and for their children and grandchildren as well) by thinking through and working on the to-do items in this book. When you use wise strategies to build a child's future education, career, and financial foundation, you're building something that will likely outlast you. You're building something that has the potential to bear fruit for 100 years after you're gone. I hope this encourages you that time spent on each of the checklists in this book is *time well spent.*

CHECKLIST

7th Grade or Earlier

1. Model the joys of living a frugal life.

2. Ask close relatives to reconsider gift giving. (Remember to read and share the free online bonus content I have provided on this subject at JeannieBurlowski.com/LAUNCH.)

3. Open a Upromise account, but be careful as you do so.

4. Schedule monthly meetings where you take steps to make your personal financial situation more stable.

5. Provide for your own retirement every single month.

6. Start a college savings plan as soon as you've achieved the above goals.

7. Plan and save for an expensive college, but be completely OK with a less expensive one.

8. Help your child find opportunities to serve others in a focused and consistent way.

9. Read (or listen to) the book *Parenting Teens With Love and Logic.*

10. Empower your middle school child to manage all of his own household chores and schoolwork.

11. Help your middle school child to apply for at least one college scholarship.

12. Require your middle school child to take a college study skills class.

13. Check my book updates page at JeannieBurlowski.com/LAUNCH to see if I have made any recent updates to this chapter.

14. Always consult your financial planning professional before making any big financial decisions.

15. Make a note in your calendar to come back and read the next chapter of this book when your child is in May of 8th grade.

Be the first to hear about updates to the material in this book by reading my free weekly email newsletter every week. Anyone can subscribe to it at any time at JeannieBurlowski.com.

Section 2
8th and 9th Grades

4 | *May of 8th Grade*

Congratulations on getting your child to May of 8th grade!

I hope you're benefitting greatly from chapter 3, "7th Grade or Earlier." It's time now to go ahead with additional tasks that will help you raise a child who graduates from college in under four years, remains debt-free, and moves directly into a career he or she excels at and loves.

HOW TO USE THIS CHAPTER

Start by just reading through this chapter. As you read, don't worry about committing to any of it. Decision time will come at the end of this chapter, when I give you a clear, at-a-glance checklist of every task I'm suggesting you consider right now.

Remember, you won't have to use every strategy I suggest; just choose the ones you think will work for your family and either modify or discard the rest.

PLAN A SPECIAL DINNER OR AN OVERNIGHT GETAWAY

Early in the summer after 8th grade, you as a parent will have some very important topics to discuss with your son or daughter.

These things are so important that I suggest you create a contract-like document, print the document out, and have parents, step-parents, and the child sign and date it. Then, post the document on the inside of a kitchen cupboard door so the entire family can see and refer to it frequently.

Right now, in May of 8th grade, let's plan ahead so you can make this document signing part of a much anticipated "right-of-passage" event. It could be a special sibling-free dinner, or it could be an overnight getaway for just the former 8th grader and his parents. Select a date for this event and put it on your calendar now.

So you can prepare ahead for this special event, let me explain in depth the six topics I suggest you cover during this meeting. Once I've explained these topics to you, I'll summarize them in a written contract-like document that you can download from my website and then tweak and modify for your individual family situation.

Note that if your child has an IEP or is under the care of a medical professional or therapist, show this chapter to that person before implementing these ideas.

Parent, here are the six topics I suggest you discuss with your child in this upcoming meeting.

[1] *YOUR LIVING SITUATION AFTER HIGH SCHOOL GRADUATION*

Imagine saying this: "Honey, let's talk about what your living situation is going to look like starting the day after your high school graduation—which is just four years from now."

Mom and Dad, I know you've heard the horror stories. You've heard of loving mothers and fathers who sacrifice for years only to find themselves in their 50s, stressed and anxious over unkempt 20-something children still living in their childhood bedrooms, sleeping in past noon, helping themselves to food from their parents' refrigerators, and then staying up long hours into each night gazing into the flickering blue screens of online video games. You know that there are hundreds of thousands of parents living this nightmare every day, right?

What are you going to do to avoid becoming that parent?

What are you going to do to help your daughter feel excited and eager to do well in high school? How will you motivate her to want to jump immediately into college or technical school, and then once there organize herself

and study strategically so she succeeds at it and graduates in the minimum amount of time possible? What's your plan for enhancing the possibility that she'll move from college or technical school directly into a career she excels at and loves?

Part of this will happen naturally two years from now, when you take some practical steps to help her figure out a career goal that makes perfect sense for her. (Chapter 13 explains this in detail.) When your daughter has just finished 8th grade, though, how can you light a fire under her that makes her eager to one day leave her childhood home behind, move into her own place, and start successfully supporting herself?

Some children will naturally do this without any prodding or firm boundaries or encouragement from anyone. But some children will not. And you never know for sure which child you have until they're 30 years old and the entire story of their 20s has been written.

Parent, you stand a much better chance of achieving your goal of independence for your adult child if you take time *now* to clearly articulate the following things concerning the living situation for any high school graduate living in your house.

"Living in our home is tied to job training."

Imagine telling your child this: "Jason, we'll be happy to provide you with free room and board after your high school graduation, as long as you are enrolled in (and making successful progress through) a full-time academic or job-training program."

If your son has committed to attend a certain technical school, college, or university by signing the necessary paperwork in early May of his senior year of high school (which is the customary way to commit to a college), he may live with you rent-free until classes begin the following fall. After that he may continue to live with you rent-free during school breaks as long as he remains enrolled in a full-time academic or job-training program.

> **WE'LL PROVIDE YOU WITH FREE ROOM AND BOARD AFTER YOUR HIGH SCHOOL GRADUATION, AS LONG AS YOU'RE ENROLLED IN A FULL-TIME ACADEMIC OR JOB-TRAINING PROGRAM.**

"Don't want college or job training? Here's the plan."

Imagine explaining to your son that if he decides at any point to *stop* being enrolled in a full-time academic or job-training program, he can still live with you under the following conditions:

» He works at a job that he finds himself, covers all of his own expenses, and pays you, his parents, fair market rent.

Tell your 8th grader plainly that if he decides he's just not interested in college or job training after high school, you will expect him to pay you rent at a rate equivalent to the market rate typically charged for a one-bedroom apartment in your city.

In the Minneapolis area, this rental fee would be $935 per month as of this writing; in the Chicago area it would be $1,692 per month. Calculate now how much a one-bedroom apartment costs in your state on average, so that your 8th grader can plan ahead. If you live in Chicago and he plans not to be serious about college or technical school, he'll have to work 51 hours a week at the Illinois minimum wage in order to afford that rent.

» He provides his own transportation.

This could be a bike or a bus pass, or it could be car payments, gas, insurance, and all necessary auto maintenance on whatever kind of car he'd like. It's up to him.

» He lives under your family's house rules.

Tell your son that you'll expect him to cheerfully help with grocery shopping, meal preparation, and an adult level of household chores. He will need to keep his room clean, come home each night by 11:00 p.m. or else call you so you won't worry, and he will have no overnight guests without prior permission.

"Wait—kids aren't going to want that!"

"Are you kidding?" I can hear some parents bellowing. "What 18- to 24-year-old kid is going to want to live under those conditions?"

Exactly.

Our goal is to treat our children with tender love at every point in their growing-up journeys, but at the same time make Mom and Dad's soft, padded nest just uncomfortable enough that the little birds can't wait to fly.

"What if our child refuses to comply?"

Just to make sure we've got recourse if a child chooses not to comply with these very reasonable requests, let's add this:

"Son, if you choose not to honor these boundaries, we'll give you four kind warnings, spaced one week apart. If, after four warnings, you're still not in compliance with these rules, we'll kindly pack your belongings in cardboard boxes, place them at the end of our driveway, and change the locks on the doors of our house."

Does this sound drastic? Yes, it does. It sounds firm and final. Exactly what we want in your child's mind as he makes his choices, plans, and decisions during the next eight years of his life.

[2] *HOW YOU'LL PAY FOR YOUR COLLEGE OR JOB TRAINING*

Imagine saying this: "Sweetheart, let me clarify that it's *your* job, not ours, to pay for all of your own schooling after high school. However, if you'll let us, we'd like to help you find clever ways to get these costs reduced way, way down."

Explain to your daughter that over the next eight years, people are going to be looking at her and deciding whether they should give her *free money to help her pay for college.* Some of these people will be on committees handing out private scholarships, and some of these people will be officers in her college's admissions offices who will look at her as an individual and decide whether to

give her tuition discounts and free money merit aid.

How can students can get free money to help pay for college?

When a student applies to college, each college's admissions office will likely give that student an "admissions ranking" of one, two, three, four, or five. If the student can do some simple things during high school to boost her admissions ranking from a two to a four, that can greatly increase the tuition discounts, free money merit aid, and financial aid that this school will give her if she attends there.

Explain to your daughter that there are five main ways to make scholarship committees and college admissions and financial aid officers feel excited about giving her free money.

» Get decent grades in high school.

We're not talking straight A's here; we're talking about consistently organizing herself and trying hard so she's maintaining a respectable level of academic proficiency. Millions of dollars in tuition discounts, merit aid, and academic scholarships are given out to kids who are not straight-A students. She must never, ever, write herself off as "not a candidate for free college money" because she thinks she isn't smart enough. The important thing is to consistently, every school year, organize herself and *really try.* Any student, no matter his or her level of natural intelligence, can do this.

» Show commitment over the long term to a cause that helps the world in some way.

No scholarship committee or college financial aid officer wants to give free money to selfish children who spend their lives lavishing the resources of the world on themselves.

But these people love to give money to students who have hearts that break for injustice, to students who move with consistency toward a cause they care deeply about, to students who invest their time, their money, and the energy of their lives into helping others. Parent, I want you to place the expectation on your child that she will identify the cause she wants to work for early on, and step up and be this person.

SHOW COMMITMENT OVER THE LONG TERM TO A CAUSE THAT HELPS THE WORLD IN SOME WAY.

Let your daughter know that you want her to start thinking now of an injustice in this world that she has the power to help correct. She doesn't have to do this work alone. She can team up with others who care about this cause—including you, her parent. Let her know you'll be the first to come alongside her and support her as she works on behalf of this cause.

I must emphasize this: *it's completely OK if her heart doesn't break for any cause right now.* What we want is for her to start by selecting a cause *out of obligation.* Just because *it's the right thing to do.* If she does this, and if she will then begin working on behalf of this cause, I promise—the caring and the broken heart will follow.

To help her decide her cause, I suggest that in the early part of summer following 8th grade, your family use the Internet to create a list of what you believe to be some of the greatest injustices of our time. Be sure to include on the list injustices that have affected someone you know of or someone you love, but also include injustices you've only just heard about.

Start with human trafficking, hunger, homelessness, children with special needs, people in prison, families of people in prison, issues related to life-threatening food allergies, environmental issues, and international issues such as lack of health care, families in refugee camps, kids not being able to attend school because of not having shoes, people persecuted for their faith, poverty that can be corrected with micro-loans through organizations such as Kiva.org, women being raped while walking miles each day to get clean water, and disaster relief. Watch Gary Haugen's gripping, inspiring TED talk about the International Justice Mission by typing this shortcut into your web browser: Bit.ly/2gvA4fW, and have your daughter consider *that* being the cause she fights for. Don't stop there, though. Have your family make its own list, with each item on it more specific than the last. Then think about the list. If you are a person of faith, pray about the list. And then choose a cause to work for.

I want your daughter to select one cause from this list, and then work on behalf of it in some way starting the summer after 8th grade, and then to one degree or another every single year throughout her entire high school career. This does not have to take a tremendous number of hours. If she does this (keeping track of what she does and when), then when the time comes for her to apply for scholarship awards and free money merit aid—believe me—she will be an absolute standout.

As a side note, I strongly recommend that although the cause she chooses may have a faith element to it, the cause should not be a predominantly religious one. Instead, it should be primarily humanitarian in nature, helping the desperate needs of real people, perhaps with faith-building woven in as a part of that cause. Why is this?

The reason is that most likely, your child's volunteer and service résumé is going to one day be evaluated by scholarship and admissions committee staff who don't understand authentic life-changing faith and how it truly helps people. These committee members may interpret religious service ("I did 95 percent of my volunteer work at my church" or "I spent hundreds of hours knocking on doors and distributing literature") not as service to the world, but as doing something for one's self or for one's own faith family. Please *do* continue to volunteer at church, but remember—almost every faith on earth calls us to also reach out beyond our walls and help a world in great need. Let your child know: you want that part of her faith to be most evident as she chooses the cause she will be a part of throughout high school and college.

It's the students who've done consistent and caring humanitarian service over time who are awarded the largest amounts of free college money. When that finally happens to your daughter, though, it won't be the money that matters to her anymore. It will be the character and the quality of heart she's developed over four years of caring about someone besides herself—that's what will be most valuable to her.

» Show long-term, focused commitment to one main nonacademic activity.

College is all about working hard over four years to develop skill, ability, insight, and leadership on a certain subject (a "major"), right?

The greatest scholarship and merit awards tend to go to students who prove throughout their high school years that they already have the ability to concentrate on a topic and develop skill, ability, insight, and leadership in it over a long stretch of time.

What we want is for your son to demonstrate that he has the character to stick with an activity, keeping at it until it builds something of worth within him over a period of years.

What can your son do to prove he has this capability?

> **IT'S THE STUDENTS WHO'VE DONE CONSISTENT AND CARING HUMANITARIAN SERVICE OVER TIME WHO ARE AWARDED THE LARGEST AMOUNTS OF FREE COLLEGE MONEY. WHEN THAT FINALLY HAPPENS TO YOUR SON, THOUGH, IT WON'T BE THE MONEY THAT MATTERS TO HIM ANYMORE.**

One of the best ways is for him to take some time prior to 9th grade to look carefully at his school's list of extracurricular activities. Ask him to mark all the activities he would love to do if time were not an issue. (If it's unclear what some of the activities on the list are, have him call the school office and ask.) Then, when he's carefully considered all the options, ask him to narrow that list down to his top two or three favorites. Ask him to attend meetings for these two or three activities and start participating in them, singling out one he likes so much that he could participate in it for all four years of high school.

What activity might he genuinely like well enough to tackle at this advanced level?

Marching band? Choir? Speech team? Debate? Creative writing? Math team? Mock trial? Peer leadership? School newspaper or yearbook? Robotics competitions? Theater? Spanish or French club?

He can be involved in as many sporadic "here-and-there" activities as he genuinely wants to be, sure, fine. But I want him to choose one special activity and stick with it—every year of high school—moving into greater and greater levels of skill, responsibility, and leadership within it. That will be tremendously impressive to the people who hand out the free money for college. And it will also build something of value within him that he could never get by hopping like a frog from lily pad to lily pad of frantic and scattered high school activity.

"Wait, wait, wait," I can just hear parents, teachers, and guidance counselors objecting, waving their hands to stop me from saying this. "Jeannie, surely this isn't true. I've always heard that colleges and scholar-

ship committees are looking for kids who are 'well rounded'—kids who do a little bit of everything (or a whole lot of everything) rather than doing one thing with any kind of depth. Isn't this true? Aren't the high-end college admissions, and the scholarship money, and the merit aid money going to insanely busy, perennially exhausted students who run themselves ragged for four years doing it all?"

My first response to this question is, "Do you know how many students in the United States fall into the category you've just described? Hyper-busy, exhausted kids, desperately packing their résumés with hundreds of activities they don't care about in futile attempts to impress people they're never going to actually meet? U.S. colleges and universities can pack their freshman classes a hundred times over with students like these. Exhausted, overcommitted students are ordinary. They're unremarkable. They're run-of-the-mill. Their college applications are yawners. Here's the truth: it's the student who's taken at least one thing and gone after it with depth and passion and commitment who's going to stand out from the crowd like a superstar and impress everyone."

Here's another way to think about this. College admissions committees rifling through piles of college applications are trying to build an interesting, well-rounded *class*, not just attract another well-rounded *applicant*. College admissions people are looking for a few bright intellectual stars for every department, some talented actors, musicians, and artists, a few exceptional athletes, a handful of wealthy kids whose parents can fund the construction of the new science building, *and* kids just like yours who are marked by long-term commitment to seemingly ordinary things like marching band, speech team, debate, school newspaper, yearbook, Spanish club, theater, and robotics. When it comes to this kind of very interesting student, the admissions committee may very well send an email to the college financial aid office that says, *"Do whatever you have to do to get this kid here."*

EXHAUSTED, OVERCOMMITTED STUDENTS ARE ORDINARY. THEY'RE UNREMARKABLE. THEY'RE RUN-OF-THE-MILL. THEIR COLLEGE APPLICATIONS ARE YAWNERS. HERE'S THE TRUTH: IT'S THE STUDENT WHO'S TAKEN AT LEAST ONE THING AND GONE AFTER IT WITH DEPTH AND PASSION AND COMMITMENT WHO'S GOING TO STAND OUT FROM THE CROWD LIKE A SUPERSTAR AND IMPRESS EVERYONE.

The college applicant who looks vaguely nice on paper but is not really special in any one category is going to have a much harder time making a great impression. The applicant who *stands out* in one of these areas will have a much easier time getting free money merit aid from the college to help cover college costs.

One important caution here: I strongly suggest that students not choose sports as their one "long-term, committed, focused nonacademic activity."

It's OK for your daughter to play sports if she truly enjoys it, but I urge you: don't in any way look at sports as your child's ticket to a free college education. Contrary to popular belief, college sports scholarships are incredibly difficult to get and even harder to keep. Many collegiate athletes find that the inordinately demanding schedule of athletic practices, travel, and games can make it nearly impossible to succeed at college academic work. Plus, if your daughter sustains a career-ending sports injury (all too common in college sports due to overuse), her involvement in the sport will end abruptly and so will the flow of scholarship money. I strongly suggest that your child focus on a nonathletic activity as her one special "long-term, committed, focused, nonacademic activity." If she wants to play sports in college, great. Many successful college students I know join college-level intramural "club" sports teams, and in doing so enjoy all the fun of their sport without intense and highly pressured practice, travel, and game schedules.

Ask your child to take some time to decide: "What will be the non-sports extracurricular activity I'll throw myself into with all my heart—and try to stick with for all four years of high school?"

» Keep careful track of it all.

In the consulting work I do with medical school applicants at GetIntoMedSchool.com, I'm continually astounded at how few premed high school and college students keep records on the volunteer and service work they've completed. Pre-med students are some of the most driven, high-achieving students on the planet, and they usually know how critically important clinical volunteer work is for a competitive med school application. Yet they will shadow or volunteer for hundreds (or thousands) of hours and never record the dates and hours they put in, who supervised them, or what they saw and experienced. When I'm working with these students, we have to work with sketchy clues to piece all of that together, and it's a lot of work.

What I'd prefer is that all students (no matter their ages, majors, or career goals—even students as young as age 14) set up profiles on LinkedIn.com where they keep track of all of their accomplishments, achievements, work experiences, school and scouting awards, scholarship awards, job-shadowing experiences, and volunteer service hours and experiences.

The best time to set up an account on LinkedIn? The summer after 8th grade, with a parent's direct help. The best time to update it? Regularly over the years that follow—every time there's an additional hour of volunteer work to add.

Yes, I know that this student is not yet even in high school. Yes, I know that the job title will read something like: "Quinn Ackerman, 9th-Grade Student, John Marshall High School." Yes, I know there will not be much work experience to put on it. That is completely OK. Help your child to create this LinkedIn profile now, this summer, and then sit down with your child regularly throughout high school and college to check the profile over and make sure it's updated.

I wish I didn't have to say this, but parental involvement is absolutely necessary if a student between the ages of 14 and 22 is to create and regularly maintain a detailed LinkedIn profile. Because of where adolescents are in regard to brain development, even the most

high-achieving student under age 22 is not likely to either create this profile or keep it updated, unless a parent leads the way by (a) setting aside the time, (b) sitting the student down, (c) completing the log-in process, and (d) scrolling through and asking questions about what might be added.

Why are students so unlikely to do this on their own? One reason is that students tend to feel as though anything they have to offer is not "interesting enough." They feel niggling fear and worry that their little accomplishment is pale and puny compared to what other students have accomplished.

Students' inability to see the value in what they've accomplished is a huge reason families hire a consultant to help students apply to law, medical, business, or grad school. I spend vast amounts of time every day telling highly accomplished, brilliant college students that indeed, what they've done is excellent and well worth putting on a med school application. Why can't they see this for themselves? I think it's because they're like barbers trying to cut the hair on the backs of their own heads. They're just too close to their own situations to be able to see what I can see so clearly.

The little things entered on a LinkedIn profile really do add up. The profile becomes more and more impressive as the years go by. The information entered on your child's LinkedIn profile over time is a gold mine, making it easier and easier to fill out scholarship applications, college applications, and even eventual medical or grad school applications.

Plus, having an updated presence on Linked

In helps your child with one other very important mission as well.

> **THE INFORMATION ENTERED ON YOUR CHILD'S LINKEDIN PROFILE OVER TIME IS A GOLD MINE, MAKING IT EASIER AND EASIER TO FILL OUT SCHOLARSHIP APPLICATIONS, COLLEGE APPLICATIONS, AND EVEN EVENTUAL MEDICAL OR GRAD SCHOOL APPLICATIONS.**

» Connect to those in authority in such a way that you can locate them later.

In years to come, your child is going to need letters of recommendation and personal connections to move forward through college and career life. Where will these connections come from? Most students look mainly to teachers and guidance counselors. I encourage your family to get much more creative than that.

Do you realize that every day since your son was a toddler, he's been bumping into and forming relationships with professional people who have careers in many different sectors of the job market?

Your son or daughter may already know a VP for the Target Corporation, a top five technology company software engineer, or the owner of a successful home building company, and you don't even realize it. Who are these people? They're your friends, Mom. They're your golfing buddies, Dad. And as your child has grown into late elementary school and middle school, he's made even more professional contacts: his friends' parents, his volunteer sports coaches, and the adults who lead his Scout troop and chaperone his church youth group retreats. All of these adults have professional identities outside of their child-rearing, their volunteer sports coaching, their Scout leading, and their church youth group volunteering. Your son or daughter can connect to all of these people, creating lifelong valuable contacts with them on LinkedIn.

Parent, every time you sit down with your daughter to help her update her LinkedIn profile, see if there are more adults she might know personally she can link to. Here are her top two most outstanding resources for this: (1) her *parents' friends* and (2) her *friends' parents.*

As your daughter gets older, she'll add teachers, college professors, those with whom she did research, fellow high school and college students, and colleagues she's worked alongside at volunteer and paid positions. Any one of these connections could one day turn into a future employment connection.

Just imagine the day your son is looking for a serious professional paid summer internship in January of his sophomore year in college, and he uses LinkedIn to send this message to a powerful VP at a top-five software company: "Hi, this is Quinn Ackerman, and I used to play baseball with your son, Jake, when I was in middle school. I'm at the University of Illinois, Urbana-Champaign working on a computer engineering degree now, and I'm wondering if you might possibly be able to help me get connected to a great internship at your company for this next summer."

Genius. Sheer, unadulterated genius.

Very few students are doing this, folks. If you're reading this book, you have a phenomenal opportunity to start very early to set your child up for every kind of career success.

Make creating the LinkedIn profile one of your priorities for the summer after 8th grade.

[3] *HOW YOU'LL GET MONEY FROM US TO PAY FOR COLLEGE OR JOB TRAINING*

Imagine saying this: "Honey, we've got a little bit of money we've been saving in an account to help pay for your college. We want to tell you right now what you'll need to do to get that money from us."

Explain to your child that shockingly, some college students don't grasp what an incredible privilege a college education is.

Sadly, there are some students on every college campus who allow their parents to sweat and scrape and sacrifice and save to pay high college bills, but then the students don't even care enough about this gift to get up and go to class in the morning.

Some of these uncaring students don't even bother to organize themselves so they've got a reliable system for getting their work done on time and in a quality manner. Some of these students even choose to drink themselves into oblivion rather than making sure they've got their test material mastered and their papers ready to hand in.

Explain to your child that if you were the parent of one of these kids, you would not want to pay one penny for their college.

That would be understandable, right?

Explain that if your son or daughter is working hard and succeeding at college, you want to get behind that and do all you can to help pay for it. But if your son or daughter is making rotten choices and washing out academically, you'd like that to be on their dime.

Explain that you'd like your child to have some "skin in the game" every single semester that he is in college.

Try saying this: "Jason, if you'd like us to chip in money for any of your college or job training, we'd like to ask you for something in return. We'd like to ask you to give us a $1,000 deposit out of your own money at the beginning of each semester that we help you.

"At the end of each semester, you log us into the computer and show us the official record of the grades you earned. If your college grades are mostly A's with maybe one B, we'll return that $1,000 deposit to you—and you can put that same money on deposit with us for the following semester. If your grades *aren't* at that kind of high level, though, we'll keep your $1,000 deposit and you can dig into your savings and come up with another $1,000 deposit as security for us for the following semester. If you play your cards right, you'll be able to make it all the way through four years of college on just one deposit and get your $1,000 back permanently once you graduate. But if you have a few bad semesters and have to fork over three or four $1,000 deposits to us, that won't be so bad. Because

$4,000 of your own money is a small price to pay for a $160,000 college education!

"Jason, this will not be that difficult for you. You'll tackle college seriously, you'll organize yourself, you'll follow each professor's directions exactly, and you'll seek out the professor's help or get one-on-one tutoring the minute you start to get stuck on anything. We have every confidence that you can do this."

[4] *SAVING AND INVESTING MONEY IS EXCITING*

Researchers tell us that the brains of middle school students are growing at an explosive rate, faster than at any time since infancy. New connections are being formed, less-used pathways in the brain are being pruned away, and new experiences are imprinting deeply, vividly, in ways that will not be forgotten even in adulthood and old age. For this reason, May of 8th grade is a prime time to have a conversation with your child that brings to life ideas about earning, budgeting, saving, and investing money.

Imagine saying this: "Honey, it's our goal to give you a true adult understanding of how money works, so we want to tell you about something we think is really exciting. It's called the Roth IRA."

THE BRAINS OF MIDDLE SCHOOL STUDENTS ARE GROWING AT AN EXPLOSIVE RATE, FASTER THAN AT ANY TIME SINCE INFANCY.

I can just hear the chorus of parental objections now. "Really, Jeannie? The Roth IRA? Shouldn't we start by lecturing our son about his responsibility to pay for college and push him to mow lawns to fatten up his college fund?"

My answer to this is, ah, no.

Let's just look for a moment at how effective that would be.

It's utterly discouraging to a teenager to spend a hot, sweaty afternoon mowing and trimming lawns, only to realize that he'd have to spend 3,600 afternoons just like that one to pay for just one year of college tuition and living expenses at NYU. (He's had his middle school math classes; he's got the quantitative ability to figure this out.) If afternoon lawn mowing were going to get a kid through four years of a college like NYU, he'd need over 14,400 afternoons of it, which would take him about 39 years.

This is demoralizing, it's paralyzing, and it makes a kid not want to work at all.

Let's not start there.

Instead, I suggest you start by telling your son that you have an ingenious idea for how he can make over $60,000—and get to spend it on himself rather than on taxes or college bills.

That should get his attention.

Start out by giving your son a thumbnail sketch of how paying for college actually works. In October of his senior year of high school, colleges are going to take a small snapshot of how much money your family has. They're going to look mainly at (a) parent and student income earned during the year stretching from January 1 of his sophomore year of high school to December 31 of his junior year of high school and (b) the sum total of your family's assets (including savings accounts) on the day you fill out financial aid forms. From that information, a decision is going to be made about how much your family can probably afford to pay for college. Whatever it's determined that your family *can't* pay, colleges will try to come up with a plan for covering. Their plan, though, will most likely include a lot of loans that your family *doesn't want.*

START BY TELLING YOUR SON THAT YOU HAVE AN INGENIOUS IDEA FOR HOW HE CAN MAKE OVER $60,000—AND GET TO SPEND IT ON HIMSELF RATHER THAN ON TAXES OR COLLEGE BILLS.

Then lean in, look your son in the eye, and tell him, "Son, they're going to be looking at all of Mom and Dad's money, and they're going to figure that we can fork out about 5.64 percent of almost everything we have to pay for your college." Then lean in even closer toward your son and drop the bomb. "But when it comes to your money, son, they're going to ask you to fork over almost all of the money you've saved up. They'll figure it's only fair for you to use that money to pay your own college bills. Are you excited about that?"

(He obviously will not be.)

Then continue. Tell him that there is a safe, legal, ethical place for him to put his money, so no one will come after it and try to get him to use it to pay college bills.

It's called a Roth IRA.

Explain that starting right now, your son has a golden opportunity to make himself a boatload of money by putting a little money each year into a Roth IRA account.

This is a great opportunity for your son for three reasons.

First, anything your son puts into a Roth IRA by the day of filling out financial aid forms (on or about October 1 of his senior year of high school) will be safely and legally squirreled away—and no one will ask him to use it to pay college bills.

Second, after at least five years go by—if your son chooses to—he'll be able to take up to $10,000 (tax-free and penalty-free) out of his Roth IRA and use it toward a down payment on a house. If he puts money into a Roth IRA by age 15, he could be pulling it out for a down payment on a house as early as age 20! And if he has the good luck to marry someone who also had this same idea? The two of them would have double the amount of money to use toward a down payment on their first home—by their early 20s.

Third (and perhaps most exciting), if your son chooses to leave the money in the Roth IRA, it will be invested, enjoy the happy miracle of compound interest, and grow and grow, until finally when your son is between 60 and 65 years old, he'll have an astounding chunk of money to pull out tax-free and spend in any way he wants to.

To illustrate this and make it real, sit down with your son and go to the Bankrate's Roth IRA earnings calculator on the Internet. You can get directly to it by typing this shortcut into your web browser: Bit.ly/2eUPRow.

Use the little form provided to run a few "what if" scenarios. What if your son found ways to earn and sock away $500 each summer from now until he begins 10th grade, and about $100 per month during each month he's in school during that time? It would amount to about $2,300 total. But if he put that money into Roth IRA contributions, just look at how much money he could have at age 65.

Run the figures in the little form on the Bankrate IRA calculator and let him see it on the screen with his own eyes: if his account earns 7 percent interest, he could have $69,607, tax-free, at age 65. Far *more* money if he continues this strategy from 10th grade until the day before you and he fill out financial aid forms in early October of 12th grade.

Then hand him the smartphone and let him play with the numbers. What would happen if he worked just a little harder and invested $3,000 in a Roth IRA when he was 15 years old? Even if he never put in another penny in his life, which is unlikely, he would have more than $82,500 (tax-free) at age 65.

Sit there for just a moment and let that sink in. This moment could be life changing for your teen.

Conclude by saying, "Son, we are so proud of you—you're going to be taking a huge step toward adulthood this summer: thinking about finding work, working hard, saving for the future! This is one of the most grown-up things you can possibly do. We want to help you as much as possible with this. So tell you what. When you're ready, we'll help you research and come up with some interesting ways you can earn money this summer.

"We'll also get you started keeping careful records of exactly what you earned and how you earned it, because you can only put money into a Roth IRA if you've earned that amount of money yourself. And you know what's super cool about this whole concept? Someday you'll be able to write essays that tell colleges all about your savings and investments. And you know what they might say? 'Wow; this kid's amazing! We've got to have him here. Let's give him an extra $20,000 to pay his college bills if he'll agree to come to our school!'"

As you read this, parent, do you find yourself concerned that your family might make too much money for you to be allowed to have a Roth IRA? Don't worry. No matter how high your household income, your child can still have a Roth IRA—as long as he can prove that his own earned income is going into it. This proof can come from official W-2s, or it can come from keeping track of photos of the checks and cash that people give your child for babysitting and raking leaves. (I'll provide a method for keeping track of this information later in this chapter.) Don't miss this opportunity to teach your child about strategically building wealth through disciplined earning, saving, and investing. Vanguard,

Charles Schwab, E*Trade, Scottrade, T. Rowe Price, and TD Ameritrade all allow minor children to open Roth IRA accounts. Charles Schwab in particular allows minor children to open Roth IRA accounts with as little as $100.

"Nice idea, but my kid doesn't want to save any money."

I understand. To increase your child's desire to save money, you might offer to "match" the money your child earns and saves in a Roth IRA. One way to accomplish this is to capitalize on your child's desire to own a car.

Rather than just buying a car for your son and handing him the keys, imagine saying, "Joe, I'll tell you what. For every $10 you earn and put into a fund to buy yourself a car, I'll also put $10 into that fund to help you buy your car. Plus, I'll go one step further than that. For every $10 you earn and save up to buy yourself a car between now and October 1 of 12th grade, I'll also send an additional $10 to Schwab for your Roth IRA. How does this sound? You work hard next Saturday and earn whatever money you can for your car fund, and when you come home that night and show me what you've earned and put into car savings, I'll put that same amount of money into your car fund, and that same amount of money again into your Roth IRA. What do you think?"

This IRA contribution strategy works for one main reason: it doesn't matter who puts money into a child's Roth IRA, as long as the total amount put into it is (a) equal to or less than the amount the child earned in that year and (b) under $5,500 per year (as of this writing).

> **FOR EVERY $10 YOU EARN AND PUT INTO A FUND TO BUY YOURSELF A CAR, I'LL ALSO PUT $10 INTO THAT FUND TO HELP YOU BUY YOUR CAR.**

And if your child doesn't want to save for a car and insists on blowing 100 percent of the money he or she earns on movies and pizza?

You as a parent *can* choose to match your child's earnings and simply make the IRA contribution yourself. For example, if your daughter earns $2,000 at a summer job and blows it all before she starts school the following fall, you as her parent are allowed to make her $2,000 IRA contribution with your own money. The IRS doesn't care who actually *makes* the Roth IRA contribution, as long as it doesn't amount to more than your child's "earned income for the year." (Be aware, though, that when you put your money into your child's Roth IRA, it's *your child* who receives any tax deduction—not you.)

To accomplish all this, you'll need to keep careful records on what your child earns, right down to recording photos of the cash paid to him or her by neighbors who hand over a $10 bill in exchange for snow shoveling. One great way to do this is to use Evernote, a highly recommended cross-platform app that organizes your notes and photos and then archives them in a way that's instantly searchable. If you've never used Evernote before, google "beginners guide Evernote." You'll find many helpful posts and videos on how to get started. I suggest you start by creating one virtual "notebook" in Evernote that you label "[Child's Name]'s Earned Income." It'll be easy and fast for you to add a photo or a note to this "notebook" every time this child earns more money.

If you can afford it, the matching plan I've described can work well on many fronts. One reason it's helpful is that it's beneficial for you to stash as much of your "cash on hand" as possible into retirement accounts before October 1 of your child's senior year of high school. Your child's Roth IRA account is a great place for you to do this.

And what if your daughter doesn't save up enough money to buy herself a car even with your matching program, but you still need her to drive herself back and forth to school? I suggest that you enthusiastically buy an ugly but reliable used car for yourself. (The uglier the car, the more your daughter will feel the natural consequence of not working harder so she could drive a nicer car.) Make it clear that you are the sole owner of this car, and leave it sitting in the grass to the left of your garage at all times unless it's ferrying a child somewhere you believe it's absolutely necessary for that child to be.

Some parents at this point will ask me, "What if we want to put additional money into our child's Roth IRA *after* October 1 of 12th grade?" You can do that. It's a good idea. The key thing to remember is to put the money into your child's Roth IRA account on the most ideal date each year. Because you will be filling out financial aid forms on or about October 1 every year that you have a child in college the following fall, the most ideal dates to make large contributions to your teen's Roth IRA account will be

»   late September of the senior year of high school

»   late September of the freshman year of college

»   late September of the sophomore year of college

»   late September of the junior year of college

These are the ideal dates because you'll be emptying family savings accounts and safely squirreling money away where it won't be scrutinized for financial aid purposes just days before filling out financial aid forms each October 1.

"Can I hire my child and put the income I pay her into her Roth IRA?"

Yes, you can, but employing a child beyond the "help around the house" level can get complicated when it comes to filing and paying taxes.

It will generally *not* work to simply hire your child as an independent contractor and try to slide through by issuing her a 1099 form by January 31 of the following year.

If you're seriously considering hiring your child, read through the valuable online information the A/N Group provides on this subject. You can get directly to it by typing this shortcut into your web browser: Bit.ly/2fS3DoR. I like this resource because it's updated every day, Monday through Friday. After you've read it, talk with your own certified public accountant about the tax implications of employing your child.[7]

[5] *WHAT ADULT LIFE AFTER AGE 18 ACTUALLY COSTS*

Try saying this: "One of the things Mom and I want to do for you is give you a good idea of what adult life actually costs. This will help you as you're planning for your future."

Prior to the age of 22, most students haven't the vaguest idea of what adult life actually costs. To a high school or college student, $24,000 a year seems like unbelievable riches. Your child likely believes that he or she will be able to live in high style on that income and have no trouble affording debt.

Help your daughter to see exactly how much it will *actually take* to live the lifestyle she'd like to have someday. Get out your computer and go to the outstanding reality check tool provided by the Jumpstart Coalition for Personal Financial Literacy. You can get directly to it by typing this shortcut into your web browser: Bit.ly/2fC5sVu.

> **TO A HIGH SCHOOL OR COLLEGE STUDENT, $24,000 A YEAR SEEMS LIKE UNBELIEVABLE RICHES. YOUR CHILD LIKELY BELIEVES THAT HE OR SHE WILL BE ABLE TO LIVE IN HIGH STYLE ON THAT INCOME AND HAVE NO TROUBLE AFFORDING DEBT.**

Using the one-page tool on this website, help your daughter to check off (a) the living situation she'd most like after college; (b) the kind of car she'd like to drive someday; (c) what she plans for her cell phone, Internet, cable TV, travel, and restaurant budgets to look like; and (d) 28 other financial obligations related to adult life. Then, with one click, get a "reality check" telling your daughter what kind of income and career will be necessary for her to achieve this lifestyle.

This is an outstanding exercise for families, churches, and schools to do with students. I recommend it highly.

[6] *USE OF DRUGS AND ALCOHOL*

Imagine saying this: "As we wrap all this up, we want to have a clear, caring talk with you on the topic of drug and alcohol use. This isn't fun to talk about, I realize, but it's something that's very important to your future."

Parent, are you hoping your child will be able to sidestep all the risks related to alcohol abuse, tobacco use, and drug addiction in high school and through college? If so, I encourage you to frankly and openly *tell* your child that. Say it right out loud.

Do you doubt that drug and alcohol use can potentially impact college and career success? Think for a moment: How many adult men and women do you know whose entire college and career lives were derailed (and perhaps even destroyed) by drug or alcohol use? This is an important topic for parents

---

7   "Putting Your Younger Children on the Payroll," Small Business Taxes and Management, accessed November 15, 2016, http://smbiz.com/sbfaq022.html.

and students to be talking about and tackling head-on, and now is the perfect time to do it.

DESIGNING YOUR OWN 8TH-GRADE "CONTRACT"

The principles I've explained in this chapter are so helpful to a student's future that I recommend parents create their own contract-type document that *clearly expresses these boundaries.*

I suggest that you print this "contract" out, and then kindly, lovingly, and clearly explain its terms to the 8th grader. Afterward, have all parents and stepparents and the child sign it.

Once the contract has been signed, I recommend posting it on the inside of a kitchen cupboard door where it can be seen often.

Signing this contract won't *guarantee* clear, wise thinking on your child's part, of course, but it will help lessen the likelihood that your child will go through the next eight years thinking, as many teens and college students in our culture do: "Oh, I can just slough off in high school and not accomplish much, have my parents fork out all the cash I need to pay for college, attend random college classes for a while but spend most of my time partying, and then quit college halfway through so I can move back into my parents' house where I'll live rent-free and spend my 20s working part-time at a coffee shop."

If you'd like a sample contract template to use as a starting point when you create your own 8th-grade contract, I provide one for you to modify and tweak in the following bonus online content.

BONUS ONLINE CONTENT:
Download the article "The 8th-Grade Contract: How to Set Your Kid Up for Maximum College Success With Just a Few Pieces of Paper, a Pen, and One Well-Timed Dinner Conversation" at JeannieBurlowski.com/LAUNCH.

CHECKLIST

May of 8th Grade

1. Choose a date for a special student/parent dinner or overnight getaway. Make all necessary reservations.

2. Meet as parents to decide exactly what your particular contract is going to say. (You will find a sample contract to tweak and modify in the free bonus online content for this chapter located at JeannieBurlowski.com/LAUNCH.)

3. If divorce is a part of your family story, see if it might be possible for both *parents* and *stepparents* to read this chapter and collaborate on creating this contract.

4. Print out two copies of the contract that say exactly what you want them to say.

5. Note in your calendar that at your special dinner or overnight getaway, your goal will be to talk gently and kindly with your child about the terms of the contract. Afterward, have the child and all involved parents and stepparents sign it.

6. Tape a copy of the contract up inside a kitchen cupboard door.

7. Check my book updates page at JeannieBurlowski.com/LAUNCH to see if I have made any recent updates to this chapter.

8. Always consult your financial planning professional before making any big financial decisions.

9. Make a note in your calendar to come back and read the next chapter of this book early in the summer after your child completes 8th grade.

Be the first to hear about updates to the material in this book by reading my free weekly email newsletter every week. Anyone can subscribe to it at any time at JeannieBurlowski.com.

5 | *Summer After 8th Grade*

I know it seems like a stretch to be thinking about college and career during the summer after 8th grade, but believe me—the groundwork you are going to lay this summer is going to pay off for your young teen over and over again for years down the road.

The tasks I'm suggesting for this summer won't take a lot of your time, but they'll give your child a huge jump start on getting through college debt-free and into a job he or she loves afterward.

HOW TO USE THIS CHAPTER

Start by just reading through this chapter. As you read, don't worry about committing to any of it. Decision time will come at the very end of this chapter, when I give you a clear, at-a-glance checklist of every task I'm suggesting you consider right now.

Remember, you won't have to use every strategy I suggest; you'll just choose the

ones you think will work for your family and either modify or discard the rest.

[1] *Set aside a block of time to help your child brainstorm some interesting ways to earn money this summer.*

You could write out a list of odd jobs that your child knows how to do, and then offer to help him or her create a paper flyer advertising these services. Canva.com provides a great, easy way to create beautiful, professional-looking, full-color flyers (and other types of advertising) for as little as a dollar.

[2] *Get free Evernote accounts for both you and your child. (Evernote works on any device.)*

Over the next eight years, I'm going to be asking you and your child to keep track of some critically important details. The best way I know to do this effectively is to use the Evernote app. Evernote allows you to easily organize and archive all kinds of information and access that information at any time on any of your devices.

With Evernote, you organize the details of your life into virtual "notebooks" that are easily searchable. As soon as you download the Evernote app, I suggest that you immediately create a notebook for keeping track of all of your child's earned income—starting now. Why? Because if either you or your daughter is going to be putting money into a Roth IRA in her name, you need proof that she earned that amount of money herself. An Evernote notebook will give her one consistent place to record (a) each date she is paid for working, (b) the amount she earns each time, and (c) what work she did to earn the money. She can even attach a photo of her paycheck, of the direct deposit made to her bank account, or of the pile of cash she just earned from babysitting or lawn mowing.

You as a parent will also be using Evernote later on, when I ask you to start keeping track of every single college-related expense you incur so you'll know exactly how much money you can pull out of your child's 529 savings plan each year.

If you'd really like to maximize Evernote and get the most possible good out of it, I highly recommend the free Evernote help provided by best-selling author Michael Hyatt. You can find a handy index to all of Michael's free online Evernote help by typing this shortcut into your web browser: Bit.ly/2g8Z3Wp.[8]

[3] *Help your daughter set up her first account on LinkedIn.*

Include in her LinkedIn profile any awards she won at the end of 8th grade, as well as any work experiences, job-shadowing experiences, and volunteer and service hours she's had so far. Make sure she has the password to her LinkedIn account, and emphasize that it's important for her to keep the number of hours she's completed in all of these areas continually updated. Finally, help her link to some of her parents' friends and some of her friends' parents on LinkedIn.

[4] *Help your son decide the humanitarian cause he will work on behalf of throughout high school.*

I went over this with you in chapter 4, but it bears repeating here. One way to do this is to create a list of what you as a family believe to be some of the greatest injustices of our time. Be sure to include on the list injustices that have affected someone you know of or someone you love, but also include injustices you've only just heard about. Start with human trafficking, hunger, homelessness, children with special needs, people in prison, families of people in prison, children in substandard third world orphanages, issues related to life-threatening food allergies, environmental concerns, and international issues such as lack of health care, families in refugee camps, kids not being able to attend school because of not having shoes, people being persecuted for their faith, poverty that can be corrected with micro-loans through

---

8   Michael Hyatt, "A Handy Index to All My Evernote Posts," MichaelHyatt.com, August 6, 2011, https://michaelhyatt.com/a-handy-index-to-all-my-evernote-posts.html.

organizations such as Kiva.org, need for clean water, and helping with disaster relief.

Don't stop there, though. Make your own list, with each item more specific than the last. Then think about the list. If you are a person of faith, pray about the list. Then have your son or daughter choose the cause that he or she will work to help to some degree each year throughout high school.

[5] *Design and complete one very small project on behalf of this cause before your son begins 9th grade.*

Do this project as a family. Be sure to have your son keep track of the hours he's worked on this, and enter that information on his LinkedIn profile.

[6] *Open a Roth IRA for your daughter, and help her put her first $100 into it.*

One of the best, easiest-to-understand explanations of what a Roth IRA is and how to get started investing in one is available from best-selling author and syndicated radio host Dave Ramsey at DaveRamsey. com. You can get directly to Dave's Roth IRA explanation by typing this shortcut into your web browser: Bit.ly/2gbR1t7.

Remember, even if your daughter earns some money and then immediately blows it on movies and pizza, you can still put *your own money* into her Roth IRA as long as the amount you put in doesn't exceed the amount she earned herself in the year you make the contribution.

If this amount seems very difficult to save

up, try a smaller amount to start. Anything will help.

[7] *Parent, think seriously about whether you might be ready for a job change by the end of August this year.*

Are you an accountant, a food service professional, a salesperson, a marketing professional, a groundskeeper, a custodian, a receptionist, a career counselor, or an administrative professional? Or do you have a master's or PhD credential that could allow you to teach on a university campus? Many colleges and universities provide free or reduced-price college tuition for the children of their employees. There may be a small catch, however: you may have to be employed by that institution for four whole years before you take advantage of this benefit.

> **COULD YOU LEAVE YOUR PRESENT COMPANY AND GET A JOB ON A COLLEGE CAMPUS NEAR YOUR HOME FOR THE NEXT EIGHT YEARS? IF SO, YOU COULD END UP GETTING FREE COLLEGE TUITION FOR YOUR CHILDREN AS ONE OF YOUR EMPLOYEE BENEFITS.**

Is there any chance you could leave your present company and get a job on a college campus near your home for the next eight years? If you do this, you could end up getting free college tuition for your children as one of your employee benefits, saving your sons and daughters over $80,000 each in eventual college debt. A generous employee benefit like this is likely to be completely free, no strings attached, and tax-free. (The benefit to you and to your family of just this strategy alone may be worth thousands of times the price you paid for this book.)

"But what if my son doesn't want to go to college there?"

That may not be a problem. Many colleges have exchange programs that grant students of eligible employees free or reduced tuition at a number of different affiliated colleges and universities.

One of the largest exchange programs in the world is the 678-member tuition exchange program you can find at Tuitionexchange. org. If you as a parent are an eligible employee at one of the 678 Tuitionexchange.org member colleges, your child can receive free or reduced-price tuition at any one of the 678 institutions in the exchange.

You can find additional tuition exchange programs by googling "tuition exchange programs."

Tuition discounts for dependents of college employees can be significant. At many colleges parents are able to take advantage of this benefit even if they *can't* work there for four full years before their child starts attending. I suggest that you set up a recurring reminder in your calendar that pops up in June each year from now until your child finishes college. The entry might say, "Could I think about getting a job at a college by this coming August?"

[8] *Finally, parent, start quietly keeping track of every dollar you spend for your child that doesn't fall into the category of groceries or household utilities.*

Create a new notebook in Evernote or a special column in your checkbook register where you record every dollar you spend on this child for hot lunches, football fees, clothes, shoes, cell phone service, amusement park admissions, pizza out with friends, and other teen life-related expenses. Record both the amounts you spend and what the money is spent on. Do this for one entire year, because next summer at this time, I'm going to give you a brilliant idea for influencing your child to be strategic with money. You'll have the easiest time with this strategy if you know with relative certainty what expenses this teen incurs in a given year.

Would you like to get an advanced look at this strategy? Jump ahead to chapter 11 and get a sneak peek at the fun that is to come.

CHECKLIST

Summer After 8th Grade

- [ ] 1. Help your daughter think up a good way to earn money during summers and during the school year.

- [ ] 2. Get yourself and your son set up with the Evernote app, so you and he will have a good way to keep track of earned income. (This will be important if he's going to be making Roth IRA contributions.)

- [ ] 3. Help your daughter set up her first account on LinkedIn, and help her use it to start connecting to other adults she knows.

- [ ] 4. Help your son choose the humanitarian cause he will work on behalf of (to one degree or another) throughout all four years of high school.

- [ ] 5. Help your son complete one small project on behalf of this cause prior to starting 9th grade.

- [ ] 6. Open a Roth IRA for your daughter and help her put her first $100 into it.

- [ ] 7. Think about whether you might be ready for a job change this coming August.

- [ ] 8. Start keeping track of every dollar you spend on your child that is not groceries or household utilities, along with what that money is being spent on.

- [ ] 9. Check my book updates page at JeannieBurlowski.com/LAUNCH to see if I have made any recent updates to this chapter.

- [ ] 10. Always consult your financial planning professional before making any big financial decisions.

- [ ] 11. Make a note in your calendar to come back and read the next chapter of this book when your child is in September of 9th grade.

Be the first to hear about updates to the material in this book by reading my free weekly email newsletter every week. Anyone can subscribe to it at any time at JeannieBurlowski.com.

6 | *September of 9th Grade*

The first few weeks of 9th grade will likely be a rough time for your child, whether he or she admits that to you or not. There are many adjustments to be made during this time, and each one comes with its own amount of stress and anxiety.

If you can, try to keep home life routine calm and predictable during this time. Plan for wide-open afternoon and evening time that will allow your child to decompress, organize, and get ahead on schoolwork, and if possible, plan to have a warm, comforting, sit-down dinner with the family each night. Try to keep corrections and demands minimal, and treat your son or daughter with a little extra kindness and gentleness during this transition.

HOW TO USE THIS CHAPTER

Start by just reading through this chapter. As you read, don't worry about committing to any of it. Decision time will come at the very end of this chapter, when I give you a clear,

at-a-glance checklist of every task I'm suggesting you consider right now.

Remember, you won't have to use every strategy I suggest; just choose the ones you think will work for your family and either modify or discard the rest.

Here are some strategies to think about during September of 9th grade.

[1] *Help your teen to gain a healthy, realistic perception of what real friendship is.*

For some students, anxiety over whether they'll be "popular" in high school can make it nearly impossible to concentrate on anything else. For girls especially, routine morning clothing choices may cause increased heart rate and hyperventilation as your daughter frets over whether this shirt or that one will help her be more popular with the mean girls she's trying to be friends with at school.

Early in 9th grade, emphasize to your child that high school friendships exist on two basic planes:

Her general reputation—how she is perceived by people who don't know her well

This general reputation is easy to manage. If she will choose to be a person who, as much as possible, consistently does the right thing in every situation as it comes up, and if she will be consistently kind to all the different people she encounters at school, her general reputation will pretty much take care of itself. People will naturally tend to like her and think well of her.

Her closest friendships

It will not be generalized, massive crowds of people who will provide your daughter the genuine, nourishing relationships that will most support and carry her through the high school years. It will be her four or so closest friends, those people who know and enjoy her for who she really is, who are loyal to her, who bring out the best in her. As your daughter starts 9th grade, one of her most important tasks is to carefully choose who these closest friends will be. Encourage your daughter to watch for and choose friends who are kind, who are emotionally safe to be around, who have excellent character and make smart choices, who she enjoys, who will influence her to be the best she can be. Then, the best thing your daughter can do is make her own personal life choices and decisions so she's the kind of person these quality people would want as a friend. If she does this, she'll never have to worry about "popularity."

[2] *Check with your teen about what organizational system she'll be using for getting academic work done in a quality manner and handed in on time.*

If your daughter floundered academically in middle school, emphasize to her that 9th grade is a fantastic opportunity to start over with a clean slate.

For a review of the six critical questions all students must be able to answer about organizing academics, see chapter 3.

[3] *Emphasize the importance of keeping a squeaky clean online reputation.*

Remind your child that every single thing posted online either by her or about her is public and can never be erased. Increasingly, employers and grad school admissions committees are performing extensive and in-depth online searches before hiring or accepting candidates. Scholarship committees may look closely at students' online reputations before awarding money. Online search tools are only going to become more sophisticated in the next 4–10 years, so embarrassing things posted by or about your daughter are only going to become easier for others to find and view. Your child should never post anything, anywhere that she wouldn't be happy having broadcast at a national news conference.

[4] *Have your son or daughter carefully go over the list of clubs and non-sports extracurricular activities available at his or her high school.*

If it's unclear what some of these activities are, ask the high school office for descriptions.

Have your son go through this list and highlight in yellow all the activities that seem most interesting to him. Then have him choose the top two or three activities that look *the most* attractive to him, attend meetings for those activities, and begin participating in them with an eye toward choosing one to be increasingly active in throughout all four years of high school.

If there's an activity the high school provides that sounds fascinating, but student participation is low and the organization is not well run, your son could join it and one day be the leader who brings it up to superstar status.

As part of this process, I suggest having your son or daughter check out the clubs and activities listed on the websites of other large high schools across the country. Your daughter may scroll through the website of a high school far from her home state and notice that the school has a "Red Cross high school club." Wondering what that is, your daughter googles "Red Cross high school club" and finds information like this posted on the website of a school located thousands of miles from her:

> Working closely with friends, having fun and learning new things about yourself, your peers, community and the world can all happen in a Red Cross high school club.

You can acquire new skills in leadership, get engaged in grassroots service, and lend a helping hand to those in need. As part of the high school club working with the local Red Cross chapter, you can become a lifeguard, learn how to perform CPR or become a trained instructor who teaches others. You may organize a blood drive, help U.S. military members, help to eradicate measles and much more. This is a club for students committed to making their school, their community, and the world a better place. Your acquired skills build a solid foundation of personal tools which are important to succeeding in college and any number of future careers. Take the first step in making a difference in your life and the lives of others by starting a Red Cross high school club![9]

Taking initiative, your daughter could ask her school administration what it would take for her to become the founder of this organization on her high school campus. Many times all it takes is completing some paperwork, finding a willing adult advisor, and publicizing an initial meeting. If your daughter does this, she'll be able to add "Founder of _____ High School's Red Cross High School Club" to the résumé she's building for herself on LinkedIn. Impressive!

The goal is for your child to choose one main activity to participate in all the way through high school, from freshman year through senior year. We want her to participate in it wholeheartedly, eventually becoming a leader in it.

---

9   "Red Cross Clubs," American Red Cross, accessed November 19, 2016, http://www.redcross.org/local/ohio/buckeye/local-programs/clubs.

We want her to be instrumental in expanding the organization to its maximum. We want her to find ways for the students in this extra-curricular activity to serve the community, whether the activity is typically thought of as a service organization or not. (Even the Accounting Club, the Chess Club, and the Drama Club can think up creative ways to use their skills to serve the community.)

We want your daughter to keep careful notes on what the group does and accomplishes, entering the details on her LinkedIn profile. Someday, your child's committed long-term activity might be part of what gets him or her a lucrative merit-based scholarship or a preferential financial aid package at a college you could never otherwise afford.

[5] *Talk to your son about how many hours he'll be able to work to earn money each week during this school year.*

Take into consideration his school, homework, and extracurricular schedule during 9th grade. When will be the best times for him to work? After school? Evenings? Weekends? Make time for that.

In addition, be sure he is entering his work hours into LinkedIn and his work earnings into Evernote.

[6] *For the next 15 months, become very serious about meeting regularly as parents to implement the strategies that will lead to your child's debt-free college graduation.*

The 9th-grade year and the six months

following it are *by far the most important months* in your child's life when it comes to strategizing for debt-free college graduation, especially if you aren't planning to save up money to pay for college. There are certain decisions that absolutely must be made during these months. They cannot wait. If you miss taking some necessary strategic steps during this critical window of opportunity, you and your child will end up paying thousands of dollars more than is necessary for college.

Don't be among the millions of parents who are going to wait to think about college until December of their child's 11th-grade year, and are then going to say, "I'd give anything if I had just thought this through two years ago!"

> **THE 9TH-GRADE YEAR AND THE SIX MONTHS FOLLOWING IT ARE** *BY FAR THE MOST IMPORTANT MONTHS* **IN YOUR CHILD'S LIFE WHEN IT COMES TO STRATEGIZING FOR DEBT-FREE COLLEGE GRADUATION**

If you haven't been taking the strategies I'm prescribing for families very seriously up to this point, now is the time to become dead serious about them.

[7] *If you haven't done so already, start quietly keeping track of every dollar you spend for your child that doesn't fall into the category of groceries or household utilities.*

As I mentioned in chapter 5, create a notebook in Evernote or a special column in your checkbook register where you record every dollar you spend on this child for school lunches, football fees, clothes, shoes, cell phone service, amusement park admissions, pizza out with friends, and other teen life-related expenses. Record both the amounts you spend and what the money is spent on. Do this for this entire school year, because next summer I'm going to give you a brilliant idea for influencing your child to be strategic with money. You'll have the easiest time with this strategy if you know with relative certainty what expenses this teen incurs in a given year.

Would you like to get an advanced look at this strategy? Jump ahead to chapter 11 and get a sneak peek at the fun that is to come.

CHECKLIST

September of 9th Grade

☐ 1. Have a talk with your teen about what real friendship is.

☐ 2. Talk to your daughter about what system she'll be using to organize her academics this year.

☐ 3. Emphasize the importance of keeping a squeaky clean online reputation.

☐ 4. Have your son carefully go over his school's list of available extracurricular activities with an eye toward eventually picking one to commit to.

☐ 5. Brainstorm with your daughter about what will be the best times for her to work for money during this coming school year.

☐ 6. For the next 15 months, become very serious about meeting regularly as parents to implement the strategies that will lead to your teen's debt-free college graduation.

☐ 7. If you haven't done so already, start quietly keeping track of every dollar you spend for your child that doesn't fall into the category of groceries or household utilities. You'll need this for later.

☐ 8. Check my book updates page at JeannieBurlowski.com/LAUNCH to see if I have made any recent updates to this chapter.

☐ 9. Always consult your financial planning professional before making any big financial decisions.

☐ 10. Make a note in your calendar to come back and read the next chapter of this book when your child is in October of 9th grade.

Be the first to hear about updates to the material in this book by reading my free weekly email newsletter every week. Anyone can subscribe to it at any time at JeannieBurlowski.com.

7 | *October– January of 9th Grade*

Ninth grade is now well underway. Your family is settling into its school-year routine, complete with focused homework times, after-school activities, and friend and family times that will one day serve as sweet and stabilizing memories for your child.

Take time this fall and winter to stand still and breathe deeply of this time of life. Even though your days may be harried and stressful, this season of life is a *gift.* Purposely take as many moments as you can to stand still and savor it.

HOW TO USE THIS CHAPTER

Start by just reading through this chapter. As you read, don't worry about committing to any of it. Decision time will come at the very

end of this chapter, when I give you a clear, at-a-glance checklist of every task I'm suggesting you consider right now.

Remember, you won't have to use every strategy I suggest; you'll just choose the ones you think will work for your family and either modify or discard the rest.

After the first few tumultuous weeks of 9th grade are over with, work on completing the following tasks before January 31 of the 9th-grade year.

[1] *Consider starting a high school, church, or homeschool co-op "club" for parents who want to get their kids through college debt-free.*

Your high school has a PTO, right? It's an

organization that brings parents together for evening meetings so they can think of practical ways to help students and teachers. This is the same type of thing, except this club's focus is on providing parents support so they can get their kids through college debt-free and directly into jobs they love afterward.

To start an organization like this, all you need to do is ask your church or high school what it takes to start up a new parent organization. Then get your friends on board, schedule a room at the church, at the high school, or at a local library, and advertise the first meeting using social media and other means.

On meeting night, have the parents all introduce themselves and tell the ages of their kids. Once this step is completed, you can conduct the rest of the meeting in one of two ways: if you've got a large group, have the parents break off into smaller groups based on their oldest kids' ages. The goal for each smaller group will be to go over the checklist(s) in this book that apply to that age group and talk through how they're doing with the tasks I suggest.

If you've got a smaller group, simply pose the question, "How are you doing with the checklists suggested for your kid at this time? How can we help you?" Allow parents to discuss their thoughts and their progress with the principles I've outlined. Your goal will be to applaud small victories, set small reachable goals for parents who are struggling, and brainstorm

together ways around the obstacles you encounter.

[2] *Brainstorm with your child about what he will do this year to help the humanitarian cause he's adopted as his own.*

Make a plan and schedule it in. If your son pulls friends in to help him with this cause, he gets points for *leadership* as well as for service.

You can greatly inspire yourself *and* your child about heartfelt service to others by watching a short inspiring video about WE Day, the one-day event where thousands of students come together to celebrate having given themselves to one local and one global act of service during the previous year. I strongly suggest that you and your child go to the WE Day website, watch the short video, and then click on the links on the top of the page. There you'll find high-quality resources that schools, religious organizations, families, and students can use to mobilize others for service. You can get directly to the WE Day website by typing this shortcut into your web browser: Bit.ly/2fxgZWR.

> **IF YOUR SON PULLS FRIENDS IN TO HELP HIM WITH THIS CAUSE, HE GETS POINTS FOR** *LEADERSHIP* **AS WELL AS FOR SERVICE.**

Be sure to help your son keep track of

everything he does in regard to service in his profile on LinkedIn.

[3] *Using the federal government's student aid website, get a ballpark estimate of what your child's future federal student aid will likely be if your current financial situation continues.*

You can get directly to this website by typing this shortcut into your web browser: Bit.ly/2gecyBD.10

Are you currently above the cutoffs for receiving need-based financial aid? If so, there may be steps you can take to make your family more eligible for financial aid. You won't have to do anything about this until your child's sophomore year of high school (and if you are following the checklists in this book, I will remind you to plan for this carefully before then), but knowing where you stand right now can be helpful.

[4] *If he'd like to go, register your 9th grader for an upcoming summer camp.*

Some (not all) 18-year-old college freshmen suffer from overwhelming homesickness during their first semester away at college. This can wreak havoc with academics. If your child is accustomed to being away from home at summer camp, though, it can make the transition to college much easier. If you're in Minnesota or another nearby state, try TroutLakeCamps.org.

Register for summer camp in January or before; spots for students ages 14 and up fill fast.

[5] *Brainstorm with your daughter about how she'll earn money this coming summer.*

I know it seems like this is too far away to think about right now, but I encourage you to work with your daughter to get everything ready ahead of time so that after her last final exam of 9th grade, she'll be ready to relax for one week and then hit the ground running earning money for Roth IRA investing. (For a reminder of how Roth IRA investing can work for teens, see chapter 4.)

[6] *In January, have your child ask two of her 9th-grade teachers for letters of recommendation to be used for future scholarship applications.*

This coming summer I'll be suggesting that your daughter create one scholarship application essay and then tweak and modify it to apply for 10 different scholarships. If your daughter has the necessary letters of recommendation all ready to go, the process will be relatively fast and easy for her.

When a teacher writes a letter of recommendation for your child, I *strongly* suggest that afterward you send that teacher a handwritten thank-you note containing a generous gift card to a store that carries practical items. Your note might say: "We value what you do so much; I just wanted to thank you in a tangible way."

---

10   For more information, go to https://studentaid.ed.gov/sa/fafsa/estimate.

Teachers work hard on these very important letters; there is no reason to expect them to do this work for free.

[7] *Be aware of the best time for your child to take SAT II subject tests.*

SAT II subject tests are hour-long, content-based tests on specific subjects that your son or daughter has studied in high school. Strong performance on SAT II subject tests can help your child to fulfill basic degree requirements or receive college credit for certain introductory-level courses. In some cases, the presence of strong SAT II test scores on a college application can help boost an applicant's admissions ranking.

When your daughter applies to college during the summer after 11th grade, she may find some colleges she's applying to requiring zero, one, or perhaps two SAT II subject tests.

> **TEACHERS WORK HARD ON THESE VERY IMPORTANT LETTERS; THERE IS NO REASON TO EXPECT THEM TO DO THIS WORK FOR FREE.**

When is the best time to take an SAT II subject test? Immediately after the student has finished a high school class focused on that subject matter. Your daughter will need a maximum of two, but taking additional SAT II subject tests may help boost her up out of some introductory courses she'd rather not have to take (or pay for!).

Any time your daughter finishes up a class on one of these subjects, have her consider taking an SAT II subject test immediately afterward. You can find free SAT II practice materials by typing this shortcut into your web browser: Bit.ly/2gvLk8B.

SAT II subject tests are available on the following subjects:

Literature	Physics	Italian
U.S. History	French	Latin
World History	French with Listening	Chinese with Listening
Math Level 1	German	Japanese with Listening
Math Level 2	German with Listening	Korean with Listening[11]
Biology (Ecology)	Spanish	
Biology (Molecular)	Spanish with Listening	
Chemistry	Modern Hebrew	

---

11 "Test Dates and Deadlines," Collegeboard.org, accessed September 24, 2016, https://collegereadiness. collegeboard.org/sat-subject-tests/register/test-dates-deadlines.

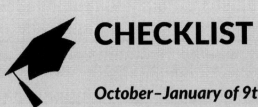

CHECKLIST

October–January of 9th Grade

1. Consider starting a church or school club for parents who want their kids to graduate from college debt-free.

2. Help your child brainstorm what small project she could complete this year to help the humanitarian cause she's adopted as her own.

3. Use the online calculator recommended in this chapter to estimate the need-based financial aid your child will likely receive under your family's present financial circumstances. Be ready for me to give you strategies next year that may very well change those numbers.

4. If he'd like to go, register your 9th grader for an upcoming summer camp.

5. Brainstorm with your daughter about how she'll earn money this coming summer.

6. In January, have your child ask two of her 9th-grade teachers for letters of recommendation to be used for upcoming scholarship applications.

7. Over the next two years, be aware of the best time for your child to take SAT II subject tests.

8. Check my book updates page at JeannieBurlowski.com/LAUNCH to see if I have made any recent updates to this chapter.

9. Always consult your financial planning professional before making any big financial decisions.

10. Call your child's school and ask this question: "When do you expect to register 9th graders for 10th-grade classes?" Make a note in your calendar to come back and read the next chapter of this book approximately one month before then. (Registration for 10th-grade classes may take place as early as January of 9th grade, or in some cases even earlier.)

Be the first to hear about updates to the material in this book by reading my free weekly email newsletter every week. Anyone can subscribe to it at any time at JeannieBurlowski.com.

8 | *Before Registering for 10th-Grade Classes*

Your child is now approximately one-eighth of the way through high school. It seems unbelievable, doesn't it? Time is flying. It seems like just a few days ago this child was waving good-bye to you from the bus steps on the first day of kindergarten, and now he's a teen with just 44 months to go before his first day of college.

If you think his life has gone fast so far, brace yourself. The pace is about to pick up. The next 44 months are going to go by in the blink of an eye. To reassure yourself that you've laid an extraordinarily strong foundation for what you're about to build next, I suggest that you go back and skim through the checklists attached to chapters 3, 4, 5, 6, and 7. Congratulate yourself on all the preparatory steps you've taken so far. Identify

some steps you originally skipped that you might be able to take care of in the next few months. And then hold on tight. The next 23 breathless months are going to be some of *the most important* for getting your kid through college debt-free and into a job he or she loves afterward.

Let's do it together.

HOW TO USE THIS CHAPTER

Start by just reading through this chapter. As you read, don't worry about committing to any of it. Decision time will come at the very end of this chapter, when I give you a clear, at-a-glance checklist of every task I'm suggesting you consider right now.

Remember, you won't have to use every

strategy I suggest; you'll just choose the ones you think will work for your family and either modify or discard the rest.

[1] *See if your state will pay for your child to take a technical college class in 10th grade.*

In some states, 10th graders are allowed to take one course at a technical college at state expense and have it count for high school and college credit at the same time. (This option replaces the "shop" classes you may remember from your high school days.) In Minnesota, for instance, a 10th grader is allowed to take a one-semester, technical college class at state expense, and if she gets a C or better in it, she's allowed to take a second one, also at state expense.

If this option is available in your state, I urge you to have your child jump at the chance. Show your daughter the course catalog for the technical college nearest your house, and have her select a course that looks interesting to her. Accounting? Auto Body Collision Technology? Cabinetmaking? Carpentry? Electronics Technology? Graphic Design? Landscaping and Horticulture? Law Enforcement? Plastics Engineering Technology? Fashion Merchandising? Welding and Metal Fabrication? Exposing her to these kinds of diverse career fields early on may influence her to one day choose an unconventional career that she truly loves. Or it might just put additional college credits in her pocket and give her another interesting entry on her LinkedIn profile.

> **SHOW YOUR DAUGHTER THE COURSE CATALOG FOR THE TECHNICAL COLLEGE NEAREST YOUR HOUSE, AND HAVE HER SELECT A COURSE THAT LOOKS INTERESTING TO HER.**

Either way, you'll need to plan for this in the winter of 9th grade, well before registering for 10th-grade high school classes. Work with your child's school counselor to (a) get that technical school class into her 10th-grade high school class schedule, and (b) plan your child's transportation to and from that technical school location.

[2] Encourage your child to also register for an Advanced Placement (AP) class or two, but *not* because you're hoping that AP will help her earn inexpensive college credit.

AP is *not* the best way to earn inexpensive college credit in high school. (You'll find out why in the next chapter.)

Still, AP courses can have some value for students because they're rigorous. They build self-discipline and intellectual muscle. They can look more interesting than ordinary courses on future college applications. And in *some* cases, taking AP classes can even result in students actually earning some amount of inexpensive college credit. If a student passes just four AP tests with scores of 4 or 5, for instance, there are some colleges that will grant the student an entire year of college credit in exchange for that work, instantly knocking 25 percent off of the student's cost of attending college. *Or*, alternatively, giving the student flexibility to take lighter course loads throughout four years of college, leaving more time during the academic years for extra internships, study abroad, work, travel, research, or additional targeted volunteer work.

The *problem* with AP is that it's not a *dependable* source of college credit.

Sometimes hardworking students get the college credit they expect from AP—and sometimes they don't. Because of this uncertainty, I tell students, "Take AP courses during the sophomore year of high school (and maybe afterward) because they're rigorous and they stretch you. But plan to use other, better strategies for amassing college credit during high school and graduating from college debt-free."

We'll dive into these other, better strategies in the next chapter.

Note that if you'd like to have your child stretch herself by taking one or more AP courses, but her high school doesn't offer them, you can ask the school to arrange for her to take an AP course at a neighboring high school or online.

CHECKLIST

Before Registering for 10th-Grade Classes

☐ 1. Go back and skim through the checklists attached to chapters 3, 4, 5, 6, and 7. Congratulate yourself on all the preparatory steps you've taken so far. Identify some steps you originally skipped that you might be able to take care of in the next few months.

☐ 2. Check to see if your state will pay for your child to take a technical school class in 10th grade.

☐ 3. Work with your child's school counselor to (a) get that technical school class into her 10th-grade high school class schedule, and (b) plan your child's transportation to and from that technical school location.

☐ 4. Encourage your child to sign up for an AP class or two for next year, but not because you're depending on AP to help her earn inexpensive college credit.

☐ 5. Check my book updates page at JeannieBurlowski.com/LAUNCH to see if I have made any recent updates to this chapter.

☐ 6. Always consult your financial planning professional before making any big financial decisions.

☐ 7. Make a note in your calendar to come back and read the next chapter of this book when your child is in February of 9th grade.

Be the first to hear about updates to the material in this book by reading my free weekly email newsletter every week. Anyone can subscribe to it at any time at JeannieBurlowski.com.

9 | *February–April of 9th Grade*

This chapter is an exciting one. Why? Because in this chapter I get to explain the #1 best way to keep college costs way, way down: *earning real, transferable college credit during high school.*

The ever-popular College Board AP program is not the best, most reliable way to do this. Read on for alternate strategies that could easily save your child $50,000 or more on college costs.

HOW TO USE THIS CHAPTER

Start by just reading through this chapter. As you read, don't worry about committing to any of it. Decision time will come at the very end of this chapter, when I give you a clear, at-a-glance checklist of every task I'm suggesting you consider right now.

Remember, you won't have to use every strategy I suggest; you'll just choose the ones you think will work for your family and either modify or discard the rest.

[1] *During the winter of 9th grade, figure out all the varying ways that students in your community can dependably earn real, transferable college credit during high school.*

Explore every early college option available in your state, in your homeschool co-op, at local colleges or universities, and in your local high school.

Students who graduate from high school with multiple college credits already under their belts have several advantages over those who wait until they're 18 to start working on college-level material:

» They increase their chances of being admitted to the colleges they'd most like to attend, since college admissions committees see that they've already opted to take the tougher academic road in high school.

» When they're high school seniors,

they're stronger candidates for the free money merit aid that colleges extend to highly qualified applicants they're especially hoping to attract.

» When they get to college, they aren't usually asked to sit through (or pay for!) expensive remedial classes that give them no actual college credit.

» They walk onto their eventual college campuses with confidence. They know how to organize themselves to accomplish college-level work, because they've already had substantial experience with it.

» They may be able to move an entire year (or two) sooner into the more advanced, more interesting college courses that apply most directly to their future career fields.

» They will have the option of being able to take somewhat lighter class loads each semester they're in college and still graduate in four years or less. They'll still qualify as full-time students, but they won't need to pack every semester tightly with classes in order to earn all the credits necessary to graduate on time. They'll end up with more time each semester to work on their more advanced classes, and they'll also have more time available for the committed volunteering and interning in their career field that is so important to their future career success. (I describe this in detail in my book for students entitled *FLY: The 6 Things You Absolutely Must Do to Be Brilliant in College and Get a Job You Love Afterward*.)

» They typically save massive amounts of money on college costs.

Start asking questions about these early college credit options when your child is in 9th grade. This way you'll be ready when these opportunities start presenting themselves in the 10th- and 11th-grade years.

[2] *Understand that of the three main ways to earn college credit in high school, the fastest and least expensive is CLEP testing.*

Some consultants you find online talking about debt-free college actually suggest that students complete entire college degrees using programs such as CLEP. I would *never* advocate that.

What I do suggest is that CLEP be used to earn a moderate number of inexpensive college credits for subjects a student has already covered fairly thoroughly in middle school or high school.

EARNING CLEP CREDIT FOR MIDDLE SCHOOL AND HIGH SCHOOL WORK

Imagine for a moment that you're a 9th grader who's worked hard and gotten A's in both Algebra I and Algebra II. You're standing in your kitchen looking down at your final trimester Grade 9 report card, and it dawns on you that there are college students at the university across town learning this exact same material, but they're getting college credit for it. What could you do to get real college credit for the material you've just mastered?

Voilà! The CLEP program.

Well respected since the 1960s, the CLEP program is administered by the College Board (the same people behind the SAT exam and all AP testing). CLEP allows students who've learned college-level material on their own (or in middle school or high school) to take a 90- to 120-minute multiple-choice examination where they demonstrate sufficient knowledge of the material to be able to earn college credit for it. Once a student has achieved a high-enough score on a CLEP subject test (usually by getting just over 50 percent correct), he or she can get college credit for that knowledge at one of 2,900 colleges and universities nationwide. CLEP tests are available in 33 different subject areas.

IF YOUR DAUGHTER HAS HAD A SOLID MIDDLE SCHOOL OR HIGH SCHOOL CLASS ON A SUBJECT TESTED BY CLEP, SHE MAY BE ABLE TO PASS A CLEP TEST ON THAT MATERIAL WITHOUT MUCH TROUBLE.

Many middle school and high school students never attempt a CLEP test because they assume they couldn't possibly know enough to pass it. Millions of students, though, have been able to pass CLEP tests simply by studying for them on their own, without taking any kind of a formal class on the subject at all. If your daughter has had a solid middle school or high school class on a subject tested by CLEP, she may be able to pass a CLEP test on that material without much trouble. I strongly suggest she look at an online list of all 33 CLEP tests and choose just one to try.

If she'd like to do this, here are the steps to take.

Look at a list of all the available CLEP tests.

Start by going to the official CLEP website and looking through a list of all 33 available CLEP tests. You can get directly to the page you need by typing this shortcut into your web browser: Bit.ly/2fximox.

Help your daughter choose a CLEP test that she's likely to do well on. (Students who've done well in English Literature classes often like to start with the Analyzing and Interpreting Literature CLEP exam.)

Have your daughter take a free CLEP practice test just for fun.

Once she settles on an exam she'd like to try, have your daughter locate one of many free CLEP practice tests on that subject online. To get directly to one of my favorite sources of free CLEP practice tests, type this shortcut into your web browser: Bit.ly/2fxqXaP.

Have your daughter take a practice test, see how she does, review her wrong answers, and get an idea of where her knowledge gaps are. No pressure here; she can even pause a CLEP practice test if she needs to.

Access some free or inexpensive CLEP prep if necessary.

If your daughter needs a little more help to pass, you can locate free CLEP practice materials online by typing this shortcut into your web browser: Bit.ly/2gBPyjL. You can also find CLEP study guide books at your local library.

Commercial (paid) online CLEP prep is also available at websites such as Instant-cert.com and Study.com. In addition, sites such as Quizlet.com, Varsitytutors.com, Proprofs.com, Cram.com, and Amazon.com have CLEP flashcards that can be downloaded onto any smartphone instantly. Have your daughter study the topics she's weak in, and then register to take the actual CLEP test on that subject and see what happens.

Register your daughter to take a CLEP test.

Registering to take a CLEP test is officially referred to as, "purchasing a CLEP exam." You can get directly to the website where this is done by typing this shortcut into your web browser: Bit.ly/2g9luXM.

Give your daughter her best chance of success on the actual CLEP test day.

Have her eat protein right before she tests so she's able to do her clearest, most focused thinking. If she's unsure of a certain question, she should eliminate answer choices that are probably wrong and guess from among the rest. (There is no penalty for wrong answers on CLEP.)

Trying to pass a CLEP test, especially when a student has already had a middle school or high school class on the subject, is absolutely worth a shot. The only thing the student risks losing is the testing fee, which is currently under $100. If a student fails a CLEP test, colleges need never find out,

and students can retake a CLEP test in six months if they'd like to.

Just look at the potential financial benefits of doing this. If a student were to pay full price for the three college credits she could earn by passing just one $100 CLEP test, here's what she'd plan on paying:

» At a four-year private college: $3,956 (plus interest, if the student has to take out student loans to pay for this college)

» At a four-year state university, where it may be a struggle to graduate in just four years: $1,275 (plus interest, if the student has to take out student loans to pay for this college)

» At a two-year community college: $535

These numbers don't tell the whole "cost story" of taking a full-length college course versus taking a CLEP test, though. A student who enrolls in and sits through an entire college course sacrifices hundreds of hours to do so. This is time that can't be used for volunteering, interning, or working for money. Many college classes are absolutely worth this time investment—but for the ones that *aren't,* I'd like for your daughter to check them off of her degree plan quickly by using CLEP.

TRYING TO PASS A CLEP TEST, ESPECIALLY WHEN A STUDENT HAS ALREADY HAD A MIDDLE SCHOOL OR HIGH SCHOOL CLASS ON THE SUBJECT, IS ABSOLUTELY WORTH A SHOT.

Taking a CLEP exam that covers something a student has already studied in middle school or high school in particular is a clear, winning strategy in terms of time, energy, and money.

CLEP tests have *no upper or lower age limits* and are administered at over 1,700 test centers on college campuses across the U.S. and around the world. The CLEP credits your child earns are banked for 20 years with the College Board, and the College Board will send transcripts of all the CLEP credits your child has earned to the college of her choice for a low $20 transcript fee.

Many students who do well on one CLEP test quickly realize that they can probably do well on more of them. As their confidence grows, some students will select a CLEP subject they've never studied before, learn the material on their own using a CLEP study guide or online CLEP prep, and then take and pass a CLEP test on the subject, amassing even more college credit as they do so.

When students with CLEP credits finally get to college, they have the distinct advantage of being able to leap right over (perhaps less appealing) introductory classes, and right into the advanced classes that interest and engage them most.

If your daughter doesn't find a CLEP test on the subject she's looking for, try searching for the same subject on a list of DSST tests.

Because DSST tests are sometimes believed to be more difficult than CLEP tests, I'd like to direct you to an online DSST test list that is arranged somewhat in order of difficulty.

You can get directly to it by typing this shortcut into your web browser: Bit.ly/2gda9aE.

MAXIMIZING CLEP—SHOP CAREFULLY FOR COLLEGES TO APPLY TO

Students who've earned college credit through CLEP, DSST, and the College Board's AP program will need to shop carefully for the colleges they'll eventually apply to.

Although CLEP and DSST credits are accepted at 2,900 colleges nationwide, colleges vary as to how many of these credits they'll allow one student to transfer in. In my local area, one well-respected private college allows its enrolled students to transfer in up to 32 of these "credit-by-examination" credits. Several good colleges near me allow students to transfer in 20 of them. Harvard University allows its students to transfer in 12 CLEP credits. One private Christian college in downtown Minneapolis (North Central University) accepts 72 CLEP credits (a gold mine for homeschooling families who make a CLEP exam the final exam for nearly every homeschool class they teach). Another private liberal arts college 60 miles from where I live is one of the few that does not allow any credit-by-examination credits at all.

When first considering a college to apply to, one of the most important questions for a student to ask will be, "How many of my CLEP, DSST, and AP credits will you allow me to transfer in here?" If the answer is a smaller number than you'd like, *apply elsewhere*. If this college doesn't want to recognize the college credits your daughter's already earned in high school, there are hundreds of other similar colleges that *will*.

Some students have used CLEP to test out of many, many college classes. There are, as a matter of fact, at least two colleges in the U.S. that will allow students to "graduate from college with degrees" after having earned 100 percent of their college credits through CLEP and other credit-by-examination programs! I strongly discourage this path. Although it can be helpful to leapfrog right over the more basic college classes that are—to some degree—a repeat of high school, there's great value in a student actually attending and participating in his most challenging college classes. Working through complex topics in the company of other students and professors who are focused on the same subjects can deepen your daughter's understanding in ways that reading on her own never could—and that's what makes college worth the money.

If you're looking for an educational consultant who specializes in helping families to maximize CLEP credit, I recommend Cheri Frame, online at Creditsbeforecollege.com. She is available for both individual consultations and conference speaking.

As your son nears the end of 9th grade, look over the lists of all the CLEP and DSST exams available and have him take at least one that will reward him for information he's already learned in middle school or high school. If he's reluctant to do this, pay him to prepare for and take a CLEP test if necessary. It's a tremendous way for him to start amassing low-cost college credits before he ever sets foot on a college campus.

[3] *Understand that the second-best way for students to earn college credit in high school is through state-sponsored dual enrollment programs.*

Forty-two states in the U.S. sponsor and fund programs that allow qualified high school juniors and seniors (and even some freshmen and sophomores) to take real college courses in place of their regular high school classes. Students who do this are able to earn high school credit and college credit at the same time, and best of all—most or all of the associated costs are paid for by their state.

In Minnesota, where I'm from, nearly 25,000 high school students from almost every public and private high school in the state earn college credit in this way from 31 different Minnesota private and public colleges and universities, with the state of Minnesota footing the entire bill.

Many students who've taken full advantage of programs like these have been able to walk onto the stage at their high school graduations with two years of college credits already completed—in many cases entirely at state expense. If these students continue to find additional clever, creative ways to pay for their last two years of college, they may very well be able to walk out of a quality, four-year, undergraduate institution having earned a bachelor's degree completely debt-free.

There's a good chance that you may live in (or be able to move to!) one of the 42 states that offer dual enrollment programs to high school students. To find out whether your state has such a program—and whether or not your son or daughter might qualify for it—google the name of your state along with the words "dual enrollment." See what comes up.

Don't wait to take this step. In some states (such as Alabama, Arkansas, Ohio, and South Dakota), students may be allowed to participate in dual enrollment programs as early as the sophomore year of high school if they plan early enough.

Make it a point to locate this information on your own; do not depend on your local school district or private high school to provide it for you. Some public and private high schools deliberately choose not to promote dual enrollment options for fear of losing funding for themselves.

While you're taking responsibility for finding and enrolling your child in dual enrollment courses, be sure to keep in regular contact with your high school guidance staff, conferring with them every time you sign up for new dual enrollment courses. You'll want to clear your child's dual enrollment course choices with your high school's staff so you can be sure your son is consistently meeting all requirements necessary for high school graduation.

STUDENTS CAN BENEFIT GREATLY FROM DUAL ENROLLMENT

Research shows that high school students enrolled in dual enrollment programs typically have higher rates of enrolling in a college or university after high school graduation, need fewer remedial courses once they get there, and have higher rates of earning postsecondary degrees than do their peers who do not take dual enrollment courses.

But what about students who don't drive, or rural students who live far from their nearest college campus? Or students whose parents would rather not have them on a college campus before they turn 18? In many states, students are allowed to take online college courses through accredited college and university "distance education" programs, such as the well-respected one at the University of Northwestern in St. Paul, Minnesota. These online courses tend to be of high quality, offer the exact same college credit upon successful completion as do on-campus courses, and (for qualifying in-state residents) are also paid for by the state. Dual enrollment courses may also be offered on campus at some local high schools as well.

WHAT DOES IT TAKE TO QUALIFY FOR DUAL ENROLLMENT?

Dual enrollment programs are an excellent idea, but not every high school student will qualify for one. State requirements vary, but typically a high school senior must be in the upper half of his or her class or score at or above the 50th percentile on the ACT or SAT, while high school juniors must be in the upper one-third of their classes or score at or above the 70th percentile on the ACT or SAT. Sophomores are allowed into some dual enrollment programs if certain additional benchmarks are met.

Contact your state department of education for details.

[4] *Make sure your child is well prepared to succeed at dual enrollment classes.*

I strongly advise that before starting any dual enrollment course, students get instruction from some professional person on organizing study time and preparing for and taking college-level exams.

The reason? Dual enrollment programs are not entirely without risk.

If a student takes a dual enrollment college course to fulfill a high school graduation requirement and then fails the college course, the student may not be able to graduate with his or her high school class. In addition, because all grades from dual enrollment courses are recorded on each student's permanent college or university transcript, low grades in these courses can affect overall college GPAs. Lower college GPAs can impact future scholarship awards, eventual employment, and even—many years down the line—future admission to law, medical, business, or graduate school, if that ever becomes a goal.

I urge every high school student: if you're going to take a dual enrollment course, remember that it's organizing yourself, time management, systematic review, *efficient studying*, strategic test taking, and following directions that will lead to success—not high IQ, good genes, luck, or anything else beyond your control. Organize yourself well so that you earn top grades in your dual enrollment courses right from the very beginning. If you'd like extra help from me with this, watch my free weekly email newsletter for

information on my 2.5-hour class titled, *The Strategic College Student: How to Get Higher Grades Than Anyone Else by Studying Less Than Most Other People.*

"But . . . don't those poor dual enrollment students miss out on the full high school experience?"

In the past few years, multiple high school students have contacted me, lamenting that their parents were trying to get them to do dual enrollment just part-time instead of maxing it out and getting the greatest possible number of college credits from it. Why would parents do this? The classic reason I've heard is, "We don't want our boy to miss out on the full high school experience."

Is this something to worry about? Do full-time dual enrollment students miss out on the full high school experience?

Students who've been through dual enrollment tell me emphatically, *no.* Here's why.

Dual enrollment students are still allowed to be as active as they want to be on their high school campuses. They aren't away off campus taking college math and science courses every minute of every day.

Dual enrollment students show up on their high school campuses during the school day for jazz band, for art and P.E. classes, and for marching band practice, choir rehearsals, and more. At 3:00 p.m. they're back on their high school campuses for sports practices, school play rehearsals, robotics club competitions, and bus trips to speech tournaments. Dual enrollment students are involved in all the high school clubs and organizations they want to be, and they attend school dances, pep rallies, and high school football games just like non-dual enrollment students do.

DO FULL-TIME DUAL ENROLLMENT STUDENTS MISS OUT ON THE FULL HIGH SCHOOL EXPERIENCE?

STUDENTS WHO'VE BEEN THROUGH DUAL ENROLLMENT TELL ME EMPHATICALLY, *NO.* HERE'S WHY.

One high school girl I encouraged through dual enrollment was even surprised, in her senior year of high school, to be elected homecoming queen! She was so involved at her high school that very few students realized that while they were toiling away in their high school classrooms, she was off taking all of her substantial high school classes at the community college down the street.

The happiest part of her story, though, came when her college registrar called her in for a meeting the first week after she moved into her fancy private college dormitory at the age of 18. "Next semester you'll be registering as a junior," the registrar told her. "You'll be able to register days earlier than everyone else on your dorm floor. You've only got two more years here, and you'll have your bachelor's degree all sewn up."

"Why is dual enrollment better than AP?"

Dual enrollment courses are one of the top two ways to earn college credit during the high school years. They are real college courses taught by actual college professors. They are the same level of difficulty as real college courses, and most important of all, if a student does quality work throughout a dual enrollment course and passes the exams and quizzes associated with it, he or she *will* get college credit for that work—no questions asked. Contrast this with the AP program, where students are refused college credit if they don't perform high enough on one test, on one day, at the tail end of the AP course. (Sadly, in most years, 44 percent or more of AP test takers nationally do not perform well enough on their AP exams to earn the college credit they were promised.)

One student I know of was devastated when he proudly showed a college admissions officer his list of six AP courses, all with excellent ending exam scores of 4 and 5— only to have the admissions officer sniff and say, "We aren't going to give you credit for any of those; we want you to take *real* college classes." (If I'd have been there when this student received this news, I'd have suggested that he *immediately* drop this college from his apply-to list and replace it with a better option.)

[5] Understand that AP classes are the *least* dependable way for students to earn college credit in high school.

Students hear a lot at school about AP courses. What they generally hear is that these classes are harder, but if they get a high-enough score on the test at the end of an AP course, they'll receive college credit for all the work they've put in. This is partially true. Let me provide you facts about what the AP program is and what the potential drawbacks of it can be.

AP classes are offered on high school campuses nationwide and are taught by high school teachers who may or may not have received some special AP teacher training. There are more than 30 AP courses available across 22 different subject areas, including macroeconomics, studio art, chemistry, and Japanese. The most common AP courses are English Literature, U.S. History, English Language, and Calculus. High school students sign up for these courses as part of their regular high school course load and receive high school credit for them.

In a typical year, 1.4 million students nationwide take 2.5 million AP exams, which are administered under the direction of the College Board and cost $89 each. Subsidies sometimes allow lower-income students to take AP exams at a reduced cost.

At the end of an AP course, students take a half-day test covering all the material they've learned in that course. AP tests are graded on a scale of 1 at the lowest to 5 at the highest. A score of 3 on an AP test may earn the student college credit. A score of 4 or 5 on an AP test is more likely to earn a student some college credit, but the actual credits awarded will vary widely depending on the college the student chooses to attend.

The upshot? I don't want your child to depend on AP to get his college paid for and then be disappointed. Dual enrollment tends to be a better bet than AP for students who want a dependable way to earn college credit in high school. If dual enrollment programs aren't available in your area, though, taking AP courses can offer high school students a small chance of possibly earning some college credit.

[6] *Understand the value of discounted summer community college courses.*

Many parents don't realize that most colleges will allow high school students (and older students too) to take deeply discounted college courses for college credit during summer breaks. Since community college courses are usually the least expensive to begin with, when they're discounted further the savings can be significant. In theory, if a student were to take one discounted, three-credit, community college course each summer beginning just after 9th grade and continuing through her college graduation date, she could earn a total of 21 deeply discounted credits (or more)—at the same time greatly enhancing her chances of graduating from college in just four years. (Students who know the name of their eventual four-year, degree-granting college or university should, of course, check with their regular college registrar before enrolling in any outside college class just to make sure that it will transfer back and count toward their four-year degree.)

Are you worried that your 9th grader isn't mature enough to take a summer community college course? Consider taking it *with him.*

Choose a community college course where you know he's got the natural talent to excel. If he's a born communicator, choose a public speaking course. If she's an accomplished artist, take an art course. If he's a musician, choose a music class you know he can ace. If she's a star high school volleyball player, take a college volleyball class and watch her satisfy her college P.E. requirement years ahead of time.

> **ARE YOU WORRIED THAT YOUR 9TH GRADER ISN'T MATURE ENOUGH TO TAKE A SUMMER COMMUNITY COLLEGE COURSE? CONSIDER TAKING IT** *WITH HIM.*

Consider taking time during the winter of 9th grade to contact your local community college to ask about registering yourself and your child for an upcoming summer course. If it's an academic course, be sure your daughter takes some professional college study skills training before her first day of college classes.

[7] *Did your 9th grader earn more than $400 last year? Have him file a tax return by April 15.*

Filing a tax return at this young age might be especially helpful for your 9th grader if he made contributions to a Roth IRA last year. He may get a tax refund.

Make a note in your personal calendar to have your teen complete his own tax return each year from now on, even though you're still claiming him as a dependent on your own tax return. The 1040EZ form isn't difficult to fill out. Your son has good records of what he's earned in Evernote if he's been following the instructions in this book, and he's likely to be very interested in getting every refund coming to him.

CHECKLIST

February–April of 9th Grade

☐ 1. Read this chapter thoroughly to ensure that you are clear on the best ways for students to earn real, transferable college credit during high school.

☐ 2. Understand that of the three main ways to earn college credit in high school, the fastest and least expensive is CLEP and DSST testing. (But don't try to make an entire college degree out of that!)

☐ 3. Together with your teen, look through the list of 33 CLEP tests listed on the webpage I've provided in this chapter. Find the exam that your teen is most likely to do well on with minimal preparation.

☐ 4. Have your son or daughter go online and take a free practice CLEP test on that subject.

☐ 5. If necessary, have your child do free or paid CLEP preparation on that subject using one of the inexpensive resources I suggest.

☐ 6. Register to take a CLEP exam by going to the website I've provided. Then, use the same-day strategies I prescribe in this chapter to give your teen the greatest chance of CLEP success.

☐ 7. Put a repeating note in your calendar that will remind you each June to consider having your teen take as many additional CLEP and DSST tests as possible using this same process.

☐ 8. Read this chapter thoroughly to ensure that you are clear on the benefits of state-sponsored dual enrollment programs.

☐ 9. Google the name of your state along with the words "dual enrollment" so you can learn the facts about dual enrollment programs in your state.

☐ 10. Make sure your teen is well prepared to succeed at dual enrollment classes. Have him or her take a college study skills class from a professional before starting any dual enrollment courses.

☐ 11. Understand that though AP courses can have some value to students, they tend to be the least dependable way for students to earn college credit in high school.

☐ 12. Put a repeating note in your calendar that will remind you each winter to consider having your son register for one or two discounted, summer community college courses near your home during each of his summer breaks. (Students who know the name of their eventual four-year, degree-granting college or university should, of course, check with their regular college registrar before enrolling in any outside college class just to make sure that it will transfer back and count toward their degree.)

☐ 13. If your 9th grader earned more than $400 last year, have him file a tax return by April 15. He may get a refund.

☐ 14. Check my book updates page at JeannieBurlowski.com/LAUNCH to see if I have made any recent updates to this chapter.

☐ 15. Always consult your financial planning professional before making any big financial decisions.

☐ 16. Make a note in your calendar to come back and read the next chapter of this book when your child is in May of 9th grade.

Be the first to hear about updates to the material in this book by reading my free weekly email newsletter every week. Anyone can subscribe to it at any time at JeannieBurlowski.com.

10 | *May of 9th Grade*

This month I'm going to start you thinking through some very bold, very radical decisions that could greatly increase the amount of financial aid your son or daughter eventually receives for college.

These are going to be big decisions.

I want you to start thinking these things through now, so you'll have six whole months to ponder them (and run them by your family's accountant, attorney, or financial planner) before this important upcoming deadline: December 31 of your child's sophomore year of high school.

HOW TO USE THIS CHAPTER

Start by just reading through this chapter. As you read, don't worry about committing to any of it. Decision time will come at the very end of this chapter, when I will give you a clear, at-a-glance checklist of every task I'm suggesting you consider right now.

Remember, you won't have to use every strategy I suggest; just choose the ones you think will work for your family and either modify or discard the rest.

This month, instead of immediately handing you a list of specific tasks, I want to take time to explain how families get *free money financial aid* to help their kids pay for college.

THERE ARE TWO WAYS TO GET FREE MONEY FINANCIAL AID FOR COLLEGE.

Free money financial aid is sometimes called "gift aid." It's the best kind of college aid because it's a free gift that never needs to be paid back. A student is granted this money at no charge based on information entered on financial aid application forms such as the FAFSA form.

You'll find out how much gift aid your son will be receiving when you open financial aid award letters from colleges in the spring of his senior year of high school. These letters will tell you (a) how much money each college is likely to cost for your son, and (b) how each college suggests that you pay for his particular college education. When you open these letters, I want you to feel surprised and happy at how much free money (that does not have to be paid back) your son will be receiving.

As you are looking forward to that day, know that there are two main ways to increase the amount of free money your child receives for college.

Increase the merit of your child.

If your child is a highly desirable applicant who will enrich the college experience for others, private colleges may very well try to attract him by offering him free money grants and scholarships that do not need to be paid back. (Important! Don't fall into the trap of believing that merit is all about grades and test scores. Grades and test scores make up only part of the picture when it comes to who will enrich the college experience for others.)

Other parts of this book talk extensively about helping your son take strategic steps to increase his merit in the eyes of college admissions and financial aid officers. Today, let's focus on the second half of the financial aid equation.

Increase the financial need of your family.

If you plan and strategize well at two different points (before December 31 of your child's sophomore year of high school, and then again each September before you fill out the FAFSA form), you may be able to drastically alter some things about your family finances—and as a result put your family in a much enhanced position to receive maximum free money financial aid for college.

So you can understand exactly how this works, let me take you on a trip just a little over three years into the future, to October 1 of your child's senior year of high school.

On that date (or as soon as possible after that), you will sit down to fill out the FAFSA form and any other financial aid forms required by the colleges your child is applying to. You'll do this in early October every year you have a possibility of having a child in college the following fall. Why am I strict about the timing on filling out these forms? Because submitting them early puts you first in line for free money to help pay for college.

Have you got a clear picture of this? Every family should fill out every possible financial aid form. Let me repeat this one more time for emphasis. Even if you make over $200,000 a year and you are completely and utterly convinced that your family is so wealthy that you could never, in a million years, ever qualify for any free money financial aid for college, you should still fill out every financial aid form you can. Even if you as a parent are planning to flatly refuse to pay one penny for your child's college education, you should still fill out every financial aid form you can.

You might be surprised.

The FAFSA form in particular puts your child in line for nine separate federal student aid programs, over 600 state aid programs, and most of the college-based (institutional) aid available in the U.S. Every year, people who were *sure* they were too well-off to qualify for any kind of aid are stunned to see what kind of generous help they actually qualify for at some colleges.

Remember, your household income is only one of several factors used to decide your child's financial aid eligibility. Age of the older parent, household size, number of family members attending college simultaneously, and many other complex and interwoven factors figure in too. Any one of these factors could greatly increase your family's eligibility for free money for college.

Besides that, every year there are very wealthy families whose fortunes turn suddenly and unexpectedly for the worse. These families' college-age children need to be in the financial aid system to get the help they suddenly need when they need it.

At the very least, you will want your child to qualify for the lowest-interest loans with the best terms if he or she does at some point (against all my pleading) end up taking out some loans to pay for college. The FAFSA form is the doorway not only to every need-based financial aid program in the U.S., but to the best, lowest-interest student loans as well.

When you complete the FAFSA form (and perhaps additional financial aid forms as well), here's what will happen.

The information you enter on those forms is going to be used to create a snapshot of your family's individual financial situation.

The financial aid calculations will not take into consideration what your financial situation looked like five years ago, and they will not try to forecast what your financial situation is going to look like way off in the future when your child is a junior in college. For this snapshot, the financial aid calculations will look only at two things: (1) certain assets in your family's possession on the day you fill out financial aid forms and (2) the income you and your child received during one short, 12-month period of time, from January 1 of your child's sophomore year of high school to December 31 of your child's junior year of high school. I call this period of time "the magic year."

> **THE FAFSA FORM IS THE DOORWAY NOT ONLY TO EVERY NEED-BASED FINANCIAL AID PROGRAM IN THE U.S., BUT TO THE BEST, LOWEST-INTEREST STUDENT LOANS AS WELL.**

This particular 12-month period is very, very important to you—because if happy circumstances occur that make you look far wealthier than you really are just before or during that year (you sell a business, your spouse takes a second job to bring in more cash, you get a huge sales commission at work, or you are blessed to have a generous relative give you a large financial gift), you may look as though you are far wealthier than you really are. You might look far too wealthy to qualify for much need-based, free money financial aid, even if your regular annual income is tiny and these windfalls are from unusual circumstances that will never be repeated again.

On the other hand, if circumstances occur

prior to the beginning of the magic year (that is, prior to January 1 of your child's sophomore year of high school) that bring your income and assets down to a low point, your son or daughter may qualify for additional free money financial aid to pay for college.

Here's a big question that some families ask themselves: "What if we were to deliberately bring our family income and assets down to a low point just prior to that special year when we'll be scrutinized for financial aid eligibility? Prior to January 1 of our child's sophomore year of high school? Would that help us—or not?"

It might.

If at this moment you are just a hairsbreadth away from the line of maybe qualifying for financial aid for college and maybe not, it might help you tremendously.

Whether bringing your income and assets down to a low point will actually help you or not will depend on your family's individual financial situation, and what "low point" means to you.

Many families considering this question will take some time near the end of their child's freshman year of high school to plug family financial numbers into free online cost calculators that can provide valuable answers. The free online financial aid calculator that I like best will help you determine how much your family will likely be expected to pay for college if your income and assets remain the way they are right now. You can get directly to it by typing this shortcut into your web browser: Bit.ly/2gvaxng.

If you fill out this form multiple times using different numbers, you'll be able to see how much your income and assets would need to fall to make your child a candidate for additional free money financial aid for college.

If you'd like second opinions on these cost calculations, other financial aid calculators can be found on these websites:

» Finaid.org/calculators/finaidestimate. phtml

» Webapps01.act.org/fane/docs/

» Aie.org/pay-for-college/understand-college-costs/efc-calculator/

Some families who take the time to do these calculations prior to the start of the magic year are surprised and happy to find that making just a few tweaks to their financial situation prior to December 31 of their child's sophomore year of high school can lead to much higher, free money, financial aid awards.

"Tweak our family finances? What would that look like?"

In the following pages, I'm going to list 10 "tweaks" (strategies) that other families have used to purposely bring their income down prior to December 31 of their child's sophomore year of high school.

Some of these tweaks are huge, and some are relatively minor. Before you make any final decisions on which (if any) of these strategies to implement, I strongly suggest that you seek the counsel of a qualified accountant, attorney, or certified financial planner. Bring this chapter with you to the meeting. You have until about September 15 of this year to do this, but don't wait until the last minute.

BRINGING INCOME DOWN BEFORE APPLYING FOR FINANCIAL AID

I don't know of anyone who would use *all* of the following strategies. Just look this list over and consider whether any of these strategies might help your individual family situation.

Have one parent simply quit working for a period of time.

Some families will choose to have one parent quit work, stay home with younger children during the magic year, save day care costs, and spend extra time coming up with clever ways for the family to cut expenses and live more frugally.

Have one parent take an unpaid sabbatical that could pay big dividends later.

Some families will decide that perhaps the magic year (beginning January 1 of the student's sophomore year of high school) would be the perfect time for Dad to take an unpaid sabbatical from work and go back to college to get that master's degree he's always wanted. This can work especially well if Dad's company is willing to pay for his master's degree under a company tuition reimbursement program.

Or maybe Mom could take a magic year sabbatical and use the time to research and write a book that will pay royalties for years to come.

Avoid having parents take on second jobs to bring in supplementary income.

Some families will decide that the magic year is not the best time for Mom to take on a second job to bring in extra cash, since higher family income during this time will result in lower financial aid awards later.

Have the student cut his work hours after a certain point.

Some students will look carefully at reducing the number of hours they will work for pay after December 31 of their sophomore year of high school, and instead give more time to focused, carefully chosen volunteer work and job shadowing.

Why would a student choose to work less after December 31 of his or her sophomore year of high school?

Because starting at that point, FAFSA calculations allow your teen to earn just over $6,000 each year before earnings start reducing his or her potential to receive free money financial aid for college.

If your son earns more than this amount in a calendar year after December 31 of his sophomore year of high school, his extra earnings will be viewed as fair game to be taken to pay for his college. (The FAFSA formula won't take *all* his extra earnings, of course. Just 50 percent of them. Which your son is going to think is bad enough.)

Note that the strategy of limiting student work hours does *not* apply to college students enrolled in the co-op education programs discussed in chapter 14. It also does not apply to most graduate students earning money through fellowships and assistant-ships, or to college students earning money through the federal work-study award that comes as part of some financial aid packages. These earnings will need to be reported on the FAFSA form, but they will not count against the student when calculating the following year's federal financial aid.

NOTE THAT THE STRATEGY OF LIMITING STUDENT WORK HOURS DOES *NOT* APPLY TO COLLEGE STUDENTS ENROLLED IN THE CO-OP EDUCATION PROGRAMS DISCUSSED IN CHAPTER 14.

Look ahead to see if you have any income surges on the horizon. Take them early if possible.

Income surges might include

» a planned stock sale,

» the sale of a family business or rental property,

» a large chunk of money you know will be coming into the family business from accounts receivables,

» a large sales commission or employee bonus,

» a large insurance settlement,

» income from the exercise of stock options,

» money you've been planning to take out of an IRA for some reason, or

» a large monetary gift you know is coming from a family member.

If you know that these types of income surges are coming, use whatever influence you have to get them in your bank account prior to December 31 of your child's sophomore year of high school—so they won't count as income during the year your child is being scrutinized for financial aid eligibility.

If a generous relative is planning to give your family a large financial gift, request that he or she do that in a special strategic way.

Of course you'll be deeply thankful if Uncle Jeff wants to give you or your child a large cash gift. The trouble is that if a large monetary gift goes into one of your family bank accounts during the magic year, it could reduce your child's future financial aid eligibility. To head this off, sincerely thank Uncle Jeff for the gift and then ask him to put that money into a 529 savings plan in Uncle Jeff's own name with your child named as the beneficiary.

For a reminder of exactly why this strategy is so helpful, review the free online resource I've created that gently explains to generous family members the best way to give a child money without diminishing his or her future financial aid eligibility. The strategies in the article will work whether your child is a newborn, a toddler, a teenager, or already a college student. The resource is free and you can share it with anyone.

*Start a business with 100 or fewer
employees.*

Some families will decide to use their available assets to start up a family business with
100 or fewer employees, and then invest a
large chunk of their money in that.

Why would a family want to do this? Because
since 2005, the value of family-owned businesses with under 100 full-time (or full-time
equivalent) employees doesn't get considered in federal financial aid formulas. (If you
decide to proceed with this idea, you have
a little extra time to plan. Just make sure
you've got the money stashed away in this
small business by October 1 of your child's
senior year of high school.)

*Consider turning your second home
or vacation home into a "formally
recognized business."*

If you own a second home or a vacation
home, don't bother trying to hide its value
by simply setting it up as an LLC and trying
to pass it off as a small business. I wish that
worked, but it doesn't.

If you own a home that you sometimes *rent
out,* though, read on for another possible option.

If part of the service you provide to your renters includes regular cleaning, linen changes,
or maid service, you may be able to keep that
asset from scrutiny on the FAFSA by making it
a part of a formally recognized business that
has 100 or fewer full-time employees. The official word on this is found at the FinAid website,
which says, "Rental properties are counted as
investments, not business assets, *unless* they
are part of a formally recognized business"
[emphasis mine].[11] If you are considering characterizing your second home or vacation home
as a formally recognized business, carefully
read the detailed directions on how to do so
that are provided on the Finaid.org website.
You can get directly to the page you need by
typing this shortcut into your web browser:
Mnstr.me/2gMMNLK.

If you are going to make your second home
or vacation home a part of a formally recognized business, I suggest you do that by
December 31 of your child's sophomore year
of high school. If you do it by that deadline, it
will exist and pay taxes as a formally recognized business for one full tax year before
you fill out your child's FAFSA form. Do this,
and when you're asked about your investments on your FAFSA form, you'll be able to
leave these assets off since they will be part
of your family's formally recognized business
that has 100 or fewer full-time employees.

---

11 "Small Business Exclusion: Rental Property," FinAid, accessed November 19, 2016, http://www.finaid.
org/fafsa/smallbusiness.phtml#rental.

If you're thinking of setting up your family's second home or vacation home as a formally recognized business, setting the property up as an LLC may be a part of that plan. Visit an attorney, accountant, or other qualified financial professional to get clear instructions, and make sure you understand all the tax and other implications before doing so.

If you're going to give your 9th grader a large financial gift, time the giving of that gift carefully.

If you're going to give this 9th grader a large amount of money for some reason, keep three things in mind.

First, it's more advantageous from a financial aid perspective to put that gift money into your daughter's 529 savings plan than to give the money to her outright. Second, if you are giving your daughter a large monetary gift, do it before December 31 of her 10th-grade year so it won't count as magic year income when financial aid calculations are made later. Third, plan for this large cash gift to be either *used up* or *stashed away in a 529 savings plan or in her retirement savings* by October 1 of this girl's senior year of high school. Why? Because if it's sitting around in a bank account in her name at that time, you'll have to report it on financial aid forms and that will diminish her future financial aid awards.

Sell off some of your assets and use the money to pay your debts and fund your retirement.

Some families will make a plan to sell off as many of their assets as is wise and prudent, use that money to pay off as many of their

debts as possible, and then put a substantial chunk of the remaining funds into retirement savings.

This can be a great idea. If you're going to do it, though, time the sale of your assets carefully. You don't want to accidentally give yourself a huge income surge during the magic year (December 31 of your child's sophomore year of high school to December 31 of your child's junior year of high school).

If you're going to sell off some of your assets, ask your financial advisor if it would be wise for you to sell everything you're going to sell by December 31 of your child's sophomore year of high school. If you do this, be sure to wisely *spend that money down* before the day you fill out your first financial aid forms, which will be on or about October 1 of your child's senior year of high school. Paying off high-interest debt and fattening up retirement accounts can be *excellent* ways to wisely spend down this money (especially since your debt payments and retirement funds aren't considered *at all* when your family's finances are scrutinized for financial aid purposes).

If your work with the online calculators listed earlier makes you think that liquidating (selling off) some of your assets, paying off debts, and then putting a chunk of your remaining funds into retirement might be a good idea, remember three things.

First, if you are going to stash assets in retirement savings, talk to a financial planning professional about it *well before* you first fill out financial aid forms. The timing on this will be important. If you don't time your retirement contribution carefully, you'll be required to report all the assets you were planning to transfer into retirement savings on your child's FAFSA form, and that will reduce your child's financial aid eligibility.

Second, keep in mind that on the day you fill out his financial aid forms (the first of which will be October 1 of his senior year of high school), your son's own assets will reduce his financial aid eligibility as well. Essentially, every penny your son has in non-retirement accounts in his name on the day you fill out his financial aid forms will reduce his future financial aid award. For this reason, your son may also want to sell off some of his assets now, when the financial aid application process won't see him bringing in extra income, and then transfer as much of that money as possible into his 529 savings plan or into his retirement accounts, using the same careful timing as you are.

> **EVERY PENNY YOUR SON HAS IN NON-RETIREMENT ACCOUNTS IN HIS NAME ON THE DAY YOU FILL OUT HIS FINANCIAL AID FORMS WILL REDUCE HIS FUTURE FINANCIAL AID AWARD.**

Third, these are big decisions. Seek out a qualified accountant, attorney, or financial planner to help you make them. He or she will counsel you to always maintain an emergency fund so you're ready to take care of your family no matter what kind of unexpected circumstances come up. Then, after that, he or she will guide you as you look closely at the value of your

- » cash on hand in savings and checking accounts,
- » money market funds,
- » mutual funds,
- » certificates of deposit,
- » stocks,
- » stock options,
- » bonds,
- » other securities,
- » commodities,
- » interest-producing investments,
- » installment and land sale contracts (with any debt owed on them subtracted),
- » real estate you own (other than the house you live in), and
- » accounts owned by the student.

Once this financial planning professional gets a good picture of these assets (along with a view of how close you are to the line of financial aid eligibility), he or she will be able to look at the suggestions in this chapter and recommend specific strategies for your family.

If you've never visited a financial planning professional before and feel trepidation about choosing a good one, best-selling author Dave Ramsey offers some great help on a webpage designed to help people feel confident about hiring investing professionals. You can get directly to that page by typing this shortcut into your web browser: Bit.ly/2g7JLxq.

PUTTING EXTRA MONEY IN RETIREMENT CAN BE ESPECIALLY HELPFUL

The "squirrel money away in retirement" strategy I've suggested might be a great help to you, because money you've socked away in accounts such as 401(k), 403(b), annuities, non-educational IRAs, SEP, SIMPLE, pensions, and Roth IRAs is not included in the calculation of Expected Family Contribution (EFC) for college under any methodology.

Your retirement funds will never be counted as your asset on any financial aid form—as long as that money is safely in those retirement accounts as of the day you first fill out financial aid forms (on approximately October 1 of your child's senior year of high school), and as long as it remains in those retirement accounts until at least January 1 of your youngest child's sophomore year of college.

The strategy of putting a *teen's* earnings into a Roth IRA can also be especially helpful. In 2013 I got a phone call from a sharp, perceptive high school student who happily told me that in September of his senior year of high school, he'd used online financial aid calculators to determine that if he put his entire college savings into a Roth IRA, he'd get more financial aid for college. He did this, and his Pell grant jumped from $1,000 to $5,500. Then, when he did the math and realized just how much his high school earnings were

going to be worth after gathering compound interest in a retirement account for 45 years, he hooted with joy and started actively shopping for sailboats.

Why was a Roth IRA a particularly good retirement savings choice for this student? Because although he put after-tax money into it, when he eventually withdraws the money at age 59 and a half (or later), none of it (including the earnings) will be taxed, as long as the Roth IRA has been open for at least five tax years.

The Roth IRA becomes an even sweeter option for a 15-year-old high school sophomore, if you consider the benefits when he goes to buy a house in the years after he graduates from college. I discussed in an earlier chapter how first-time home buyers with Roth IRAs are allowed to pull out up to $10,000 in profits penalty-free and tax-free, as long as the money has been in the Roth IRA for at least five tax years. If your son starts putting money into a Roth IRA at age 15 or earlier, he will be able to start pulling money out to contribute to a down payment on a house in his early 20s. If he is fortunate enough to eventually marry someone who also made this same choice, the two will have double the money available to use as a down payment on their first home.

IF YOUR SON IS FORTUNATE ENOUGH TO MARRY SOMEONE WHO ALSO MADE THIS SAME CHOICE, THE TWO WILL HAVE DOUBLE THE MONEY AVAILABLE TO USE AS A DOWN PAYMENT ON THEIR FIRST HOME.

I caution you, though, not to use a Roth IRA as a primary college savings method. Even though technically Roth IRA money can be withdrawn tax-free and penalty-free for educational expenses, money taken out of a Roth IRA before January 1 of the child's sophomore year of college *counts as income for financial aid purposes* and so will reduce his financial aid eligibility. When it comes to college savings vehicles, 529 plans tend to be far better options.

To see whether the strategies I've suggested in this chapter might be useful for your family, use one of the calculators I've provided and run the calculations both ways (first, with all of your money considered in the financial aid calculation, and second, with a portion of your money socked away for retirement). See which strategy yields the greatest return for your family. Then talk to your accountant, attorney, or financial planner and get professional guidance.

"Wow. How long would we need to keep doing this?"

When I present these strategies in the live seminars I teach, I always have a parent raise a hand and ask, "Wait a minute; to keep our need-based financial aid, we'll have to keep our income and assets low all the way through December 31 of our youngest child's sophomore year of college, right?"

That's right, but it's just a little bit more complicated than that.

On January 1 of your youngest child's sophomore year of college, you'll be able to (a) freely increase the money you earn from working, (b) take all the income surges you've been holding off on, (c) pull money out of a Roth IRA to pay educational expenses, and (d) freely use the money in the 529 plan that your child's grandma has kept in her own name with your child named as the beneficiary. This extra money will be of great help to you when it comes to paying for this child's last two and a half years of college expenses, and it won't reduce financial aid eligibility at that point. But I do have one caution about it.

On January 1 of the sophomore year of college, this child will still have one more FAFSA form to fill out. On October 1 of the junior year of college, your family will have to report once again how much money you have in money market funds, mutual funds, certificates of deposit, stocks, vested stock options, bonds, other securities, commodities, installment and land sale contracts, cash, savings accounts, checking accounts, and investments (including real estate you don't live in that is not a part of a formally recognized business). You won't want the total of these assets to be too high.

So what's the upshot? Don't plan to fill your bank accounts with a lot of extra income starting January 1 of your youngest child's sophomore year of college unless you have a plan for wisely spending that money down before you fill out your final financial aid form(s) the following October 1. One idea you might try is to call the bursar's office at your child's college or university and see how many of your child's future college bills you can pay in advance. If your money is sitting in an account in the bursar's office, it won't show on that final financial aid form.

NOW, HERE'S THE GREATEST NEWS OF THIS ENTIRE CHAPTER

If you've followed my earlier instructions about maximizing CLEP, DSST, and especially high school dual enrollment programs, your daughter may very well be graduating from college with a bachelor's degree just 24 months after she graduates from high school.

> **IF YOU FOLLOWED THE INSTRUCTIONS IN THIS BOOK, YOU MIGHT BE FILLING OUT YOUR DAUGTHER'S LAST FAFSA FORM JUST FOUR MONTHS AFTER SHE GRADUATES FROM HIGH SCHOOL.**

If this happens, then January 1 of your daughter's "sophomore year of college" may occur five months before her high school graduation date! You might be filling out her last FAFSA form just four months after she graduates from high school.

Just sit back a minute and let that sink in.

For families whose child has earned two years of college credit in high school, they may be looking at just a very short season of careful financial restriction: from December 31 of the child's sophomore year of high school to December 31 of the child's senior year of high school, plus one additional day (the day of filling out the last financial aid forms—four months after graduating from high school).

If you have just one child (or if you've strategized so that both your children attend col-

lege during the same years) this may be just two short years.

Might living under these special financial circumstances for two short years be worth it if it helps your son or daughter receive far more free money financial aid for college?

"Won't we have to update someone if our financial situation changes?"

Parents may be wondering, "If our financial situation suddenly changes radically for the better in the middle of our daughter's sophomore year of college, won't we have to update someone? The numbers we typed in on the FAFSA form just three months beforehand will suddenly be out-of-date."

Excellent question.

Let's go straight to the makers of the FAFSA and get the answer from them. The FAFSA website says this about which details you've entered on the FAFSA form must be updated if they change:

> There are certain items that you must update: You must update anything that changes your dependency status (for instance, you are now pregnant or are now in legal guardianship) except a change in your marital status. If your marital status changes, you must speak to the financial aid office to determine whether you may update the FAFSA. If (and only if) you are selected for verification, you must update your FAFSA if there is a change in the number of family members in your parents' household or in your household. If the number of family members changes as a result of a change in your (the

student's) marital status, you must speak to the financial aid office at the school you plan to attend to determine whether you may update the FAFSA.[12]

This is the definitive answer to whether or not you need to report a change in financial status. It's no. You don't have to update anyone, and as a matter of fact, you aren't *allowed* to update anyone if you wanted to.

"My goodness. Is it really OK for us to strategize to this extent?"

As you read these strategies, do you find yourself huffing in disapproval that anyone would try to "play the system" by making their financial situation look piteous during the specific times they're being evaluated for financial aid eligibility?

Do you think that the most ethical thing is to have families make all their financial decisions blindly throughout this important period of time, be stunned and shocked at how little student aid they qualify for, and then sign their children up for indentured servitude to odious student loan payments through age 50?

Let me be clear about this. The financial aid rules and policies in the United States are set up to reward families who take the steps I've outlined. Wealthy families already know about these strategies; they have lawyers and accountants to help them figure these things out. If we keep these strategies secret, we will only disadvantage the middle class and low-income families who need them most.

THINK THESE TOPICS THROUGH NOW, WHEN YOUR CHILD IS STILL IN 9TH GRADE

Why? You may be looking at making some radical changes to your family finances prior to December 31 of your child's sophomore year of high school. To give yourself maximum time to plan, start thinking about these things now. December 31 of your child's sophomore year of high school is just months away.

---

12 "What Kind of Changes Can I Make to My FAFSA Once It's Been Processed?," Federal Student Aid, accessed November 19, 2016, https://studentaid.ed.gov/fafsa/next-steps/correct-update.

CHECKLIST

May of 9th Grade

☐ 1. Read this chapter carefully, so you'll be ready to possibly take some big steps to improve your child's financial aid eligibility before this coming December 31.

☐ 2. No matter how high your net worth, commit to filling out the FAFSA form every October 1 that you have a child in college the following fall.

☐ 3. Plug your family financial numbers into free online cost calculators to see how close your child currently is to receiving financial aid for college.

☐ 4. Understand that there are 10 key decisions you can make in the next seven months that could drastically increase the amount of financial aid your child eventually receives. Discuss these strategies as a family, and seek the help of a qualified accountant, lawyer, or certified financial planner before making any final decisions.

☐ 5. Note in your calendar that on *January 1 of your youngest child's sophomore year of college*, you will be able to significantly increase your income and your assets, but plan to wisely spend down this extra money before submitting your daughter's final FAFSA the following October 1.

☐ 6. This chapter has shown you again how valuable it is to have students earn college credit in high school. Encourage your daughter to earn as many CLEP, DSST, and dual enrollment credits in high school as possible over the next three years. (Just don't try to put together a college degree made up entirely of CLEP and DSST tests!)

☐ 7. Check my book updates page at JeannieBurlowski.com/LAUNCH to see if I have made any recent updates to this chapter.

☐ 8. Always consult your financial planning professional before making any big financial decisions.

☐ 9. Make a note in your calendar to come back and read the next chapter of this book in June after your child completes 9th grade.

Be the first to hear about updates to the material in this book by reading my free weekly email newsletter every week. Anyone can subscribe to it at any time at JeannieBurlowski.com.

II | *Summer After 9th Grade*

You are making outstanding progress toward getting your child through college debt-free. You've done so many things already that many parents *never* think to do.

This chapter is likely to feel very reassuring to you. It contains important to-do items for this summer, but the first thing you'll notice is how many you already know about and already have in place. When you see this, it'll build your momentum and your confidence and energize you for the steps we'll be taking together in your child's 10th-, 11th-, and 12th-grade years.

HOW TO USE THIS CHAPTER

Start by just reading through this chapter. As you read, don't worry about committing to any of it. Decision time will come at the very end of this chapter, when I give you a clear, at-a-glance checklist of every task I'm suggesting you consider right now.

Remember, you won't have to use every strategy I suggest; you'll just choose the ones you think will work for your family and either modify or discard the rest.

[1] *Just as you did after 8th grade, schedule a meeting where you as a parent/child team go over the terms of the contract you and your son signed one year ago.*

You have it posted on the inside of a cupboard door in your kitchen, right?

[2] *Cheer your daughter on as she starts work at her summer job.*

Remember, your daughter has until roughly October 1 of her senior year of high school to pump all the earnings she possibly can into her own Roth IRA account (up to legal Roth IRA limits).

Even if your household income is so high

that you as parents don't qualify for a Roth IRA, don't worry. Children can have Roth IRAs of their own, even if their parents can't have them.

For a review of the excellent benefits of the Roth IRA to middle school and high school students (including what you as a parent can do if your child refuses to save), please review chapter 4.

[3] *Check to be sure that your son is recording all of his earnings in Evernote, including photos of each check and piles of cash he receives.*

It's important that he keep track of every dollar he earns so he can prove he has earned income to put into his Roth IRA.

[4] *Search for a list of CLEP and DSST exams, and see if there are any your daughter is now close to passing because she studied those subjects during her 9th-grade year.*

Use the instructions in chapter 9 to have her practice for and take as many CLEP and DSST exams as possible this summer. Every one she takes and passes could save her up to $5,000 in future college costs, so if she balks at doing this, you might offer to pay her to do it.

[5] *Help your child design and complete a summer project that benefits the humanitarian cause she's adopted as her own.*

Get your whole family involved if you can.

Pull in other families and friends as well. Need ideas for this? Even if you don't have a lot of time to dedicate to service this summer, google "Eagle Scout Service Projects" and you'll find hundreds of ideas for service projects you can modify and complete on a smaller scale.

[6] *Log your son into his account on LinkedIn and help him to update his profile there.*

Include in his LinkedIn profile any awards he won at the end of 9th grade, as well as any work experiences, job-shadowing experiences, and volunteer and service hours he's had so far. Help him to link to more of his parents' friends, his friends' parents, and other adults he knows on LinkedIn.

Remember, parent, because of where your son is in regard to brain development, he is unlikely to sit down and do this unless you log him in and walk him through it.

[7] *Have your daughter use the details in her LinkedIn account, her teacher letters of recommendation, and her cut and paste skills to apply for 10 private scholarships.*

Pay her for doing this if necessary.

If writing the application essays presents an obstacle for her, have her take my two-hour *Make Them Say Wow* class on writing brilliant, attention-getting scholarship application essays. Details about when and where you can access this class are found in my free weekly email newsletter.

[8] *Have you and your child previously registered to take a reduced-price community college class together this summer?*

If so, taking that class will be on the agenda for this summer as well. Express pride in your daughter that she's stepping up and tackling difficult things that most 9th graders never even consider attempting. Let her know that you see a very bright future ahead for her!

Finally, here's your most important task for the summer after 9th grade:

[9] *Tell your son that starting this summer you'll be asking him to pay for all of his own personal expenses using money you provide.*

Parent, one of your preeminent goals in life is to raise a child who is smart about managing money.

No matter your household income, your goal is to raise a child who knows the value of a dollar, who budgets and saves carefully, who thinks strategically about how to wring as much as possible out of each paycheck, who hunts for bargains, and who frequently says no to himself when he feels the temptation to buy something frivolous.

How will you raise a child like this? By giving him a great deal of experience with money management early on—while he's still safe at home under your roof. If you'll do this starting when your child is 15 years old, you'll help him learn tremendously valuable life and money lessons while the costs are still low, rather than having him learn them as an adult through the pain of home foreclosure, bankruptcy, automobile repossession, or crushing levels of student loan and credit card debt.

How to hand personal money management over to a teenager: use an allowance system.

During the summer after 9th grade, tell your son that you're ready to be done making his financial decisions for him. Explain to him that you're tired and you're busy, and he's old enough and smart enough, so you'd like him to take over that responsibility.

Take your son down to your local bank and help him open a checking account with a debit card in his own name. Explain to your son that you plan to deposit a specific amount of money into that checking account every two weeks, and that you will plan on him using that money to pay for all of his own clothes, shoes, school lunches, athletic fees, cell phone service, amusement park admissions, pizza out with friends, and all of his other teen life-related expenses. Create a written list of all the things you expect him to pay for with this money.

How will you know how much money to give him? If you've been following the instructions in this book since your child was in 8th grade, you started one year ago keeping track of how much money your family actually spends on this child per year, along with what that money is being spent on.

If you didn't keep track of those expenses that's OK, just do your best to estimate.

WHAT YOU WANT IS FOR YOUR SON TO LEARN HOW TO DEAL WITH SCARCITY. HOW TO HANDLE LACK. HOW TO STRATEGIZE TO MAKE MONEY STRETCH. HOW TO BE FRUGAL. HOW TO STRETCH A DOLLAR UNTIL IT SCREAMS.

Take the total amount you believe you spend on this child for these items in a year, divide that number by 24, and have your bank automatically transfer that amount from your bank account into your son's checking account on the 1st and the 15th of every month.

But wait just a minute. If your son has exactly what he needs to get by, that's no fun. That's no challenge. He won't learn anything from that. What you want is for him to learn how to deal with scarcity. How to handle lack. How to strategize to make money stretch. How to be frugal. How to stretch a dollar until it screams. You've got just three years to instill this skill in your son; you'd better start now.

What you want is to re-create the Great Depression in your own home.

Without saying anything about it to your son, I suggest that you give him just about 70 percent of what you know it will actually take to cover all of his personal expenses.

Watch him squirm and struggle to pay for everything he needs, just as you did when you were young and just starting out. Watch him juggle and plot and think and strategize. Watch him start saying no to paying retail at malls, and instead start shopping on clearance racks, at consignment clothing stores,

and at upscale thrift shops. Watch him fix his old tennis shoes with a rubber repair product he buys himself so he can wear them another season. Watch him start suggesting to his friends that everyone bring lawn chairs and attend free movie night in the park instead of paying $11 a head for movie theater tickets. Watch him learn valuable lessons when he runs out of money before his two weeks are up. Watch him realize that he needs to look ahead and see big expenses coming while they are still a long way down the road, so he can plan and save up for them.

And what will you do, parent, with the 30 percent of his expenses you aren't giving him outright?

Wait for a catastrophe.

Teenage son: "Mom! Prom tickets are only available through Friday, and I forgot to buy mine! Can you please lend me $150 until the 15th?"

Mom: "Oh no! You're out of money and can't afford prom tickets? That's awful! Emily will be so disappointed if you have to call off prom. I'd say this calls for breaking into your emergency fund!"

Teenage son: "Mom, I, uh—I don't have an emergency fund. I haven't saved up for that yet. Could you please just lend me $150? Just until the 15th?"

Mom (genuinely sad for him and wanting to help): "Well, I can't allow you to incur debt for that. We don't believe in debt in this family. But how about this? I will pay you $50 for every scholarship application you fill out in a quality manner. Do you think you could fill out three scholarship applications by Friday? I bet you could!"

When your child runs into a financial emergency as a result of poor planning, let him bear the consequences of his poor decision making. And if he gets so hard up for money that he has to beg you to lend you your cash, let him earn what he needs by filling out scholarship applications in a quality manner. You are the smartest parent in the world; you've already cleverly arranged your family finances so you've got the money to pay him for that.

I highly recommend using this financial management system starting the summer after your child finishes 9th grade. If you do so, you'll allow your son to learn valuable life skills that will pay off for decades into his future. You'll free yourself from having to respond to whiny requests for money every day, because your reply to every request will be, "Sure! Sounds fun! If you've got enough money to pay for that, I'm all for it!"

If you do this, though, follow the advice of my friends Joy and Patrick, who did this with their 15-year-old son. "Identify the nonnegotiable items in advance," Joy told me. "If there are certain things you absolutely want your son to buy, tell him up-front that he doesn't have to fork out his own money for those things. If you really want him to wear boots and a winter coat, use deodorant, brush his teeth, get haircuts, buy school supplies, and attend summer camp, for instance, tell him from the beginning that you'll happily pay for all of those things. If he runs out of hot lunch money, he can always make himself cold peanut butter sandwich sack lunches in your kitchen, but if he runs out of haircut money, you don't want him not visiting a barber for three years."

> **YOU'LL FREE YOURSELF FROM HAVING TO RESPOND TO WHINY REQUESTS FOR MONEY EVERY DAY, BECAUSE YOUR REPLY TO EVERY REQUEST WILL BE, "SURE! SOUNDS FUN! IF YOU'VE GOT ENOUGH MONEY TO PAY FOR THAT, I'M ALL FOR IT!"**

[10] *Use this "allowance system" to empower your son to remember to get his own household chores done on time without nagging or reminders.*

Earlier in this book, I emphasized (in chapter 3, "7th Grade or Earlier") that it's critically important for your child to learn to do all of his own household chores by himself without being reminded.

The allowance strategy I've discussed gives you exquisite leverage for enforcing that.

Let your son know that if he "forgets" to do one of his chores on time, you won't be upset. You'll just wait until he's gone to school or out with friends and cheerfully do the chore for him. It'll be no problem for you to keep track of the chores you do on his behalf along with the dates and times you complete them. Then, when it's time for you to put money in his bank account, you can just dock his pay $2 for each chore you've completed for him.

When he notices that your recent deposit to his bank account was $10 short, kindly and empathetically hand him your list of chores, dates, and charges. With genuine sadness for him in your voice, say something like, "Oh, you were so busy in the past two weeks that five of your chores didn't get done on time.

That's OK; I understand. I did them all for you, and I did a really good job. And I knew you were short on money, so I only charged you $2 for each chore instead of $3. This was no problem for me. I'm glad to do chores for you any time you're busy!"

You may want to charge a child $2 for an undone chore, or you might want to charge more or perhaps less. The amount you charge should sting, but it should not be so high that the child is disheartened and feels like giving up.

[11] *If you have a complex financial situation, make an appointment this summer with a certified public accountant or a certified financial planner who specializes in financial planning for college.*

Your own personal financial planner may have the specific, targeted expertise to be able to do this, or you can seek specialized help from one of the thousands of certified public accountants and certified financial planners who are members of the National College Advocacy Group (NCAG) at Ncagonline.org. If your income is very high or your financial situation very complicated, get help from highly respected Forbes contributor Troy Onink by signing up for one of the very valuable one-hour consultations he offers at Stratagee.com.

Whichever option you choose, take steps now to find the person who will guide you through tax and financial planning both before and during college, and then make sure that person knows about the key strategies you're following on your own using this book.

You have big decisions to make prior to this coming December 31, and it will be good to let this professional person have a voice in your decisions.

CHECKLIST

Summer After 9th Grade

1. Schedule a meeting where you and your daughter look over the terms of the contract you and she signed one year ago.

2. Cheer your son on as he starts work at his summer job.

3. Check to be sure that your daughter is recording all of her earnings in Evernote, including photos of each check or stack of cash she receives.

4. See if there are any CLEP or DSST exams that your son is now close to passing because he studied those subjects during 9th grade. Have him prep for and take those tests.

5. Help your daughter design and complete a modest summer project that benefits the humanitarian cause she's adopted as her own.

6. Log your son into his account on LinkedIn, and help him update his profile there.

7. Have your daughter use the details in her LinkedIn profile, her teacher letters of recommendation, and her skill with cut and paste to apply for 10 different private scholarships.

8. If you and your son registered to take a reduced-price community college class together this summer, attend classes and do the necessary studying.

9. Set up the allowance system where your child pays all of his or her own personal expenses using money you provide.

10. Use this allowance system as leverage to help your child learn to get all household chores done on time without nagging or reminders.

11. If you have a complex financial situation, make an appointment this summer with an accountant or other financial planning professional who specializes in financial planning for college. Show that person chapter 10 of this book. There are big decisions ahead, and you may want this person to have a voice in those decisions.

12. Always consult a financial planning professional before making any big financial decisions.

13. Check my book updates page at JeannieBurlowski.com/LAUNCH to see if I have made any recent updates to this chapter.

14. Make a note in your calendar to come back and read the next chapter of this book when your child is in September of 10th grade.

Be the first to hear about updates to the material in this book by reading my free weekly email newsletter every week. Anyone can subscribe to it at any time at JeannieBurlowski.com.

Section 3
10th, 11th, and 12th Grades

12 | *September–December of 10th Grade*

During this three-month period, I'm going to ask you to complete some tasks that may seem like they could wait until next spring. There's a reason I'm asking you to complete these tasks now. Starting in January of 10th grade, I'm going to give you some extraordinarily important, relatively complex tasks to complete—and I don't want the following tasks to get lost in the shuffle.

Complete these tasks now, and you'll have extra time and space for completing the very important tasks we're going to start working on shortly after January 1.

HOW TO USE THIS CHAPTER

Start by just reading through this chapter. As you read, don't worry about committing to any of it. Decision time will come at the very end of this chapter, when I give you a clear, at-a-glance checklist of every task I'm suggesting you consider right now.

Remember, you won't have to use every strategy I suggest; just choose the ones you think will work for your family and either modify or discard the rest.

[1] *Ask your daughter about her plan for organizing her 10th-grade academics.*

Just as you did during the first week of 9th grade, check in with your teen about what organizational system she'll be using for getting academic work done in a quality manner and turned in on time during 10th grade. If you need a reminder of the six critical questions she must be able to answer on this subject, revisit chapter 3, "7th Grade or Earlier."

[2] *Be aware that your son will likely take the PSAT and PLAN standardized tests in the fall (usually in October) of his sophomore year of high school.*

Usually, high school guidance counselors make all the arrangements.

Have your son eat protein before he tests, focus intently, and make educated guesses where he's unsure, but otherwise don't stress too much about these tests.

> **HAVE YOUR SON EAT PROTEIN BEFORE HE TESTS, FOCUS INTENTLY, AND MAKE EDUCATED GUESSES WHERE HE'S UNSURE, BUT OTHERWISE DON'T STRESS TOO MUCH ABOUT THESE TESTS.**

[3] *Brainstorm with your daughter about what she will do this year to help the humanitarian cause she's adopted as her own.*

Make a plan and schedule it. Remember, if your daughter pulls in friends to help her, she gets points for leadership as well as for service. Excellent! Be sure to help her keep track of everything she does in her profile on LinkedIn.

[4] *Encourage your son to continue with that one special extracurricular activity he's planning to stick with throughout all four years of high school.*

This year, have him think about how he can expand or enrich that activity for others. How can he move into more leadership within it? Is there a way that he and the other stu-

dents involved in the activity with him could somehow serve the community? Encourage your son to propose that. Arrange it. Execute it. Enter the details on his LinkedIn profile.

Remember, someday this committed, long-term activity might be what gets your child a lucrative merit-based scholarship or a preferential financial aid package at a college he could never otherwise afford.

[5] *When will your teen work to earn money during this school year? Help her brainstorm and plan that out.*

Your daughter has until December 31 of this year to earn and pump all the money she can into her Roth IRA account while still protecting her future financial aid eligibility.

After December 31, she'll be allowed to earn just a certain small, fixed amount of money each year without cutting into her future financial aid awards. As of 2015–2016, that amount was $6,300 per year after taxes (about $7,162 before federal, FICA, state, and other taxes are taken out), with the amount adjusted upward slightly each year for inflation. Note that this fixed amount does not include a student's earnings from college work-study programs, co-op college programs, or grad school assistantships or fellowships—which never count against the student for financial aid purposes no matter how high they may be.

Wouldn't it be a great goal for your daughter to try to earn exactly that small $6,000–$7,000 amount of money each year from January 1 of her sophomore year of high school until January 1 of her sophomore year of college? (January 1 of her sophomore year of college is the date when her earnings can no longer affect her college financial aid awards.) All your daughter will have to do to keep this $6,000–$7,000 amount of money for herself each year while she's in high school and college is be sure it's all either (a) wisely spent down or (b) stashed away in her Roth IRA or in a 529 college savings plan each September 30, just before you and she fill out her FAFSA form.

If your daughter hasn't yet started keeping careful track of all the money she's earning, have her start that in earnest now. This way she'll know when she begins to approach these cutoff points. Be sure that she's consistently noting her hours worked on LinkedIn and keeping track of her earnings in Evernote.

[6] *Continue allowing your daughter to juggle all of her own expenses using the small amount of money you provide.*

Giving your daughter an "allowance" and expecting her to cover a long list of her own expenses with that money is a great way to teach wise money management. If you haven't set this up yet, now is a great time to do so. See chapter 11, "Summer After 9th Grade."

If your daughter makes a costly mistake, offer tender empathy, but don't jump in and rescue her. If she gets truly desperate for money, offer her $50 for every scholarship application she fills out in a quality manner.

[7] *Become serious about selecting the particular dual enrollment program your child will begin in the fall of 11th grade.*

Dual enrollment programs, remember, allow

your son or daughter to take college courses in high school and have them count for college credit and high school credit at the same time—often with your state footing the entire bill. Dual enrollment is one of the best ways for a family to save $50,000 or more on college costs. (You can refresh your memory on what dual enrollment is and how it works by reviewing chapter 9, "February–April of 9th Grade.")

> **DUAL ENROLLMENT IS ONE OF THE BEST WAYS FOR A FAMILY TO SAVE $50,000 OR MORE ON COLLEGE COSTS.**

Start calling the colleges and universities that provide dual enrollment programs in your area. (Your state's department of education will be able to help you figure out the names of the colleges and universities near you that provide these programs.) Colleges providing dual enrollment programs may sponsor "information nights" for high school sophomores and their families in February of the 10th-grade year, just in time for your child to enroll in one of these programs for the fall of the junior year of high school. Call these colleges in December so you can get these information nights on your calendar.

Then, as soon as is allowed, register your child for dual enrollment courses that begin in the fall of 11th grade.

Remember, search for these programs yourself. Don't rely on high school guidance counselors to find out this information and announce it. Guidance counselors carry very heavy workloads, and in some school districts are quietly told not to publicize dual enrollment because it can negatively impact the amount of state funding received by the high school.

[8] *Consider having your son look for a discounted community college class that he can take next summer.*

Help him choose a class that's in one of his areas of natural talent and interest. Attend alongside him if that will help.

[9] *Consider registering your daughter for a professional college study skills class that will get her ready to take college-level, dual enrollment courses in the fall of her junior year of high school.*

The sooner she takes a college study skills class the better, because it will help her succeed in high school as well as in college. The 2.5-hour study skills class I teach is called *The Strategic College Student: How to Get Higher Grades Than Anyone Else by Studying Less Than Most Other People*, and information on how to access it is in my free weekly email newsletter.

[10] *In December, start planning ahead for summer camp if your son is willing to go.*

Having experience at sleep-away summer camp can reduce the incidence of debilitating homesickness in college. Senior high camps fill fast, though, so plan to register soon. If you're in the upper Midwest, try TroutLakeCamps.org.

[11] *Help your daughter come up with a plan for how she will make money during the summer after 10th grade.*

Keep in mind that she will be able to earn between $6,000 and $7,000 during that entire calendar year before her earnings start cutting into her financial aid eligibility. If possible, help her figure out how she can earn that amount of money in the fewest number of hours she can. Housecleaning, for example, can earn more money faster than babysitting or working a fast-food counter. Earning her money in the fewest hours possible will give her more time for things like job shadowing and volunteering to help the cause she's adopted as her own.

[12] *Have your child ask two teachers for fresh letters of recommendation to use for upcoming summer scholarship applications.*

As I mentioned in chapter 7, when a teacher writes a letter of recommendation for your child, be sure to send that teacher a handwritten thank-you note that contains a generous gift card to a store that carries practical items. Teachers work hard on these very important letters; there is no reason to expect them to do this work for free.

[13] *From this point on, carefully save receipts from any purchase that could qualify as a college-related expense.*

This goes for both parents, all involved stepparents, and the teen. If anyone in the family pays money for anything related to college, hold onto the receipt. I recommend that families keep track of these receipts by photographing them and recording them in a "[Child Name]'s Educational Expenses" notebook in Evernote. Be sure that each receipt gets recorded only once.

When you're noting college-related educational expenses, be sure to include the cost of the career direction work I'm going to ask you to do in January of 10th grade, as well as all the expenses related to in-state and out-of-state college visits and (in the summer after 11th grade) college application fees. Some of these costs may be tax deductible; others may be safely and legally subtracted from a child's 529 savings plan. Your job for now is to keep track of all of these receipts so a qualified professional person can help you determine later on what can be deducted where.

[14] *Remember that you have very important financial decisions to make before December 31 of your child's sophomore year of high school.*

Please go back and carefully reread chapter 10, "May of 9th Grade," where I first introduced to you the 10 key decisions that could make your son or daughter more eligible for free money financial aid for college. Make a list of the specific income- and asset-lowering strategies you plan to use, get the advice of a qualified financial planning professional where necessary, and then complete the steps you've selected no later than December 31 of your child's sophomore year of high school.

CHECKLIST

September–December of 10th Grade

1. Ask your daughter about her plan for organizing her 10th-grade academics.

2. Don't stress too much about the PSAT and PLAN standardized tests coming up this fall (usually in October).

3. Brainstorm with your child about what she will do this year to help the humanitarian cause she's adopted as her own.

4. Have your son continue with that one special extracurricular activity he's sticking with throughout all four years of high school.

5. Help your daughter brainstorm how and when she'll work for money during this school year and next summer, keeping in mind the income restrictions detailed in this chapter.

6. Continue allowing your son to juggle all his own expenses using the very limited amount of money you provide.

7. Become serious about selecting the particular dual enrollment program your child will begin in the fall of 11th grade.

8. Suggest that your son consider looking for a discounted community college course he could take next summer.

9. If your daughter has not yet had a professional college study skills class, find a good one now.

10. In December, start planning ahead for summer camp if your son is willing to go.

11. Have your son ask two teachers for fresh letters of recommendation that he can use when he submits 10 scholarship applications this coming summer. Be sure to thank each of these teachers with a handwritten note and a generous gift card.

12. From this point on, use Evernote on your smartphone to carefully save receipts from any purchase that might qualify as a college-related expense.

13. VERY IMPORTANT: Reread chapter 10, "May of 9th Grade," and carry out whichever income- and asset-lowering strategies listed there that you've decided to use. Your drop-dead deadline for getting this done is December 31 of your child's sophomore year of high school.

14. Always consult your financial planning professional before making any big financial decisions.

☐ 15. Check my book updates page at JeannieBurlowski.com/LAUNCH to see if I have made any recent updates to this chapter.

☐ 16. Make a note in your calendar to come back and read the next chapter of this book *early* in January when your child is in 10th grade.

Be the first to hear about updates to the material in this book by reading my free weekly email newsletter every week. Anyone can subscribe to it at any time at JeannieBurlowski.com.

13 | *January–February of 10th Grade*

This chapter is critically important for you if you are to have a child who will work hard in college, graduate debt-free in fewer than four years, find a post-college job that actually uses the degree she's worked for, and enjoy a satisfying, lifelong career doing work she excels at and loves.

Please start this month's tasks as early in January as you can. There's a lot to do in this chapter, and I'll want you to get all the steps completed before we go on to your next step this coming March.

HOW TO USE THIS CHAPTER

That said, start by just reading through this chapter. As you read, don't worry about committing to any of it. Decision time will come at the very end of this chapter, when I give you a clear, at-a-glance checklist of every task I'm suggesting you consider right now.

Remember, if you can't use every single strategy I suggest, that's OK. Just do the tasks you can. Choose the ones you think will work for your family, and either modify or discard the rest.

[1] *Locate an educational consultant certified to use three specific assessments to help your child get a fix on a potential career goal.*

I don't do this kind of consulting myself these days, but there are thousands of other trained professionals who do exactly this kind of work every day. At the end of this chapter, I'll explain where you can find a properly certified educational consultant for your child.

This consultant will walk your son through a series of fun, nonthreatening questions about his interests, strengths, likes, and dislikes, and about how he sees and experiences the world. This consultant will then present you and your son with a series of attractive charts, graphs, and printed information that will allow you to see and appreciate this child at a depth you've never been able to before.

The consultant will go over these documents with you, explaining in detail the kinds of things your child tends to be naturally interested in, good at, and energized by. Then you, your child, and the consultant will use this data and some other tools to figure out two main things:

» what type of career your child might be wonderfully well-suited to work in after college, and

» what types of college, technical school, or job training programs would best help your child get straight to that destination—without one bit of time or money wasted.

Does it stun you that high school sophomores can get a vision of what they would like to do with their lives, and then start making their life plans accordingly?

Don't underestimate these students. With the help of the three assessments I'm about to prescribe and a caring guide to walk them through the process, they can.

"But I told her to follow her passion. Isn't that good enough?"

Please don't tell your teen that. It's a fallacy that teens are able to somehow look into themselves, identify a passionate feeling about something, and then build a career around that feeling. This ill-advised "career-planning strategy" simply *does not work*. Most teens who are told "follow your passion" look into themselves, see that they're not really passionate about anything yet, and then secretly feel anxious and afraid, wondering if there's something wrong with them.

Most people don't actually carve out happy and fulfilling work lives by "following their passion." Instead, the path to true passionate career satisfaction opens up before us as we identify and understand our own individual strengths, talents, and abilities, and then work hard to develop those strengths, talents, and abilities into practical skill.

When we do this—and then buckle down with intense, fully involved focus and concentration to do work we're really good at—it's at that point that we begin to feel the energized, passionate sensation that psychologists call "flow," "passion," or "absorption." It's at that point that we (whether we are age 15 or age 55) are overtaken by the sense of joyous exhilaration where time seems to either fly or stand still. It's at that point that we stand up after 10 hours of hard work and say, "That felt like 10 minutes! I feel so jazzed and energized right now that I could go climb a mountain!"

This is the work life we want for your son or daughter. This is true passion. This is what happens when students are given the opportunity to (a) identify their strengths, talents, and abilities and then (b) cultivate and develop those specific strengths into practical skill.

Awareness of strength, natural talent, and ability first. Then hard work that leads to specific skill. Then passion. In that order.

WHY IDENTIFY A TEEN'S STRENGTHS, TALENTS, AND ABILITIES NOW?

Three reasons. First, we want to give your teen a six-year head start on identifying and then developing her specific God-given strengths, talents, and abilities. Second, it's important to do this now because we don't want your daughter wasting thousands of dollars and years of valuable time on a college program she's ill-suited to and will eventually abandon. We don't want her to enroll at a college or university she's only going to suffer in and eventually have to transfer out of. (Remember, the generous financial aid package you worked so hard to get from the first college will likely not transfer to the second college.) Third, and perhaps most importantly, we don't want her one day graduating from college after investing $70,000 in educational costs only to find out that there *aren't actually any real jobs in the field she's been studying.*

Trained, certified, highly qualified educational consultants help students avoid these kinds of nightmares by clarifying the bull's-eye on the target before students take aim and shoot.

On the surface, the national statistics on college completion and college graduation look completely demoralizing. Seventy percent of the bright-faced, expectant students who start college each fall do not graduate in four years. Thirty-three percent of all college freshmen drop out during their freshman year. Forty-seven percent of the students who start work on a college degree either take longer than six years to complete it or do not finish it at all.

Many adults rail against the colleges themselves for these problems, as though it's all their fault. I think that the bigger reason for this abysmal college failure rate is that students are allowed to start the hard road of college without any sense of purpose or direction. Too many freshman college students feel as though they've been thrown out into the middle of an ocean while their parents and grandparents stand on the deck of a cruise ship and shout cheerfully, "Enjoy all the possibilities out there! I hope you end up somewhere nice!"

> **HIGHLY QUALIFIED EDUCATIONAL CONSULTANTS HELP STUDENTS AVOID THESE NIGHTMARES BY CLARIFYING THE BULL'S-EYE ON THE TARGET** *BEFORE* **STUDENTS TAKE AIM AND SHOOT.**

This can be frightening and painful for students. It's no wonder that binge drinking, drug abuse, and sexual promiscuity are rampant on college campuses. Kids are desperately looking for *something to hang onto.*

If you will hire a properly certified educational consultant to take your child through the following steps, you won't feel like you're throwing your child out into an ocean on an inner tube. You'll feel like you're sending a well-trained sailor out on a sturdy sailboat with a compass and a map to an exciting destination.

THE SPECIFIC ASSESSMENTS I RECOMMEND

Parent, I hope I've fully convinced you that hiring a highly qualified, properly certified educational consultant to do this work with your son or daughter is a great idea.

As I name and describe the following assessments, let me speak directly to your child and convince him or her that this is a good idea as well.

The first assessment: StrengthsFinder 2.0

Student, imagine having a career where you do what you do best—every single day.

Imagine how you would feel, walking into a workplace where you know you're likely to do an extremely good job at whatever it is you're asked to do. A workplace where your coworkers, colleagues, and bosses look at you with increasing respect because the work you put out is consistently of extraordinary high quality.

What if you could quit spending valuable time and energy trying to fix your shortcomings, and instead concentrate your efforts on using and further developing the things you're already naturally good at? The latest research

from the positive psychology movement (led by PhD psychologists such as Martin Seligman, Shawn Achor, and Shane J. Lopez) has shown that this can happen to you, every day, if you are in a career that uses your particular set of personal human strengths.

Using your personal strengths in your daily work is far more than just a nice theoretical idea. Gallup research has found that employees who have the opportunity to use their particular set of personal strengths every day are "three times more likely to report having an excellent quality of life, six times more likely to be engaged at work," and "8% more productive" than employees who don't get to focus on what they do best.[13]

The first assessment I'm going to prescribe for you will help you figure out exactly what your top five human strengths are. The tool you will use for this will be the StrengthsFinder 2.0 assessment, a carefully researched series of questions that you answer about yourself online in about an hour. I'm convinced that there are few better investments for teens, for college students, or for adults anywhere on the planet. By the time I'm through with you, I hope you'll have every member of your family taking StrengthsFinder 2.0 and actively reviewing and discussing the results.

You can purchase this assessment right now, today—even if you haven't yet hired the educational consultant I've been telling your

---

13 Peter Flade, Jim Asplund, and Gwen Elliot, "Employees Who Use Their Strengths Outperform Those Who Don't," Gallup, October 8, 2015, http://www.gallup.com/businessjournal/186044/employees-strengths-outperform-don.aspx.

parents about. To access it, all you need to do is purchase the book *StrengthsFinder 2.0*[14] for under $20. I highly recommend that you buy the hardcover version so you can keep it on your bookshelf for easy future reference, but a Kindle version is also available. The book will provide you an Internet address and a unique access code that will allow just one person to go online to take the StrengthsFinder 2.0 assessment and view and print results. One caution: never buy a used *StrengthsFinder* book. If the unique access code in the book has been used by someone else, you will be blocked from going online to take the assessment using that code.

StrengthsFinder 2.0 is Gallup's newest, most improved strengths assessment. It can be used by anyone ages 15 and up. It's so popular with colleges and universities that more than 300 "strengths-based campuses" worldwide have every incoming freshman and every staff and faculty member take it. On strengths-based campuses, students, staff, and faculty all frame and post a list of their top five strengths in their offices and dorm rooms, and use the results throughout the academic year.

My philosophy on this topic is, "Why wait for your future college to require you to take StrengthsFinder 2.0? Give yourself a massive head start. Take StrengthsFinder 2.0 when you're in 10th grade and start building and developing your strengths three years earlier than everybody else!"

The second assessment: the Strong Interest Inventory

Student, imagine how you would feel if you could work every day at something you're intensely interested in. What if you could land a job that, even after 30 years, still appeals to you, excites you, and enthralls you?

There are people in this world who feel this way about their work, and you can be one of them.

The Strong Interest Inventory (formerly known as the Strong-Campbell Interest Inventory) is a fun, easy online assessment that asks you to respond to 291 prompts, all asking about what you personally prefer. It takes between 35 and 40 minutes to complete. When you finish the assessment online, you will receive a well-organized report bursting with valuable information that will help you sort through career options.

The Strong Interest Inventory report starts by letting you know which one or two of the following you tend to be:

» Conventional (an organizer)
» Investigative (a thinker)
» Enterprising (a persuader)
» Realistic (a doer)
» Artistic (a creator)
» Social (a helper)[15]

---

14 Tom Rath, *StrengthsFinder 2.0* (New York: Gallup Press, 2007).

15 Strong MBTI, "Strong Interest Inventory and Myers-Briggs Type Indicator Career Report with Strong Profile," Career Report developed by Judith Grutter and Allen L. Hammer, accessed November 15, 2016, https://www.cpp.com/pdfs/smp289246.pdf.

Then the inventory helps you get a grasp of your particular interests, your preferred work activities, your potential skills, and what your values are likely to be within your dominant theme or themes.

Let me give you an example.

If you score high in social, for instance, your natural interests may include people, teamwork, helping, and community service. You may prefer work activities such as teaching, caring for people, counseling, or training employees. This information can be very helpful in choosing a career. The assessment goes further, though, even listing potential skills you may already have that you could purposely develop further. In the case of the social person, for instance, potential skills might include "people skills, verbal ability, listening, and showing understanding." And values you may have as a social person could include "cooperation, generosity, and service to others." This is also very helpful to know, since you will tend to be happiest in a career that is a strong match with your most deeply held personal values.

Knowing these details about yourself can help you move toward careers that you will love and be good at, and away from careers that are likely to make you miserable. The social student reading these results, for instance, will be encouraged to steer clear of careers that are typically done alone or mostly with objects or machines, as well as careers that require little to no talking or communication with others. As one very social young woman put it to me: "The Strong Interest Inventory gave me great ammunition when my 'realistic' father was trying to pressure me to become a mechanical engineer!"

> **KNOWING THESE DETAILS ABOUT YOURSELF CAN HELP YOU MOVE TOWARD CAREERS THAT YOU WILL LOVE AND BE GOOD AT, AND AWAY FROM CAREERS THAT ARE LIKELY TO MAKE YOU MISERABLE.**

Finally, the Strong Interest Inventory (more properly called an "inventory" or a "psychological instrument" than a "test," since there are no right or wrong answers to it) will provide you with a long list of careers that you may—and I repeat, may—be interested in. Be prepared, though, that not all the careers listed will be a fit for you. This is why experts suggest that you look at the Strong Interest Inventory results in conjunction with the Myers-Briggs Type Indicator (MBTI) results, which I'll talk about next, and overlay both with strengths assessments that tell you what you are likely naturally good at.

When you first look through the long list of career possibilities on the Strong Interest Inventory, I suggest that you highlight the ones that jump out at you as being most interesting to you, and let go of all the rest. If you wonder what some of the careers listed in your results actually are and what they might pay—don't worry. I'll give you an easy way to figure that out.

Are you ready to take the Strong Interest Inventory right now? Hold on; I want to tell you one more thing before I explain exactly how to access it.

The third assessment: the Myers-Briggs Type Indicator

The final tool I'm going to recommend to you

is—in my opinion—the crème de la crème of all tools designed to help students determine career direction. This is the one you absolutely must not miss.

This is the most important tool I've found to help students uncover focused career direction, future purpose, and personal life mission. You may at some time have heard of someone referring to himself or herself as an "ISFJ" or an "ENTP." These designations come from the MBTI. The MBTI, like the StrengthsFinder 2.0 and the Strong Interest Inventory, also consists of a carefully researched series of questions you answer about yourself online. It consists of 93 questions and usually takes about 30 minutes to complete. When you finish the assessment online, a certified practitioner reviews your results with you and provides you with a well-organized, clearly laid-out report that—when viewed alongside your Strong Interest Inventory results—will give you tremendously valuable information you can use to make well-informed career decisions.

What's so phenomenal about the MBTI? It brings a whole different facet of who you are into the career discussion. While strengths assessments analyze natural talent, and interest inventories clarify which careers might most appeal to you, excite you, and enthrall you, the MBTI helps you choose careers that fit beautifully with your individual personality type—the way you naturally get energy, process information, solve problems, make decisions, relate to others, and interact with the world around you.

It'll be a tremendously exciting moment if you see the same fascinating career type coming up on both the Strong Interest Inventory and the MBTI. But when you begin to realize that the same career just happens to be perfectly aligned with the particular set of human strengths you discovered in yourself after taking StrengthsFinder 2.0—that's when you'll feel the enthralling, exhilarating sense that you might have just found the work you're created to do.

The official MBTI was first created in 1943, but in the years since, it has evolved and changed and been perfected through rigorous ongoing research and development. Millions of people have taken the MBTI. Its research database is massive, and the most recent edition of it came about after a landmark normative study that involved thousands of people and took two years of work by a team of experts specializing in psychometrics (psychological testing).

You may be able to find a free inventory on the Internet that purports to be an MBTI, but none of the free, web-based quizzes are the real thing. None have met commonly accepted psychometric standards for reliability and validity, and none are able to properly interpret the results for you when you finish. What you want is the gold standard MBTI published by CPP, Inc. (formerly Consulting Psychologist Press). It's available from CPP and its licensees in more than 20 languages.

I'll tell you where to access it at the end of this chapter.

GREAT IDEA: HAVE THE STRONG INTEREST INVENTORY AND THE MBTI COMBINED INTO ONE REPORT

CPP, the publisher of both of these two assessments, sees great value in having students ages 15 and up take both the MBTI and the Strong Interest Inventory, and then look at all the results at the same time.

To make this easy, CPP will, when asked, provide one combined report that converges your MBTI and your Strong Interest Inventory results. Best of all, the combined MBTI and Strong Interest Inventory report will emphasize *careers that are suggested for you by both assessments*. Excellent! That's exactly what we want.

These assessments are good for anyone of any age, but if a high school student can use these tools before making any regrettable, expensive education or career mistakes— that's absolutely brilliant.

I'll tell you how to access the Strong Interest Inventory and the MBTI and receive your results in a combined report, but before I do, let me tell you about one additional low-cost tool that goes along beautifully with these assessments.

> **BEST OF ALL, THE COMBINED MBTI AND STRONG INTEREST INVENTORY REPORT WILL EMPHASIZE** *CAREERS THAT ARE SUGGESTED FOR YOU BY BOTH ASSESSMENTS.* **EXCELLENT!**

DO WHAT YOU ARE

Once a student has taken the three assessments I suggest and soaked in the results, I love to have him or her buy a copy of the book *Do What You Are* by Paul D. Tieger, Barbara Barron-Tieger, and Kelly Tieger.

The authors of this book are nationally recognized experts in personality typing, and over a period of 20 years have trained thousands of career counselors, outplacement consultants, and human resource specialists to use the results of the MBTI to help people find the work they're naturally wired to do. There is an entire chapter of *Do What You Are* dedicated to each MBTI personality type, and each chapter includes dozens of potential occupations that are popular with people who have that particular personality type. (Students find it especially interesting to see how many of the occupations listed in "their chapter" of *Do What You Are* also show up on their Strong Interest Inventory report!)

And when students wonder what people in these careers actually do or what the jobs pay? It's easy to get answers. Just google "BLS" along with the name of any career you can think of. In under one second you'll get straight to a well-designed, user-friendly Bureau of Labor Statistics web page that provides a large number of interesting details about that career. In an instant you'll be able to see what people in that career do, what the median pay is, what education is required, and even what personal qualities help a person to do that job well.

One of my favorite interactions with my past clients has occurred when I turned to the appropriate chapter in *Do What You Are* and pointed to its pages and pages of career options that tend to work beautifully for people with my client's exact personality type. I love to hear students gasp as they realize that the career they've been dreaming of for a long time—maybe hardly even daring to speak out loud—is actually printed right there, a career choice thought to be beautifully aligned with how they're naturally wired.

"Excellent! So where do I go to take the Strong Interest Inventory and the MBTI?"

There's only one way to access both the Strong Interest Inventory and the MBTI and receive this valuable combined report. You will need to locate an educational consultant who has been specifically certified by CPP to administer these assessments. I am not a CPP certified consultant, so I don't provide these assessments myself, but you may find an educational consultant who is CPP certified in your community, online, in a high school or college career center, or on my "Approved Consultants" tab at JeannieBurlowski.com.

The product you want to buy from your CPP certified consultant is the "Strong Profile, College Edition + Strong and MBTI Career Report."

When you purchase this product, here's what you'll get:

1. Your CPP certified educational consultant will provide you with access codes and exact links that will allow you to take both the Strong Interest Inventory and the MBTI on your own at home. (There is no way around this. CPP's publisher policies do not allow you to take a real MBTI without the supervision and direction of a CPP certified professional.)

2. This same CPP certified educational consultant will compile your results and schedule a telephone meeting to interpret them and explain them to you. This is called an "interpretation meeting" or "an interp." Parents and students can both be on the line if you like. (You may have to schedule this phone meeting as much as a month in advance, so plan ahead.)

3. After this interpretation meeting, the CPP certified educational consultant will email you a printable copy of your very valuable Strong Profile, College Edition + Strong and MBTI Career Report. For greatest usability, I suggest that you print the report in color.

How much will this service cost you? The amount will vary depending upon the educational consultant you choose and the level of service he or she provides. Some educational consultants charge up to $850 for this service, but as of this writing there is at least one good quality, properly credentialed educational consultant online who will administer the two assessments and do the bare minimum CPP required professional interpretation of a student's Strong Profile, College Edition + Strong and MBTI Career Report for only $119.

Why the huge difference in pricing? Prices vary widely because some educational consultants only administer these assessments as part of a larger career counseling or college planning package that you buy from them. These packages can be valuable. The educational consultant may spend hours talking to a student, compiling data about him, and helping him as an individual work through all his decisions about what he wants to do with his life. This can be absolutely worth the cost. If money is an issue, though, it is OK to tell a CPP certified educational consultant, "I'm not looking for professional career counseling at this time. All I really want you to do is just spend 30 minutes with me 'verifying type' on the Myers-Briggs. Then, if I need you for career counseling later, I'll get back to you." Many CPP certified practitioners will be willing to simply administer necessary assessments and then just verify type on the Myers-Briggs for a fee of $150 or less.

If you are looking for a CPP certified educational consultant online, you may be able to find one on the Independent Educational Consultants Association (IECA) website at Iecaonline.com, but be careful. IECA consultants vary dramatically in quality, experience, focus, certification, and credential, so you must interview them carefully before you hire.

PARENTS BEWARE—DON'T HIRE THIS KIND OF EDUCATIONAL CONSULTANT

As you look toward hiring the kind of CPP certified educational consultant I've described, beware. Do not hire an educational consultant who pushes every child toward the Ivy League and "top-ranked schools" as though expensive, elite private education is a sure and guaranteed route to career success and happiness. It isn't, especially when students take on exorbitant student loan debt to pay for it. (If you need a reminder of how true this is, please go back and reread the first two chapters of this book.)

What you really want is a CPP certified educational consultant who specializes in two things: (1) helping families use every tool possible to reach the goal of debt-free college graduation and (2) administering the assessments I've prescribed in order to identify students' potential career goals and resulting "best fit" colleges, majors, and career preparation strategies. For greatest effect, I advise that this be done when students are in 10th grade—well before they start choosing colleges to apply to. But if your child is currently well past 10th grade, don't worry. It's not too late. Even age 45 or 50 is not too late to clarify career goal and plot an effective path to a great future.

If you interview a consultant who can't immediately point you to 40–50 strategies for helping you toward debt-free college, or if you interview a consultant who says, "I don't use assessments with students; kids usually figure out their own career goals once they get to college," run away as fast as you can and don't look back.

"OK . . . but isn't 10th grade way too early to be thinking about career?"

The answer is an emphatic yes—10th grade is way too early to be thinking about career goal if the only tool you have to figure it out is wild guessing. But if the student is able to access high-quality, research-backed assessments and then work through the assessment results with a trained and caring educational consultant, then a student absolutely can get a sense of potential career goal as young as 10th grade.

IF YOU INTERVIEW A CONSULTANT WHO SAYS, "I DON'T USE ASSESSMENTS WITH STUDENTS; KIDS USUALLY FIGURE OUT THEIR OWN CAREER GOALS ONCE THEY GET TO COLLEGE," RUN AWAY AS FAST AS YOU CAN AND DON'T LOOK BACK.

And if your son one day refines this career goal and shifts focus to some degree? That will be no problem. At least he'll have spent years in high school and college developing and honing strengths and abilities and talents he naturally has in abundance in the first place. This will equip him well for whatever opportunities may come his way in the future.

Tenth grade is the optimal time to do these assessments and this career clarification work. Students who do this will tend to go through the rest of high school excited about a bright future ahead. They will tend to choose technical schools, colleges, academic programs, and college majors with a strategic eye toward what they plan to do after college. They will be able to begin volunteering and job shadowing in their eventual career fields far earlier than other students, getting a jump start on building not just a solid and focused résumé, but skills and abilities they'll be using for years to come as well. They'll transfer schools less. They'll finish college faster. They'll pay far less for college than do students who wander aimlessly through college and grad school without a clear sense of focus or direction.

If you have any worries about finding the money to pay a CPP certified educational consultant for this critically important,

tremendously valuable service, save up the money over a period of three months. Having this kind of consulting service for your college-bound student is, in my mind, a *nonnegotiable*. Neglect it, and you may end up paying far more for college than is necessary—as well as suffering unnecessary heartache along the way.

[2] *With the help of your CPP certified educational consultant, write down in one sentence the type of education required for a person to reach your child's career goal.*

Once the consultant has helped your child arrive at a sense of a possible career goal based on assessment data, let this same consultant help your family determine what kind of college, university, technical college, or job training program would best prepare your son or daughter for that specific career.

The sentence you write down might say, "She'll need a two-year degree from a technical college that has a program in respiratory therapy," or "He'll need a four-year degree from some college or university that has a direct path toward teacher licensure in Colorado," or "It's possible to become a chiropractic assistant by just working for a chiropractor—no college or technical school degree is even required," or "What would be awesome for her would be a biology degree from a four-year college located where she can find three exciting internships over the four years—plus work a part-time job that gives her tuition reimbursement as one of her employee benefits!"

If you all find yourselves mystified as to what kind of education gets you to some particular, very unique career goal, call up five different people currently doing that work and ask them how they got there. One 10th-grade boy came up to me after hearing me speak in 2015 and asked me, "I really want to work in computer animation. Where do I go to college for that?" My reply was, "I don't exactly know that myself. But if I were you, I'd call up Disney and Pixar and ask if you can talk to someone who works in computer animation there. Ask the person how they got there. Ask them to connect you to other people who work in their same department. Most adults are happy to help kids with questions about career. And in the meantime, keep drawing, and jump at the chance to take any local computer animation class you can get your hands on."

[3] *Don't be thrown if it turns out that a two-year degree is all your child needs.*

As you and your child do this very important how-do-I-get-there work, please don't be taken aback if the assessments show that your son or daughter might be a great candidate for a career that requires only a two-year technical college degree.

For many students, a two-year technical college degree is an outstanding option. If your daughter can attend two years of technical college, finish her education at age 20 with zero debt, and then jump immediately into a highly skilled, well-paying career that she excels at and loves, that's much better than accumulating $50,000 in debt in a liberal arts program she despises and then struggling to find a job that uses that education afterward. And if she someday decides she wants a particular career that requires a four-year bachelor's degree? The four-year colleges will always be there waiting.

> **PLEASE DON'T BE TAKEN ABACK IF THE ASSESSMENTS SHOW THAT YOUR SON OR DAUGHTER MIGHT BE A GREAT CANDIDATE FOR A CAREER THAT REQUIRES ONLY A TWO-YEAR TECHNICAL COLLEGE DEGREE.**

You can find out about other exciting career options by reading through the course catalog of the technical college nearest your house. Remember, if you wonder what some of these careers are and what they pay, google "BLS" along with the name of the career you're wondering about. You'll instantly see pages of well-organized information on that career.

If a CPP certified educational consultant helps your child take the assessments I've prescribed and it appears that one of the careers on this list might be a fit for your son or daughter, don't let the short education time scare you off. Many jobs that require only a two-year degree pay *more* than those requiring a bachelor's or a master's. Why would you want to go through additional years of schooling and accumulate more debt and then end up in a job that doesn't pay as well?

There are a significant number of well-paying careers that require only two-year associate's degrees, earn average salaries of between $40,000 and $60,000 a year, and have excellent job outlooks. Here are a few examples:

Air traffic controller
Registered nurse
Construction manager
Aerospace engineering and operations
   technician
Nuclear medicine technologist
Cardiovascular technician
Radiation therapist
Construction equipment operator
Physical therapy assistant
Brick mason
Occupational therapy assistant
Crane operator
Radiologic (x-ray) technologist
Magnetic resonance imaging (MRI)
   technologist
Diagnostic medical sonographer
Carpenter
Intensive care unit nurse
Nuclear technician
Dental hygienist
Boilermaker
Rotary drill operator for the oil and gas
   industry
Wind turbine technician
Millwright
Industrial machinery mechanic
Commercial diver
Computer support specialist
Computer network support specialist
Website designer
HVAC technician
Graphic designer
Environmental engineering technician
Paralegal

Diesel mechanic
Executive pastry chef
Aircraft mechanic
Electrical and electronics drafter
Sheet-metal worker
Pile-driver operator
Funeral director
Avionics technician
Electrical and electronics engineering
   technician
Automotive mechanic
Solar panel consultant and installer
Electrical technician
Auto body repairer
Mechanical engineering technician
Master plumber, pipefitter, or streamfitter
Geological and petroleum technician
Welder
Police detective

On this same topic, I'd like to add this: just imagine your daughter at age 22, with zero debt, looking back at two years of work experience where she earned over $100,000 and made zero payments to creditors. This could be your child, if the assessments show that one of these great careers might be an excellent fit for her.

> **REMEMBER, IF YOU WONDER WHAT SOME OF THESE CAREERS ARE AND WHAT THEY PAY, GOOGLE "BLS" ALONG WITH THE NAME OF THE CAREER YOU'RE WONDERING ABOUT.**

[4] *Write out a description of what kind of a college, technical school, or job training program would be a dream fit for this child based on the career goal you've just landed on.*

List the specific attributes you'll want your daughter's college to have if she is to (a) be happy and well adjusted throughout college and (b) get to her specific career goal at the lowest possible cost and as near to debt-free as possible.

Think: if you and your daughter could create and build the perfect post-high school education for her *and for her specific goals,* what would that look like?

We will be working on this description more two months from now, but for now just start by jotting down some general ideas. To get you started on this, here are three examples of what these initial ideas might look like for three very different students.

Meredith's college description

The consultant's assessments and conversations with Meredith showed that she loves science, public speaking, organizing information, large groups of people, and schedules and routines that have predictable structure. It seems like it might be a natural fit for her to one day become a high school biology or chemistry teacher. If she is to do this, she'll need to someday get a high school teaching license. This will require that she attend a college that offers both a four-year bachelor's degree and a major that will specifically prepare her for high school science teaching.

We want the college she attends to be very familiar with teacher licensing requirements for our state, so it will be a good idea for this college to be located right here in our home state.

Meredith can easily achieve her career goals without attending an expensive, big name private university; our primary goal is to prep her for this career while allowing her to graduate college in under four years, completely debt-free.

We want this college to be located in a place with convenient, safe, public transportation so that Meredith can save money by not taking a car with her to college. There are many different colleges that could fulfill these requirements for Meredith.

Terry's college description

Terry has a tremendous natural bent toward leadership. The larger the group or organization Terry leads, the more excited and energized he gets. He loves to strategize about the best ways to solve large-scale problems and get big things done, and his dream is to work with people—strengthening them, developing them, and maximizing their potential so they can perform as superstars.

At the same time, Terry is very interested in business. He's been reading the business section of the newspaper every day since he was eight.

Terry might be a great fit for a future career in business management. He may even eventually want to apply to top business schools and earn an MBA. This means that for Terry, the best college choice would likely be a four-year undergraduate college or university located in (or very near) a big city where many large companies have their corporate headquarters. This will make it easy for Terry to hop on a bus or a subway and go somewhere fantastically interesting to job shadow, volunteer, or intern.

This college needs to have a great undergraduate business major—preferably with special classes that teach leadership. It would be great if this college had a leadership certificate program, or a special leadership track. We want this college to be big enough to have some great campus organizations for Terry to be a part of and possibly lead, and we want it to give Terry credit for the 12 CLEP credits he earned in high school. We'd love for this college to be a nationally known prestigious college

with a big name, as long as we can strategize ahead of time so that Terry graduates from it completely debt-free. (The Harvard Extension School might end up being one great option for Terry. I'll provide information on HES in chapter 14.)

Casey's college description

Casey loves the outdoors, has a lot of experience fishing and hunting with his dad, and has always wanted to live as far away from the big city as possible. The assessments show him to be highly *Investigative*, and this may be one reason why he really likes the idea of law enforcement. These two things together make it look as though "game warden" might be a great lifetime career for Casey.

Casey dislikes being cooped up inside of buildings, so he wants to get any necessary college over with as quickly as possible.

Fortunately for Casey, the main educational requirement for a game warden is a two-year community college degree in wildlife law enforcement. Casey and his parents jot down his ideal college description: "Has a two-year wildlife law enforcement program, is located far from any big cities, and allows Casey to get through *fast*."

A peek at what happens to Casey

The story I'm about to tell you is fictional, but it illustrates well what kinds of things can happen when parents and students think, "OK, we've got a career goal based on quality data from career assessments, not on guessing. Now, what's the fastest, least expensive way to get this kid to that career goal?"

The first thing that happens is that the whole family gets excited about the possibility of Casey graduating from college in far less time than most people do.

Just for fun, 10th-grade Casey and his parents quickly research community colleges that offer degrees in wildlife law enforcement. They find one that sounds perfect, at Vermilion Community College (VCC) in Ely, Minnesota. VCC is a two-year college located way out in the sticks, four hours from the nearest big city, right on the edge of northern Minnesota's 1,700-square-mile Boundary Waters Canoe Area Wilderness. The VCC degree even includes a 420-hour park ranger training program and options for internships with Minnesota state or federal wildlife agencies. This sounds great. But will VCC accept the CLEP and dual enrollment college credits that Casey earned while he was still in high school? Why just sit home guessing about it?

Casey's dad calls VCC on the phone and reaches someone in the registrar's office. "Hey," he says, "I read your information online, and I see that for VCC to grant a degree in wildlife law enforcement, the student needs to take college courses in criminal justice, sociology, investigations, computer science, report writing, emergency response, psychology, environmental interpretation, and natural resources law. Tell me, would it be possible for my high school junior son to take his criminal justice, sociology, psychology, and computer science courses at a community college near our house in Minneapolis while he's

still in high school, and then transfer those credits to you so he can graduate from VCC faster?"

"Yes," the registrar replies. "No problem at all with that. Just check with us before your son enrolls in anything, and we'll make sure it's the exact course he actually needs."

Casey's dad hangs up the phone and says to Casey, "I have an idea. How would you like to take a little trip to Ely, Minnesota, next week?"

Tenth-grade Casey and his dad notify the VCC admissions office that the two of them are planning a campus visit, and a week later they arrive for an appointment in the VCC registrar's office. Father and son have just had a tour of the campus courtesy of the VCC admissions office, and now they're ready to get their big questions answered. Casey's only 16, so his dad speaks first. "Can you show me a list of all the courses necessary to earn a VCC degree in wildlife law enforcement?" Dad asks. Then, with that list in front of him, he opens up the Normandale Community College course catalog on his iPad. "Now," he says to the registrar office staff person, "can you put in writing for me exactly which Normandale classes will fulfill these VCC requirements?"

The next morning as Casey and his dad drive out of Ely past the North American Bear Center on Highway 169, Casey looks over the printed list of Normandale Community College courses he'll be allowed to take to fulfill degree requirements for his wildlife law enforcement degree at VCC. "Next thing we'll do," his dad says, "is take this list of Normandale courses to your high school guidance counselor, and ask her which ones you can take at Minnesota state expense during high school to fulfill your high school graduation requirements. The state won't pay for all of them, of course, but that's OK. Mom and I will be glad to pay for a few discounted Normandale summer classes for you. You can bike from our house over to Normandale and take them during the summer after 10th, 11th, and 12th grade. You do this, and you'll not only save a ton of money on room and board costs, you might also be able to graduate from college debt-free at age 19 after only one or two semesters of living up in Ely!"

Parent, do you see how working with a consultant and creating a college plan in 10th grade worked in Casey's favor in tremendous ways? Can you imagine the personal, financial, and career disaster that could have occurred if Casey's parents had forced him to sit through four years of high school courses and then (to satisfy their own need for all things elite and prestigious) had pushed him to attend an expensive, elite, private, East Coast college for four additional years? Can you imagine a miserable Casey at age 24, $80,000 in debt, finally realizing that what he really wants is to be a game warden—only to find he can't do that because the salary isn't enough to pay his exorbitant student loan payments?

[5] *Print out hard copies of all the documents you've been working with this month and put them carefully in a three-ring binder.*

Don't leave any of the documents you worked on this month on the hard drive of your computer. Print out all three assessment results, all the notes you took during this process,

and the short description of what kind of a college, technical school, or job training program you and your child are thinking might be a dream fit for him or her.

Snap all these important papers into the binder, and then carefully put the binder in a good, safe spot where you won't forget where it is. The papers in this binder are going to be a gold mine when your child starts to wonder, "What in the world would I ever write about in a scholarship application essay?"

> **THE PAPERS IN THIS BINDER ARE GOING TO BE A GOLD MINE WHEN YOUR CHILD STARTS TO WONDER, "WHAT IN THE WORLD WOULD I EVER WRITE ABOUT IN A SCHOLARSHIP APPLICATION ESSAY?"**

CHECKLIST

January–February of 10th Grade

- [ ] 1. Read this chapter thoroughly so you understand why it's critically important for students to determine career goal early on. Have your 10th grader read this entire chapter too.

- [ ] 2. Use my instructions to find and hire a CPP certified educational consultant who will administer and interpret the three assessments I prescribe.

- [ ] 3. As soon as possible (even before your first meeting with this educational consultant), purchase the book *StrengthsFinder 2.0* for under $20 and have your child take the StrengthsFinder 2.0 assessment.

- [ ] 4. Once your child has his StrengthsFinder 2.0 results, have him read only the five chapters in the *StrengthsFinder 2.0* book that explain his top five strengths. (It'll be a fast, easy, fun read.) Have your son underline or highlight the parts of these chapters that he thinks really sound like him.

- [ ] 5. Following your CPP certified educational consultant's instructions, have your son or daughter take the Strong Interest Inventory and the Myers-Briggs Type Indicator. Ask that the results be presented to you in a combined report.

- [ ] 6. Meet with your CPP certified educational consultant for the required MBTI interpretation meeting. This meeting will help your consultant ensure that the MBTI type indicated by the assessment is indeed accurate.

- [ ] 7. Get a copy of the book *Do What You Are* by Paul D. Tieger, Barbara Barron-Tieger, and Kelly Tieger.

- [ ] 8. Read (and have your child read) the chapter of *Do What You Are* that pertains to your child's MBTI personality type. Ask your child to highlight any of the listed careers that look interesting to him.

- [ ] 9. Do you and your child wonder what certain careers involve or what they pay? You can go straight to a tremendously helpful Bureau of Labor Statistics page on any career by googling "BLS" along with the name of the career.

- [ ] 10. Once your CPP certified educational consultant has helped your child arrive at one to three possible career goals, write down in one sentence the types of education required for each of those career goals. If you find yourself mystified as to what kind of education gets you to some very unique career goal, call up several people currently working in that career and ask them how they got there.

11. Reassure your child that she doesn't *have* to do any of the career goals indicated by these assessments. She can always change her mind and shift direction later if she wants to. For now, though, she's clarifying a bulls-eye on a target so she can take careful aim before she shoots.

12. Take a baby step toward choosing future colleges by helping your child write out a short description of what sort of a college, technical school, or job training program would be a dream fit based on all you've just learned.

13. Put all the hard-copy printouts I asked you to make into one 3-ring binder, and put that binder in a good, safe spot where you won't forget where it is.

14. Check my book updates page at JeannieBurlowski.com/LAUNCH to see if I have made any recent updates to this chapter.

15. Always consult your financial planning professional before making any big financial decisions.

16. Make a note in your calendar to come back and read the next chapter of this book when your child is in March of 10th grade.

Be the first to hear about updates to the material in this book by reading my free weekly email newsletter every week. Anyone can subscribe to it at any time at JeannieBurlowski.com.

14 | *March–April of 10th Grade*

Parent, this month you'll be doing a lot of thinking about college options on your own, without your child present.

Our goal will be for you to take the massive, roiling ocean of college possibilities out there, and reduce that ocean to the size of a nice, big swimming pool. This strategy will give your daughter plenty of college possibilities to explore and choose from—just not so many that she gets lost or drowns.

By the time you're finished with the thoughtful exercises I'm going to have you work through this month, you'll have clear ideas about what specific kinds of colleges, universities, or technical schools might be fantastic options for getting your child through college debt-free and into a career he or she is going to love afterward.

This pre-work will give you a great base of knowledge from which to respond thoughtfully when your son tells you, "I'm going to XYZ University. The brochures and the sweatshirts and the football team are like, so cool!"

I know it seems terribly early to start thinking about which colleges your child will apply to 15 months from now, but it's important to do it now so you will have lots of time for the in-person college visits that will occur during 10th and 11th grades.

HOW TO USE THIS CHAPTER

Parent, start by just reading through this chapter. As you read, don't worry about committing to any of it. Decision time will come at the very end of this chapter, when I give you a clear, at-a-glance checklist of every task I'm suggesting you consider in the next few months.

Remember, you won't have to use every strategy I suggest; just choose the ones you think will work for your family and either modify or discard the rest.

[1] *Understand the first rule of choosing colleges: your local four-year state university may not be your bargain choice.*

Some parents tell me, "Oh, I don't think we're going to need much help picking colleges to apply to. My wife and I looked at the tuition costs; we're just gonna send our kid to a local state university where the sticker price is cheap. Decision done."

Please don't jump to this conclusion.

Before you conclude that your local state university is going to be your child's bargain choice, quickly look up that university on CollegeData.com. There you'll be able to instantly view the university's freshman satisfaction rate, average student debt after leaving the university, percentage of students receiving valuable free money merit aid, and (tremendously important) the university's four-year graduation rate.

If the university's four-year graduation rate is low but the average student debt there is high, think about what that means. Many students are leaving that university after one to four years of study without degrees—but with large student debt loads that they need to pay back anyway. A college or university with a high four-year graduation rate and a low student debt rate may be a far better option for your child, even if that college appears at first glance to have a higher sticker price.

Knowing four-year graduation rates is extremely important. A low four-year graduation rate may indicate that students are having such problems getting into courses required to graduate that they're taking five

and six years to finish. Years of full-time income can be lost this way, plus, of course, free money financial aid and merit aid awards don't stretch to cover extra years of college. Students pay full price for their fifth and sixth years of college, often by taking out additional higher-interest loans or running up excessive amounts of credit card debt.

I suggest that your child apply to only one or two carefully chosen, in-state, four-year state universities, just to give these schools a fair shot at wowing you with their financial aid packages.

> **IF THE UNIVERSITY'S FOUR-YEAR GRADUATION RATE IS LOW BUT THE AVERAGE STUDENT DEBT THERE IS HIGH, THINK ABOUT WHAT THAT MEANS.**

To fill out the rest of your child's potential "apply to" list, let's add on some other kinds of colleges and universities that may give your child an extraordinary college experience for a truly rock-bottom bargain-basement price.

[2] *Understand the second rule of choosing colleges: community colleges can be fantastic bargain options.*

Community colleges, though state-funded, are generally ideal bargain choices, especially when a student does well for the first two years and then transfers the credits earned to a carefully chosen "good fit" four-year institution. A great many high-quality, four-year colleges and universities will even extend generous free money scholarships to students coming to them with community college experience.

Put the community college nearest your house on your child's potential apply-to list.

I'm not saying that your child has to go to community college—I'm just suggesting that you always have one on the apply-to list as a possibility.

> **DO NOT FALL FOR THE LIE THAT YOUR CHILD MUST ATTEND A "TOP-RANKED" SCHOOL STARTING AT AGE 18 IN ORDER TO GET A GOOD JOB WHEN SHE GRADUATES.**

If you find yourself worrying that community college might mark your daughter for life as a person "not smart enough to get into a real college," please dismiss this thought from your mind right now. Two years of strong grades earned in community college and then transferred to a "great fit" four-year college or university can be the foundation for an extraordinarily successful life.

In the over 20 years I've been helping students apply to highly competitive law, medical, business, and graduate schools, I have not seen community college keep even one student from achieving great things in life. Not one. Do not fall for the lie that your child must attend a "top-ranked" school starting at age 18 in order to get a good job when she graduates. If you need a reminder of why this is true, please go back and reread the first two chapters of this book.

And if your daughter *doesn't want* to consider community college? Completely fine. She can demonstrate her avid interest in attending a four-year college by filling out 20 scholarship applications each year and bringing the cost of her four-year college down to the price of a community college.

[3] *Understand the third rule of choosing colleges: an honors program at a private university (or at a public university in your home state) can be a fantastic bargain option.*

Increasingly, students accepted at prestigious Ivy League universities are turning down Ivy League admission and instead enrolling in honors programs at state universities in their home states. Why is this? Because the education in state university honors programs can be of quality equal to or better than the Ivy League, tuition prices are far lower, and finishing within four years is attainable since honors students are usually given the privilege of registering for courses first— giving them fewer problems getting into the courses they need to graduate and so increasing their four-year graduation rates.

Now that we've covered applying to state-funded colleges and universities, let's look at adding some private colleges and universities that may be even better options to your child's potential apply-to list.

[4] *When choosing colleges to apply to, carefully consider which financial aid form(s) each college requires.*

As you start to create a large and fluid list of possible apply-to colleges, strongly consider the over 3,000 U.S. private colleges that look only at a student's FAFSA financial aid form and *not* at his CSS/Profile. (CSS/Profile is a highly detailed financial aid form administered by the College Scholarship Service, the financial aid division of the College Board. The CSS/Profile will ask you about income and other financial details that may not help you in your quest to get maximum financial aid for college.)

Private colleges and universities that look only at the FAFSA may award your child so much free money financial aid and merit aid that a degree from one of them ends up being less expensive than a degree from your local state university.

Let me explain how this works by building on some principles I touched on earlier, in chapter 10. Some of what I'm about to say will be review for you, but that's OK. It's important that you have the following facts front and center in your mind right now.

About 18 months from now, on or about October 1 of your child's senior year of high school, you will fill out the financial aid forms that will likely get your family some help paying college costs. (You'll want to fill these out as early as possible in October each year, so you are always putting yourself first in line for financial aid money.)

These financial aid forms will ask you for details about your family income and assets during two specific periods of time: first, the 12-month period of time that stretched from January 1 of your child's sophomore year of high school to December 31 of your child's junior year of high school, and second, the specific day you fill out the FAFSA form in October of your child's senior year of high

school. A quick snapshot of just that brief 12-month period of time plus one day will be used to make many decisions that will affect your child's finances for years to come.

The information you enter on these forms will be used to determine how much it is believed that your family can afford to pay out of pocket for college. (This out-of-pocket amount is called your Expected Family Contribution or EFC.)

Once your family's EFC is known, individual college financial aid offices will come up with a plan for helping you to cover the portion of the Cost of Attendance (COA) that it has been determined your family cannot cover. Most colleges will meet just about 80 percent of this need by awarding your student a combination of grants and tuition discounts (free money that never needs to be paid back), work-study programs (flexibly scheduled paying jobs during the academic year that students should always accept), tax credits, possible military scholarships, and (hold your nose here) subsidized and unsubsidized student and parent loans.

"Only 80 percent?" I can hear you asking incredulously. "These financial aid offices plan to give us only 80 percent of what they know our family actually needs? Where's our family supposed to come up with the other 20 percent?"

The one place I hope you *won't* look to fill this 20 percent gap is signing up for more student loans.

I hope that your family will be prepared well ahead of time with dozens of clever and creative strategies that will allow you to pay cash for everything the financial aid office thought you were going to have to get loans for.

One of the best strategies you can use to reduce the amount you'll have to pay with loans is to do everything you can to keep your family's EFC as low as possible. The more you're able to do this, the more belief there will be that your family has great need, and the more help colleges are likely to give you to help your child cover educational costs.

Here's the important thing you need to know now if you want to keep your EFC *as low as possible* in the future: there are two different financial aid forms.

THE FAFSA FORM

You as a family will always fill out the relatively simple FAFSA form. This is the Free Application for Federal Student Aid available online at Fafsa.ed.gov. You will fill out this form in early October every year that you have one or more children in college the following fall. I want you to do this, without fail, every year, even if you have a very high personal income and feel certain you will never qualify for any federal financial aid for college. One big reason for this? If your child does (against all my pleading) end up taking out some student loans, I want them to be *Federal Direct Loans*. The only way your child can get *Federal Direct Loans* is for you to fill out the FAFSA form every October that you have a child in college the following fall.

Over 3,000 U.S. colleges and universities require only this one simple form as their entire financial aid application. This is a tremendous boon for families, because the FAFSA form determines your EFC without requiring you to disclose the value of your family's multimillion-dollar, family-controlled small business (as long as it has fewer than 100 full-time employees), the value of the home you live in, your non-qualified annuities, or the money your child's grandparents have saved for his college. In addition, the FAFSA form won't require you to disclose the income and assets of your wealthy ex-spouse and his new wife, as long as you're the parent the student has lived with the most during the 12 months before you fill out the FAFSA form.

Most families, of course, are going to look poorer and needier if the system tries to determine their ability to pay for college without looking at line items like these.

THE CSS/PROFILE FORM

Fewer than 400 out of 7,000 colleges and universities across the U.S. will ask families to fill out the more extensive CSS/Profile financial aid form in addition to the FAFSA form.

The CSS/Profile form will require you to disclose far more about your family assets, including the following:

» The value of your family-controlled small business (even if you do have fewer than 100 full-time employees)

» The value of the home you live in

» The value of your non-qualified annuities (Some salespeople might try to tell you that if you pack all your liquid assets away into annuity and insurance products, you'll be able to "hide" them from all financial aid calculations. This isn't true. All of your non-qualified annuities are considered as your family assets on the CSS/Profile financial aid application.)

» In some (but not all) cases, the money in any 529 savings plans owned by your child's grandparents

» The income and assets of your ex-spouse (and your ex-spouse's new husband or wife!), even if your ex is *not* your child's main custodial parent and there's been what was believed to be a rock-solid pre-nuptial agreement stating that this new stepparent will not be helping with any college costs. (Prenuptial agreements are always ignored by every financial aid calculation process.)

When you include these valuable assets in the financial aid analysis, you're naturally going to end up looking wealthier, and so your EFC will likely go up—up—up accordingly.

"Well," you might be thinking, "I just won't let my son or daughter apply to any of those colleges that want us to fill out the CSS/Pro-file form. Those schools are going to think we're rich and not offer us much financial aid!"

Please don't jump to this conclusion.

I do still want your son or daughter to apply to two to four good-fit schools that require the CSS/Profile form. Why? Because in some cases it may be a generous, well-endowed CSS/Profile school that ends up bringing in your child's college education at the very low-

est cost. It may look on the surface as though these schools would never offer you a bar-gain education because they have a clearer picture of how high your family assets really are, but you never really know until you fill out the forms, allow the individual financial aid offices to crunch their numbers, and then look at the reports that show the actual out-of-pocket costs you would see as an indi-vidual family.

Do you hesitate to believe that colleges and universities might still want to give your child financial aid, even if your family has high income and substantial assets? Believe it. It's true. At some of the most expensive colleges in the U.S., students can qualify for a significant amount of financial aid, even if their parents earn over $200,000 per year and have substantial assets.

This is great news. Every year there are stu-dents who are stunned and thrilled to realize they are going to be able to graduate from an expensive CSS/Profile private college for a lower price than it would have cost them to attend a local state university.

AT SOME OF THE MOST EXPENSIVE COLLEGES IN THE U.S., STUDENTS CAN QUALIFY FOR A SIGNIFICANT AMOUNT OF FINANCIAL AID, EVEN IF THEIR PARENTS EARN OVER $200,000 PER YEAR AND HAVE SUBSTANTIAL ASSETS.

To maximize the chances that you will one day find yourself looking happily at the best possible college financial aid package, here's the strategy I recommend to parents, students, guidance counselors, and college consultants.

While you're choosing good-fit colleges and universities to apply to, try to include only two to four CSS/Profile schools on the apply-to list, and make sure that the other six to eight colleges on the apply-to list are schools that look only at the FAFSA form. This is the most efficient way for parents to determine what kind of school is going to give their child a college education at the lowest possible out-of-pocket cost.

I suggest that if your child's career goal (based on the three assessments I strongly recommend in chapter 13) means that she will definitely need a four-year college degree, have her apply to at least two "stretch" schools that seem like they may be harder for her to get into, at least two "safe" schools that seem like they'd be fairly easy for her to get into, and at least two colleges that fall somewhere in the middle. Spread these schools out across these categories:

» Two to four good-fit CSS/Profile schools

» One to two good-fit four-year state schools that look only at the FAFSA form

» One community college located near your home

» Five to six good-fit private schools that look only at the FAFSA form

You can easily tell whether a college requires the CSS/Profile form (and consequently non-custodial parent financial information) by

typing this shortcut into your web browser: Bit.ly/2fFGKXD.

Of course, if the three assessments your child completed with the help of her educational consultant make it clear that no CSS/Profile schools are good fits for your child's particular career goal, it's perfectly OK for your child to just stick to all FAFSA schools.

Every family's assets are different, so a book like this can't advise you personally on which financial aid forms or which colleges will get you the best financial aid result. What I've found, though, is that if your son applies to mostly FAFSA schools and just two to four CSS/Profile schools, he will maximize his chances of getting the strongest, most generous financial aid packages when final financial aid decisions are made.

[5] *Use the following strategies to come up with a massive "maybe" list of colleges worth considering.*

Don't show this list to your daughter while you're working on it; it'll feel too overwhelming to her. Just quietly make this list for your own reference.

I suggest that you lay out your maybe list this way: When a college or university pops out as looking like even a remote possibility, write down its name and geographic location in a spiral notebook. Leave 10 lines of space underneath. Use the blank space for jotting down solid, logical reasons why you like that college. (For example, "It's especially well known for its accounting program," "It's 15 minutes from Grandma's house," or "It gives ROTC students free room and board.")

It's OK if this list ends up having a huge number of colleges on it. The purpose in making this list is to see which colleges and universities end up having the longest list of solid, logical reasons to like them.

Got your pen and notebook ready? While you're sitting alone, with your child out of the room, let's start making a massive "maybe" list of colleges and universities that might be worth considering.

Start by googling "good colleges for" along with the college major your child is considering.

When you've got your spiral notebook ready, google "U.S. News top colleges" along with the major your child will probably be looking at based on the career assessment work prescribed in chapter 13.

Look at several of the sites listed in your search results. This is a good way to very quickly find a high-quality list of well-respected colleges that excel at teaching exactly what your child wants to learn. Many of the schools that result from this search may be relatively expensive CSS/Profile schools, but that's OK. Two to four of the schools your child applies to are going to be CSS/Profile colleges, right?

When I recently googled "U.S. News top colleges" along with the word "robotics," a long list of results showed me many colleges that I expected to find in this category: MIT, Carnegie Mellon, University of Pennsylvania, and others. But I also found Indiana State University and UT Austin listed as top colleges for robotics. Wow! If I were a parent of a prospective college student interested

in robotics, I'd think, "This is great! As state schools, ISU and UT Austin may well end up being less-expensive college options, especially since when I google 'CSS/Profile participating institutions,' I see that both these schools are FAFSA schools that don't require me to bare my soul in the CSS/Profile financial aid application. It's true that my child would be attending as an out-of-state resident, but it still might be worth it. Especially if my child could get into an honors program there. Hmm. I wonder if our family could *move* there in time for my child to qualify as an in-state resident? I'll call their admissions office and ask about the residency requirements. Just before I do, though, I'll use CollegeData.com to check their four-year graduation rates."

As you go through this process, keep your eye out for private colleges and universities that are well respected for the education they provide in your child's prospective career field, but they aren't big name nationally ranked schools. Lower-ranked private schools may give your son a highly desirable preferential financial aid package that contains more grants and fewer loans, along with a wonderful "big fish in a small pond" experience during the years he attends there.

Don't shy away from private colleges located far away from your home state.

Add some of those to your list too. Why? In an astounding number of cases, private college admissions personnel are working hard to create incoming freshman classes that are impressive due to their geographic diversity. "We have students here from every state in the U.S. and 15 countries!" admissions staff chirp happily to parents during campus tours. If this particular private school is in Oregon and your child is one of that school's only applicants from Florida, the school may bend over backward to offer your kid preferential financial aid and free grant money in order to attract him. It's true that you'll need to buy a plane ticket to get this child home for Thanksgiving, but the lower cost of attending college may be well worth this trade-off.

Note that this "geographic advantage" strategy works best for lower-ranked (but still good quality) private colleges and universities. Top 20 colleges have no trouble attracting students from every state, and state universities far from your child's home won't be so eager to offer him discounted tuition. Instead, they'll charge him extra.

Strongly consider co-op college programs. These programs are so outstanding that some students decide to apply only to co-op college programs.

Conventional college students sometimes spend four straight years taking notes and taking tests in classrooms, get little to no practical work experience in their fields, struggle to find jobs after college, and then despair when they realize that they detest the work they've just spent $100,000 training for.

Not so with students taking classes in brilliant and innovative co-op college programs.

A student in a co-op college program typically takes college classes for about six months, then waves good-bye to the classroom in order to go to work at a com-

pany that's part of her university's co-op program. The student works full time at this company, gaining six months of work experience and additional income ranging from $11,000 to $18,000. She then returns to the college campus to take another six months of classes. She repeats this cycle again and again over five years until she graduates from college with four things: a four-year degree, a boatload of focused and substantial work experience in her field, an astounding number of networking connections and potential job offers, and up to $46,000 in additional income that can be used to pay college expenses and graduate debt-free.

> **CONVENTIONAL COLLEGE STUDENTS SOMETIMES SPEND FOUR STRAIGHT YEARS TAKING NOTES AND TAKING TESTS IN CLASSROOMS, GET LITTLE TO NO PRACTICAL WORK EXPERIENCE IN THEIR FIELDS, STRUGGLE TO FIND JOBS AFTER COLLEGE, AND THEN DESPAIR WHEN THEY REALIZE THAT THEY DETEST THE WORK THEY'VE JUST SPENT $100,000 TRAINING FOR.**
>
> **NOT SO WITH STUDENTS TAKING CLASSES IN BRILLIANT AND INNOVATIVE CO-OP COLLEGE PROGRAMS.**

Nearly 50,000 employers participate in co-op college programs—including multinational corporations, government agencies, small businesses, and nonprofit organizations. More than 80 of the top 100 Fortune 500 companies employ students in co-op college programs.

One of the best things about co-op college programs, though, is that co-op earnings don't count as student income on the FAFSA form the way some other college student summer and school-year earnings do. The result? Potentially higher financial aid awards for co-op college students.

And as if this weren't enough, college co-op programs can also provide tax advantages for families with investment income.

How so?

If a co-op college student is able to earn enough money in a given tax year to provide more than half her own support (something extremely likely to happen in a co-op college program), she gets around "kiddie tax" laws requiring her to pay taxes on certain portions of her investment income at her parents' higher tax rate. Having extra co-op money in her pocket will mean that she's allowed to pay taxes on all of her investment income (interest, dividends, and capital gains) at the lowest "child rate." She can sell an investment for more than she paid for it, perhaps worrying that she'll have to pay high capital gains taxes on the profit, and then be delighted to find that she's required to pay capital gains tax only in the lowest tax bracket. For some families, this can save a bundle.

Parents and grandparents take note: if the co-op college student in your life qualifies for need-based financial aid, don't gift assets to him or her prior to January 1 of the sophomore year of college just to take advantage of this tax strategy. You'll only diminish his or her chances of qualifying for need-based financial aid later. If it's clear that your co-op

college student *isn't* qualifying for need-based aid anyway, though, go ahead and give. Gifting this child with assets in this case won't damage his or her future financial aid eligibility in the least.

For wealthy families, this strategy can be worth $5,000–$15,000 in tax savings per year per child. Combine these tax savings with the student's college co-op earnings and any additional merit-based aid he or she gets, and it can add up to $110,000 or more per student. Not only that, but it's also possible to use the student's personal exemption, standard deduction, and the American Opportunity Tax Credit on her tax return to wipe out the federal tax owed on tens of thousands of dollars of income. Plus, of course, because students in co-op college programs have earned income, they or their parents can put that amount of money into regular and Roth IRAs as well.

Here's a list of colleges and universities I know of that have co-op college programs. Students at the ones I've marked with an asterisk may be eligible for a generous World Association for Cooperative Education (WACE) scholarship (which I'll talk about a little later).

Azusa Pacific University

Brigham Young University

California State University

Calvin College

Central Piedmont Community College

Charles Sturt University

Clarkson University*

College of Lake County

Cornell University

County College of Morris

DePaul University

Drexel University*

Eastern Kentucky University

Endicott College

George Mason University

Georgia Institute of Technology

Georgia State University

Glendale Community College

Harvard University

Hinds Community College

Howard University

Indiana University— Purdue University Indianapolis

Iowa State University

Johnson & Wales University*

Kettering University

LaGuardia Community College

Lane Community College

LIU Post

Long Island University

Macomb Community College

Massachusetts Institute of Technology

Merrimack College

Miami Dade College

Michigan State University

New Mexico State University

Northeastern University

Northwestern University

Old Dominion University

Pacific Lutheran University

Post University

Purdue University

Queens College

Robert Morris University

Rochester Institute of Technology*

Rowan University

South Dakota School of Mines & Technology

Spelman College

State University of New York at Oswego*

The Culinary Institute of America

University of Arizona

University of Central Florida

University of Cincinnati*

University of Louisville J. B. Speed School of Engineering

University of Massachusetts Lowell*

University of Michigan

University of Mississippi

University of North Dakota

University of Tennessee

University of Texas at Austin

University of Toledo*

University of Waterloo

Wentworth Institute of Technology*

Worcester Polytechnic Institute

Students who've been accepted to one of the nine schools I've marked with an asterisk in the list on the previous page can apply for one of 160 generous merit-based WACE scholarships, many of which are renewable for four years and valued at $24,000. WACE is "the only international professional organization dedicated to developing, expanding, branding, and advocating for cooperative and work-integrated education programs within industry and educational institutions."[16] You can find WACE online at Waceinc.org.

The scholarships noted above are based on merit only and do not require financial need. In theory, your family could have millions in assets and your child could still qualify for one of these WACE scholarships. WACE has awarded over $34.9 million in merit-based scholarship money since 2003.

Students who want to apply for a WACE scholarship are advised to do so early in their senior year of high school or early in their sophomore year of community college by going to Waceinc.org/scholarship. (If you keep reading this book, I'll remind you of this when your child is in 12th grade.) The WACE scholarship application requires only a 3.5 GPA and a 300-word essay on why the student desires cooperative education. No letters of recommendation are required.

If your child enrolls in a co-op college program, it's likely that the college's co-op staff will assist her at every step, beginning with sitting down with her to define her work skills and goals. They will show her lists of potential co-op employment positions, assist her in applying for those positions, help her to prepare for interviews, assist her as she selects among the job offers she receives, and work alongside her and her employers to ensure that her work experiences are consistently linked to her courses and career development.

According to WACE, college co-op programs are available in most professional fields including (but not limited to) the following:

Chemicals and Petroleum	Manufacturing	Public Relations
Health Services	Education	Government
Communications	Media and the Arts	Retail Trade
Hotel and Restaurant Management	Environmental Services	Transportation
Computers and Electronics	Public and Private Utilities	Financial Services

---

16 "About WACE and CWIE," WACE website, accessed September 24, 2016, http://www.waceinc.org/about.html.

During the quarters that co-op students are away from campus working at their co-op jobs, they are still considered full-time students for the purposes of keeping student loans in deferment and qualifying for their insurance. However, because they are not registered for the minimum six credit hours of coursework while they are away, they do not qualify for financial aid during these time periods. This usually turns out OK, since their colleges are not usually charging them full tuition during that time. Usually, all that is charged during those months is a smaller co-op fee that covers the cost of administering the co-op program.

Co-op students who have received private scholarships will need to check with their donors to confirm whether they can continue to receive scholarship money while gone from campus during co-op quarters, or whether the flow of scholarship money will stop temporarily and start up again when regular classroom study resumes. (Now you know why, way back in chapter 3, I suggested that you keep careful track of the contact information for each organization sponsoring the scholarships your child applies for and wins.)

If you're convinced that an Ivy League education will be critically important for this particular child, consider the Harvard Extension School.

If you'd like your child to have a Harvard University education but not the nerve-wracking admissions pressure or astronomical tuition cost, you might seriously consider the bachelor of liberal arts (ALB) degree at the Harvard Extension School (HES), where the Cost of Attendance (COA) is under $25,000 per year, including tuition, housing, food, books, sup-

plies, personal expenses, and transportation (with financial aid available to those who apply and qualify).

Yes, the bachelor of liberal arts degree from HES is a real Harvard bachelor's degree. HES is one of 12 schools at Harvard University, and Extension School students are allowed to choose from among 600 degree courses, many of which are taught by Nobel Laureates and other distinguished Harvard faculty members who are renowned experts in their fields. (If your daughter someday wants to take Genetics to beef up her med school application, she'll be delighted to find that at HES, Genetics is taught by a renowned Harvard med school professor worthy of mention on her AMCAS personal statement.)

> **EXTENSION SCHOOL STUDENTS ARE ALLOWED TO CHOOSE FROM AMONG 600 DEGREE COURSES, MANY OF WHICH ARE TAUGHT BY NOBEL LAUREATES AND OTHER DISTINGUISHED HARVARD FACULTY MEMBERS WHO ARE RENOWNED EXPERTS IN THEIR FIELDS.**

HES students don't live on Harvard's campus, but if they rent apartments with roommates in Cambridge, attend their Harvard classes in person in historic Harvard Yard, they will likely feel exactly like (and have nearly all the benefits of) traditional Harvard University students paying an additional $120,000 over their four years of college.

HES students are assigned Harvard email addresses, and are given the official Harvard student ID card that allows them access to Harvard research opportunities, to Harvard career and grad school counseling services, to the computer facilities at 53 Church Street, to all campus events (including football games, the Winter Ball, and student performances in Sanders Theater), to academic workshops, to the Writing Center in Grossman Library, to the Math Question Center in Sever Hall, to the Harvard Library Portal (which allows access to more than 3,000 electronic databases and journals), and to the Grossman Library, one of the largest academic libraries in the world. At commencement, HES students march into Tercentenary Theater and receive their degrees along with every other Harvard graduate.

But is the HES education of good quality, and well respected? Are its graduates well regarded?

Patrick Engleman, an HES grad who is currently a partner with Direct IT (a network management company based in Waltham, MA) said this about his HES experience:

> Overall I feel that I received the best undergraduate education possible. It was a great honor to study and then be a TA under Tom Hayes and run the Physics 123 lab. I think it's entirely possible that Tom is the best introductory circuit design teacher in the world, and I know I am in great company. It was also a great honor to study cyberlaw at the Berkman Center of Harvard law as an undergraduate. I was able to take more IP, patent, copyright, and digital law classes than are available at most law schools, including Larry Lessig's former class, "The Technology and Politics of Control."[17]

Engleman went on to recount how tremendously privileged he felt to be able to study number theory, probability, topology, calculus, linear algebra, and group theory under some of the greatest, most brilliant minds in the country.

If anyone tries to argue that HES offers some kind of inferior education, a statement like that should shut them right down.

An unnamed lawyer commenting on a blog post about HES said this: "HES offers both undergraduate and graduate degrees for a fraction of the cost of 'traditional' Harvard degrees. Same profs, same syllabus, same books, same exams, but no postgraduate debt in the tens of thousands of dollars that'll take decades to repay. Now you tell me, who is the smarter student?"[18]

ENGLEMAN WENT ON TO RECOUNT HOW TREMENDOUSLY PRIVILEGED HE FELT TO BE ABLE TO STUDY NUMBER THEORY, PROBABILITY, TOPOLOGY, CALCULUS, LINEAR ALGEBRA, AND GROUP THEORY UNDER SOME OF THE GREATEST, MOST BRILLIANT MINDS IN THE COUNTRY.

---

17   Quote used with permission of Patrick Engleman. Any unauthorized duplication is strictly prohibited.

18   Anonymous, comment on "New York Times Front Page Extension School Article," *Harvard Extended, the Original, Unofficial Harvard Extension Blog*, founded and owned by Ian Lamont, December 11, 2007, http://harvardextended.blogspot.com/2005/11/new-york-times-front-page-extension.html.

Most HES courses are available only on campus in Cambridge, but some are offered online. Currently, more than 200 of HES's 600 degree courses are offered online, and official policy requires that HES students take only 16 credits on campus at Harvard in order to earn the HES bachelor of liberal arts degree. This is the one aspect of the HES policy that I'm not in favor of. While I believe that it's fine to take a few courses online if distance prevents a student from taking them in person, I don't believe that taking the majority of HES classes online approximates the true Harvard experience.

If your child decides to earn a bachelor's degree from HES, I say it's a brilliant idea. It will give her a world class education while saving your family a jaw-dropping amount of money. But if your child is going to do it, encourage her to rent an apartment in Cambridge, get some roommates to split the costs, and make full use of that official Harvard ID to boldly access every club, research project, summer activity, extracurricular activity, and career service her heart desires.

Would your child ever consider exchanging military service for a large college scholarship and guaranteed employment after college? If so, consider ROTC.

The U.S. military awards generous four-year scholarships to students who are U.S. citizens between the ages of 17 and 26, have high school diplomas or the equivalent, meet certain physical standards, have scored at certain minimum levels on the SAT or ACT, have a high school GPA of at least 2.5, and can agree to accept a four-year active duty commission in the military followed by an additional four years serving as part of the Individual Ready Reserve (IRR). This by itself can be a tremendous benefit to students, but it gets even better when students attend colleges that offer free room and board to ROTC students.

> **IF YOUR CHILD DECIDES TO EARN A BACHELOR'S DEGREE FROM HES, I SAY IT'S A BRILLIANT IDEA. IT WILL GIVE HER A WORLD CLASS EDUCATION WHILE SAVING YOUR FAMILY A JAW-DROPPING AMOUNT OF MONEY.**

What is college like for a student on an ROTC scholarship?

Students who attend college on ROTC scholarships have the exact same college experience as non-ROTC college students, with just a few exceptions.

ROTC students wear an Army uniform one day a week, on the day they attend "drill" (which usually takes about three hours), and ROTC students take one ROTC class and one ROTC lab per term. These classes "involve hands-on fieldwork as well as classroom work," but at the same time they are "standard college classes that fit into a normal academic schedule."[19] In addition, ROTC students usually get up very early

---

19 "Army ROTC: College Scholarship FAQ," U.S. Army, accessed September 24, 2016, http://www.goarmy.com/rotc/college-students/faq.html.

During college summer breaks, ROTC students may participate in extended training activities that take up multiple summer weeks. Here are some of the summer training opportunities offered to Army ROTC cadets:

Airborne

Air Assault

Army Internships

Cadet Troop Leader
  Training (CTLT)

Combat Diver Qualification
  Course (CDQC)

Culture and Language
  Program (CULP)

Leaders Training Course
  (LTC)

Northern Warfare

Robin Sage

Mountain Warfare

Nurse Summer Training
  Program (NSTP)

United Kingdom Officer
  Training Camp (UKOTC)

at least three days a week to participate in physical training (PT). Would your son or daughter like to know exactly how difficult Army PT is, and maybe even get a head start on getting into shape for Army service? You can download the Army PT guide by typing this shortcut into your web browser: Bit.ly/2gzz2xe.[20]

Other than the uniform, the weekly three-hour drills, the specialized classes and labs each semester, the PT, and the opportunity for additional summer training, ROTC students are pretty much ordinary college students. They have just as much fun as regular college students. They pledge fraternities and sororities at the same rates as regular college students, they participate in community service projects, and they play varsity team and individual sports.

The big difference is that ROTC students experience far fewer financial worries. (This is especially true if they've enrolled at a col-lege or university that offers ROTC students free room and board for four years.) ROTC students enjoy two-, three- or four-year scholarships that pay full tuition and fees, a separate allowance for books, and payment of certain travel expenses. ROTC students receive free clothing (including shoes and hats), good quality military-style travel bags, and a tax-free stipend of up to $5,000 a year to spend on personal expenses while they are in college. ROTC students know that they have jobs after graduation, and they enjoy the possibility that the military may pay for their grad school or med school education as well when the time comes.

After college, ROTC students complete their training at the Army's five-week Leadership Developmental and Assessment Course (LDAC) at Fort Lewis, Washington. Afterward, they are commissioned as second lieutenants in the U.S. Army and are paid as such. As of 2015, that pay was $2,784 per month (with raises up to $3,503

---

20 You can access the Army PT guide at http://www.goarmy.com/downloads/physical-training-guide.html.

per month after three years of service) plus medical and dental care, 30 days paid leave (vacation) per year, and housing and subsistence (food) allowances that could bump that total salary and benefit package up to over $50,000 per year. These grads receive specialized training in one of 17 different Army branches, and according to the GoArmy website, they "receive regular professional training . . . and many opportunities for advanced leadership positions and post-graduate education."[21] Add to that the fact that many ROTC graduates are able to leave college debt-free without being tied to $950-per-month student loan payments, and ROTC can make for a very attractive financial option.

When ROTC students finish their military service commitment, they are free to leave the military and become a part of the civilian workforce. When they do so, they bring with them a hefty résumé that lists five straight years of documented management and leadership experience. As the Army ROTC website says, "Army ROTC is one of the only college programs that teaches leadership. This training is invaluable for any career that involves leading, managing, and motivating people or fostering teamwork. Young Army officers are typically responsible for hundreds of soldiers and millions of dollars in equipment; this kind of management experience can be very attractive to post-Army employers."[22]

The application season for ROTC scholarships opens on or about June 12 each year.

High school students are advised to apply for ROTC scholarships as early as possible during the summer after their junior year of high school, and then finish all associated paperwork and updates by February 28 of the following year.

If your child applies for ROTC and is only awarded a two-year scholarship, she could ask ROTC if the scholarship could be held for her for two years while she lives at home and works her way through community college— making sure that every community college class she takes will transfer to a four-year college or university with an ROTC program. If ROTC agrees, she can transfer all the credits she's earned to that four-year college and use her two-year ROTC scholarship to pay for the remainder of her four-year degree.

Every branch of the military has slightly different ROTC requirements and benefits. Most of what I've discussed here is Army-specific, since the Army (a) has the largest ROTC program in the U.S. (20,000 cadets in 273 ROTC programs), (b) allows its cadets to major in nearly all academic areas, and (c) offers a wider range of career opportunities (in more places around the world) than any other U.S. military branch at this time. For specific information on Navy, U.S. Coast Guard, and Air Force ROTC, contact local Navy and Air Force recruiters.

Would you like to see a list of colleges and universities with Army ROTC programs, all organized by state? The army provides a great comprehensive list on its website. You

---

21 "Army ROTC."

22 Ibid.

can get directly to it by typing this shortcut into your web browser: Bit.ly/2fIErU9.

As you look at individual colleges with ROTC programs on this site, give extra careful consideration to those that offer a *room and board incentive*. Free or reduced-price room and board could save your child thousands on living expenses over four years of college.

You might consider adding colleges with ROTC programs to your list now. If your child ends up being completely sold on the idea of ROTC and loves the idea of doing it, you will eventually be able to eliminate from your consideration every college and university that doesn't offer it.

If you are located outside the United States, consider the nearly free University of the People.

Millions of qualified students around the world are prevented from attending college due to war, poverty, unstable governmental systems, or natural disasters. In a heartbreaking number of countries, education for female students is viewed as a shame and a disgrace, and is punishable by death. Students in these situations will likely never be able to afford even the most basic college costs, no matter how strategic they try to be about planning. So how can students like these get access to a fully accredited university education?

The University of the People is a fully accredited, tuition-free, nonprofit, degree-granting university that offers students in the U.S. and around the world real college degrees in two in-demand fields: computer science and

business administration. The best news? The entire University of the People bachelor's degree program is available online using the lowest-possible level of Internet connection. (No audio or video files are involved, so broadband Internet is not required.)

Courses are taught by more than 3,000 professors, including presidents, vice chancellors, full professors, and academic advisors from elite universities, such as Yale, NYU, Berkeley, and Oxford. Textbooks and materials are made available for free. Enrolled students read online lecture material and textbooks, do homework, and interact with other students around the world in small 20- to 30-person discussion-based classes. The only fees involved? Students are asked to pay $100 USD per course to cover testing expenses, but scholarships are widely available to cover even that when students can't afford to pay.

> **THE UNIVERSITY OF THE PEOPLE IS A FULLY ACCREDITED, TUITION-FREE, NONPROFIT, DEGREE-GRANTING UNIVERSITY THAT OFFERS STUDENTS IN THE U.S. AND AROUND THE WORLD REAL COLLEGE DEGREES IN TWO IN-DEMAND FIELDS: COMPUTER SCIENCE AND BUSINESS ADMINISTRATION.**

In 2014 alone, University of the People had over 1,700 accepted students studying in 143 countries, with no limit on additional available seats. The only requirements necessary to become a University of the People student are a high school diploma, sufficient English, and the most basic Internet connection. For further information on University of the People (or to donate to it), visit Uopeople.edu. To be truly inspired, you can watch Shai Reshef's TED talk about the University of the People by typing this shortcut into your web browser: Bit.ly/2gkDC1Q.

> **IN 2014 ALONE, UNIVERSITY OF THE PEOPLE HAD OVER 1,700 ACCEPTED STUDENTS STUDYING IN 143 COUNTRIES, WITH NO LIMIT ON ADDITIONAL AVAILABLE SEATS.**

Sit down with your teen for a quick, fun criteria search on Collegeview.com/ collegesearch.

At this user-friendly website, students and/ or parents can check off 20 different criteria, such as major, school type, school size, availability of campus housing, campus setting, public versus private, four-year graduation rate, sports, religious affiliation, and liberal versus conservative lean, and instantly receive a ranked list of colleges that the website believes most best fits those criteria. It's an excellent tool.

Click on each of the orange bars on the left side of the site, and each will instantly expand to become a brief questionnaire that you can answer to identify your preferences. Results pop up instantly. The more questions you answer, the more focused the results. Parents, you can then consider adding some

of these results to your "maybe" list.

If you'd like a second opinion, CollegeData. com offers a similar tool. You can get directly to it by typing this shortcut into your web browser: Bit.ly/2gMrJVV.

OPTIONAL STRATEGIES FOR EXPANDING THE "MAYBE" LIST

You may feel as though you have plenty of college names on your maybe list now and don't really want any more ideas on how to find additional colleges to consider. That's completely OK.

Our goal at this point, though, is to keep this list very large and very fluid. You and your child are about to start making in-person visits to colleges, and once you start doing that, you'll learn volumes about what kinds of colleges your daughter genuinely likes and what kinds she doesn't. You may come home from a trip where you visited three colleges only to have your daughter say, "Let's cross out all the urban ones located in really big cities. I just didn't feel safe walking down to the classroom area from that freshman dorm." Or "I really want to be able to play in a jazz ensemble in college. Let's cross out all the ones that don't let freshmen do that."

I'd like to give you nine additional strategies that will help you to further expand this maybe list. One of these nine strategies will provide you a list of over 50 colleges and universities that are known to be especially generous with financial aid and merit aid. You can access these nine additional strategies by downloading the free bonus online content below.

[6] *Now, ruthlessly knock some of the maybe college options off of your list using the following criteria.*

Once you've got a huge list of college possibilities in front of you, it's time to start crossing off schools that (for one reason or another) aren't your strongest options. Here are some criteria to consider as you think this through.

Consider eliminating from your list all schools that don't offer free money merit aid to anyone.

There are some U.S. colleges and universities that attract so many highly qualified applicants that they have no need to hand out free merit aid to entice quality students. Your son may get a generous tuition discount from one of these schools if your family income and assets are very low and you have significant financial need, but the schools on this list will not offer free money to students based on grades, test scores, service, or any other life accomplishment. Even if your son has straight A's, perfect ACT and SAT scores, and has single-handedly solved the clean water crisis in Haiti, he will still not get one penny of extra aid money from the schools on this list.

"SARAH'S JUST GOT TO GET INTO ONE OF THESE BRAND-NAME SCHOOLS," ANXIOUS PARENTS FRET, BITING THEIR NAILS WITH WORRY. "OTHERWISE SHE WON'T BE ABLE TO GET A GOOD JOB OR HAVE A HAPPY LIFE AFTER SHE GRADUATES." *THIS IS ABSOLUTELY UNTRUE.*

I worry about the thousands of smart, high-achieving students who are steered to apply only to schools on this prestigious list.

"Sarah's just got to get into one of these brand-name schools," anxious parents fret, biting their nails with worry. "Otherwise she won't be able to get a good job or have a happy life after she graduates." *This is absolutely untrue.* If you're thinking this way, please re-read chapter 2. If you cling to this false belief and have your child apply only to top colleges you can't afford, you may one day find yourself looking at 10 financial aid award letters that all require your child to take on suffocating amounts of student loan debt.

If your son or daughter is determined to apply to one or two of the colleges on this list "just to see what happens," that is fine. But unless your family income and assets are low, don't depend on these schools to help with the mission of keeping your child debt-free.

State universities outside your home state can cost $30,000 extra or more per year. Consider either removing them from your list now or carefully using the strategies on page 174 to lower their costs as much as you can.

State university tuition for out-of-state students can be astronomical. If you doubt this, visit CollegeData.com and type the name of a random state university into the search bar. Look for the resulting boxes labeled "Res. COA" and "Non-Res. COA." The figures in these boxes are costs of attendance for students who are residents and for students who are not residents of that state. See the difference?

Now ask yourself, "What is it about this college that would make it worth this greatly increased cost? Will it be worth it to pay

---

Colleges That Don't Offer Merit Aid to Anyone

(Important note: colleges I've marked with an asterisk on this list don't give out merit aid, but they are known to be generous with need-based financial aid.)

Amherst College*	Harvard University*	Trinity College, CT
Barnard College	Haverford College*	University of Pennsylvania*
Bates College	Julliard School	Vassar College*
Bennington College	Marlboro College	Wellesley College*
Bowdoin College*	Massachusetts Institute	Wheaton College, MA
Brown University	of Technology*	Williams College
Bryn Mawr College	Middlebury College*	Yale University*
Colby College	Mount Holyoke College*	
Colgate University	New England College	
Columbia University*	Princeton University*	
Connecticut College	Reed College	
Cornell University	St. John's College	
Dartmouth College	Sarah Lawrence College	
Goddard College	Stanford University*	
Hamilton College	Swarthmore College*	

years of interest on the student loans I might have to take out to send my child there?"

These schools may offer some "consortium," "regional exchange," or "reciprocity" arrangements that allow some students from neighboring states to qualify for in-state tuition. That may help. Be careful, though; read all the fine print. Ask especially whether your child will need to reapply for these special programs every year, and if so what the deadlines are.

If there's an out-of-state state university that feels like an absolute must-have for your son, it will quickly become evident to you that his Cost of Attendance (COA) would be much lower if he could magically become a resident of that state. You might ask that university's financial aid office exactly what it would take for that to happen. Rules on this subject vary from state to state. Some states require that the student graduate from high school in that state. Most states require that the student live and pay taxes within its borders for 12 to 36 consecutive months before first enrolling in college there. It's very rare that a state would allow a student to pay reduced in-state tuition rates after he or she has already enrolled in college.

If you decide to move your family to another state in order to establish legal residency and qualify for in-state tuition, great. Just get the residency requirements in writing before you pack a single cardboard box.

This is a radical strategy, I know. But if it could save your son $80,000 in increased

tuition and future student loan payments, it might be worth it.

> **IF YOU DECIDE TO MOVE YOUR FAMILY TO ANOTHER STATE IN ORDER TO ESTABLISH LEGAL RESIDENCY AND QUALIFY FOR IN-STATE TUITION, GREAT. JUST GET THE RESIDENCY REQUIREMENTS IN WRITING BEFORE YOU PACK A SINGLE CARDBOARD BOX.**

If you'd like professional help figuring out how to get your son in-state tuition at a university far from home, Instateangels.com may be able to help.

Your son will likely work a job while going to college. Would you like that job to reimburse him for part of his tuition, as well as giving him a paycheck? If so, you might cross out all the schools on your list located in places where it's unlikely he'll ever be able to work a tuition reimbursement job.

Tuition reimbursement jobs pay parts of students' college expenses, in addition to providing a paycheck. Sound like a great idea? It *is*.

Caitlin Anderson, in a blog post she wrote for Lumerit Scholar (a company that coaches students of all ages through earning their bachelor's degrees debt-free), writes with glee about how Starbucks helped her toward a debt-free college degree. She writes,

> As a former barista, the company was good to me. Not only did I get cheap health insurance, great hours, and a flexible sched-

> **Many thanks to Caitlin Anderson and Lumerit Scholar for providing this partial list of companies that provide varying levels of tuition reimbursement for students:**
>
> | | | |
> |---|---|---|
> | Aeropostale | Discover Card | Lowe's |
> | Ann Taylor | Disney | Macy's |
> | Anthem Blue Cross and Blue Shield | ExxonMobil | McDonald's |
> | Apple | Fiat Chrysler Automobiles | Nike |
> | Applied Materials | FedEx | Proctor and Gamble |
> | AT&T | Ford | Raytheon |
> | Bank of America | Gap | Siemens |
> | Barnes and Noble | GE | Staples |
> | Best Buy | Google | Starbucks |
> | Boeing | Home Depot | Target |
> | BP | IBM | UPS |
> | Capital One | Intel | Verizon Wireless |
> | CarMax | J.M. Smucker Co. | Walgreens |
> | Chase | John Deere | Walmart |
> | Chevron | Johnson & Johnson | Wells Fargo |
> | Coca-Cola | KFC | Yahoo |
> | Deloitte | Lane Bryant | |
> | | Lockheed Martin | |

ule but I got something that really helped me. Tuition reimbursement. Between my paycheck, tuition reimbursement, CLEP® savings, and some money from my parents which was quickly paid off, I was able to graduate without student loans hanging over my head.[23]

One student reported to Caitlin that Verizon Wireless contributed up to $8,000 per year for six years to help pay for his associate's,

bachelor's, and master's degrees (plus two additional certifications). "You don't have to pay Verizon back or stay with the company under any sort of contract provided you graduate with a C or better and stay employed until you finish the class," he said. "I graduated debt free with no student loans!"[24]

This is great news, but students who are really strategic can carry this one step further. They can set a goal of getting a tuition

---

23 Excerpts from article titled "33 Companies That Can Save You From College Debt" by Caitlin Anderson was originally published on CollegePlus.org February 17, 2011, https://collegeplus.org/blog/33-companies-that-can-save-you-from-college-debt, and is used with the permission of Lumerit Education © 2016 (formerly College Plus). Any unauthorized duplication is strictly prohibited.

24 Ibid.

reimbursement job working for the type of company they'd love to work for as a degreed professional one day.

Does your son love technology? What could be better than getting tuition reimbursement by working at Google for four years? (And just in case you're tempted to shoot this idea down by saying, "Well, he doesn't want to live in California for college," let me remind you that Google has offices in 40 different locations, including Lenoir, North Carolina, and Council Bluffs, Iowa. You can get directly to a list of all Google locations by typing this shortcut into your web browser: Bit.ly/2fKETkM.

IF YOUR DAUGHTER LOVES FASHION MERCHANDISING, SHE COULD APPLY FOR A TUITION REIMBURSEMENT COLLEGE JOB AT ANN TAYLOR OR GAP. IF HER GOALS ARE IN THE FINANCE INDUSTRY, SHE COULD LOOK FOR OPENINGS AT BANK OF AMERICA OR WELLS FARGO.

Don't stop with Google, though. If your daughter loves fashion merchandising, she could apply for a tuition reimbursement college job at Ann Taylor or Gap. If her goals are in the finance industry, she could look for openings at Bank of America or Wells Fargo. If your son's career goals involve aviation technology or aerospace engineering, you could find out where all the Boeing and Lockheed Martin offices are, encourage him to apply to colleges nearby, and then cheer him on as he applies

for tuition reimbursement jobs in his industry prior to his freshman year of college.

If a college on your list is located in a city where your son is unlikely to ever be able to work a tuition reimbursement job, you might want to cross that college off of your list now. If it's located in a city with lots of potential tuition reimbursement opportunity, though, you might want to put a large star next to that college's name on your list.

For each college you're considering, look at five critically important pieces of information on CollegeData.com. Eliminate colleges from your list that look increasingly unattractive when you do this.

I love CollegeData.com because it displays detailed, easy-to-find information about colleges in a standardized way. I can type any college name into the CollegeData.com search box and instantly see that college's city, state, size, gender mix, entrance difficulty, pricing information, percentage of students receiving merit aid, average student debt, freshman satisfaction rate, graduation rate, and type (public, private, or for-profit).

In addition, with just a little more digging, I can easily see whether this college takes the "Common App" application or the "Universal College App." I can do a preliminary calculation of a family's likely Expected Family Contribution (EFC) using financial data from last year, and I can estimate a student's chances of admission at this college, as well as gain ideas on how to improve his odds.

Remember, though, *your* child's chances of getting into a given college will always be *better* than these calculators report if he has a record of committed service to others over time and long-term focused commitment to one or two targeted extracurricular activities through four years of high school (as I talk about in chapter 4).

Warning from me: as you use CollegeData.com, please be sure to ignore the ad for the credit card on the home page. Credit cards can be a dangerous trap for college students and are not in any way necessary for college.

Here are the five main questions you will want to get answers to when you examine an individual college using CollegeData.com:

Question #1 for CollegeData.com: "What is this college's four-year graduation rate?"

Your goal as a parent is to get your child through college in four years or less. You are not interested in any college where it's so hard to get into the classes needed to graduate that students take five and six years to finish. This is especially important because financial aid and merit aid grants aren't extended into the fifth and sixth years of college. Eliminate colleges from your list that have low four-year graduation rates.

Question #2 for CollegeData.com: "What is this college's freshman satisfaction rate?"

This little number tells volumes about the quality of the student experience at an individual college. Low freshman satisfaction rate is a classic reason why so many students drop out of college after the freshman year and never go back. Eliminate colleges from your list that have serious problems with freshman satisfaction.

Question #3 for CollegeData.com: "Does this college give out free money merit aid?

Merit aid is free money for college that is given based on a student's merit and not on financial need. You can have $1 million in the bank and your son can still receive generous amounts of merit aid based on his own personal accomplishments.

If a college or university you're considering is not willing to give students free money merit aid in recognition of their ongoing service to others, committed and focused extracurricular involvement and leadership, strong grades, test scores, and other accomplishments—there are hundreds of other colleges that will. I suggest that you take the colleges that *don't* award merit aid off of your list.

Question #4 for CollegeData.com: "Is this college a *for-profit* institution?" If so, cross it off your list now.

I strongly suggest that your child not apply to any for-profit colleges or universities. Statistically, students at these schools have lower graduation rates, alarmingly high debt loads after college, grave problems transferring the credits they earn, unusually high rates of student loan default, and deeply concerning trouble finding jobs after they graduate.

On CollegeData.com, look at the box that says "Type." If you see the word "Profit" there, that's a college to avoid.

If you need additional convincing that for-profit colleges can be destructive for students, read the Generation Progress article entitled "Beware For-Profit Colleges: How the For-Profit Industry Is Hurting American Students and Our Economy."[25] It makes my blood boil. You can get directly to that article by typing this shortcut into your web browser: Bit.ly/2gvolLE.

Question #5 for CollegeData.com: "Will my son's service to others, grades, test scores, and other accomplishments likely put him in the top 25 percent of applicants to this particular college?"

CollegeData.com can help you estimate this too. This is helpful, because if your son's personal accomplishments do put him in the top 25 percent of this college's freshman class, he'll be far more likely to be offered free money merit aid to attract him to enroll. This will be a huge draw for you. You will gladly sacrifice a "prestigious" college name in order to get this, since you know full well that the quality of the college experience consists not in the brand name splashed across the top of the diploma, but in what your son makes of the college experience once he gets there.

While you are on CollegeData.com, click "Estimate" on the far left on any college's data bar. Enter just a few details there and

you'll be able to instantly see whether that particular college is a "stretch" school for your child, a "maybe school," or a "good bet." Study the details underneath, and you'll also get a good idea of what your son could do over the next 15 months to boost himself up into the "good bet" category.

When you read this information, parent, remember: you're not really interested in whether your son can "get in there." You're interested in whether your son could be such a superstar in that college's eyes that he will be awarded large amounts of free money merit aid to help pay for his education there. If your son looks like he might eventually end up being in the top 25 percent of applicants this school sees, he just might be that superstar.

For each college you're still considering, call its financial aid office and politely ask the following three questions. Eliminate from your list any colleges that give you answers you don't want to hear.

Question #1 for the financial aid office: If our child is awarded outside scholarships (private scholarships she finds and applies for outside of your financial aid system), will you use that scholarship money to reduce the number of loans in the financial aid package you give her? Or will you use her scholarship money to reduce the free grant money she would otherwise be getting? What is the school's official policy?"

If the policy at this school is to use your

25   Elizabeth Sohns, "Beware For-Profit Colleges: How the For-Profit Industry Is Hurting American Students and Our Economy," Generation Progress, May 15, 2014, http://genprogress.org/wp-content/uploads/2014/05/For_Profit_Issue_Brief1.pdf.

daughter's hard-won private scholarship money to reduce the free grant money she receives, you may want to take this college off of your list now.

Question #2 for the financial aid office: "Our son may be going into teaching. Does your school offer federal TEACH grants?"

If your son has used assessments to conclude that he's most likely going into teaching, consider this: Students willing to teach a "high-need subject" in a low-income location for four years after college might consider applying to colleges that offer federal TEACH (Teacher Education Assistance for College and Higher Education) grants. Qualifying for a TEACH grant can give a student up to $4,000 of free money each year to help pay for college, and your son won't even have to fill out a separate application to get it. TEACH grants are given out based on information in the student's FAFSA form.[26]

Please note that I extend this advice only for students who have completed the three assessments I prescribe in chapter 13 and feel convinced that teaching truly is their life's call. I would never want a student to go into teaching just to get this grant money. Remember, students who accept TEACH grants and then don't fulfill the necessary teaching and location requirements after college may find that their TEACH grants become loans needing to be paid back in their entirety—with interest.

If you'd like more information on TEACH grants, you can get directly to official TEACH grant details by typing this shortcut

into your web browser: Bit.ly/2fhOjAv.

> **PLEASE NOTE THAT I EXTEND THIS ADVICE ONLY FOR STUDENTS WHO HAVE COMPLETED THE THREE ASSESSMENTS I PRESCRIBE IN CHAPTER 13 AND FEEL CONVINCED THAT TEACHING TRULY IS THEIR LIFE'S CALL.**

Question #3 for the financial aid office: "Our daughter is interested in ROTC. Does your college award any special monetary benefits, such as free room and board, to ROTC students?"

You did some research on this earlier while selecting schools to apply to, but it's a good idea to get the most current information now by asking someone in the financial aid office at the college. When you ask this question, I suggest that you have the individual college's information on this subject open on your computer. You can get directly to the page where you search for that information by typing this shortcut into your web browser: Bit.ly/2fIErU9.

If your daughter is interested in ROTC and the answer is yes, the college *does* offer free room and board to ROTC students, that's a huge reason to put a big star beside the school name on your list.

For each college you're still considering, call its registrar's office and politely ask the following three questions. Eliminate from your list any colleges that give you answers you don't want to hear.

---

26   For more information, go to https://studentaid.ed.gov/sa/types/grants-scholarships/teach#eligible-programs.

Question #1 for the registrar's office: "If my child enrolls at your university, what's the total number of CLEP, DSST, and AP credits she'll be able use toward the completion of her degree plan? While I have you on the phone here, could you send me a copy of your school's 'CLEP equivalency course guide,' so I'll know which CLEP test replaces which course at your university?"

If your daughter has CLEP, DSST, and AP exams already completed, you'll want to find out now what this college's official policies are for awarding college credit for this work.

It will be interesting to find out now that Harvard University will allow your daughter to meet 12 credits of Harvard requirements with this credit-by-examination work; Carleton College in Northfield, Minnesota, will allow a flat, uncompromising zero; and North Central University in Minneapolis can potentially award her over 70 college credits for it. (This is one reason why homeschooling families who always use CLEP as their high school final exams love to send their kids to North Central University.)

> **IF MY CHILD ENROLLS AT YOUR UNIVERSITY, WHAT'S THE TOTAL NUMBER OF CLEP, DSST, AND AP CREDITS SHE'LL BE ABLE USE TOWARD THE COMPLETION OF HER DEGREE PLAN?**

If this college is not going to give your child very much actual college credit for her cred-

it-by-examination work, you might want to cross it off of your list. It won't be difficult to find other colleges to apply to.

Question #2 for the registrar's office: "If our son takes dual enrollment college classes when he is in high school in (name your state), how many of those credits will transfer to your institution? He also has additional credits from XYZ Community College as well. How many of those will he be able to transfer in? Do I need to send you some paperwork to get an official answer on this?"

There will be many colleges nationwide that will be happy to accept the dual enrollment and community college credits your son earns in high school. After all, your son is a good risk. He's already proven his ability with college-level work!

If a college on your maybe list doesn't want to give your son free college credit in exchange for the college-level work he's already done, you may want to cross that college off of your list.

Question #3 for the registrar's office: "If my child earns a two-year associate's degree from a community college before enrolling at your school, will you allow her to 'block transfer' it in?"

A block transfer occurs when the four-year college the student wants to one day graduate from agrees to accept her entire two-year chunk of community college credits as one large block, rather than picking apart her transcript and saying, "We'll give you credit for these courses, but not for these others."

The block transfer is the preferred one

because it guarantees that not one hour of your daughter's community college work will be wasted, and that she's already as far along on the path to a bachelor's degree as she can possibly be. If a college tells you, "No, we will not block transfer that degree," that may be enough to remove that college from your maybe list.

For each college you're still considering, call its admissions office and politely ask the following questions. Eliminate from your list any colleges that give you answers you don't want to hear.

Question #1 for the admissions office:
"What percentage of students at your college get by without having a car on campus? How safe and reliable is the public transportation on and near your campus?"

A student can save thousands on college expenses over four years by not taking a car to college. The only way this will work, though, is if the public transportation on and near campus is safe, reliable, and available at all different hours of the day and night.

Will your son or daughter be able to easily hop on public transportation to get to class, to activities and events, to the grocery store and movie theater, and to the airport when necessary? Will your daughter be able to easily order up an Uber car or find a Zipcar when she has armloads of heavy bags to carry? Has the school worked out a secure way for your daughter to feel perfectly safe walking back to her dormitory from the bus stop after night class?

If the public transportation on or near this campus is iffy, that might be enough to drop it off of your list.

Question #2 for the admissions office:
"Our son is considering a possible major in _____. Does your university have a special honors program available for students in that major? What are the entry requirements for that honors program?"

As I've mentioned previously, one of the greatest educational bargains out there is an honors program at a lower-priced, lower-ranked public or private college or university. What would it take for your son or daughter to be admitted to an honors program at this particular college?

At some colleges, it's simply a matter of qualifying academically, filling out a few extra forms, and taking a couple of extra high-level courses.

Honors programs can be extremely valuable—adding significant panache to scholarship applications, future résumés, and eventual grad school applications, while providing students the intimacy of a high-quality liberal arts college at low, low prices. Students in honors programs may receive special advising, have certain special classes all to themselves, be allowed to live on their own quiet dorm floors, and in some cases get first pick of classes, greatly increasing the possibility that they'll graduate from college within four years. In an honors program, your son may find himself surrounded by many high-caliber students who were admitted to Yale, Stanford, Harvard, and other elite colleges, but simply didn't want the burden of having to pay for those schools with onerous student loan debt.

Let the college's answer to this question guide you to either cross this school off of your list or give you one more reason to love it.

> **IN AN HONORS PROGRAM, YOUR SON MAY FIND HIMSELF SURROUNDED BY HIGH-CALIBER STUDENTS WHO WERE ADMITTED TO TOP FIVE COLLEGES, BUT TURNED THEM DOWN TO AVOID ONEROUS STUDENT LOAN DEBT.**

We're almost ready for our last step for this month. Just before you take our last step, do this:

[7] *Look over the college list you've just created. Review the bullet-point reasons that explain why each college might be a good one.*

It's likely still a massive, huge list—but that's OK. It's a swimming pool to explore. You've got 15 months to work side by side with your child to reduce that huge list down to

»   two to four good-fit CSS/Profile schools,

»   one or two good-fit, four-year state schools that look only at the FAFSA form,

»   one community college located near your home, and

»   five to six good-fit private schools that look only at the FAFSA form.

[8] *You've done your legwork; now find a good time to gently and respectfully pull your child into the college choice discussion.*

Parent, our goal this month was for you to take some quiet, thoughtful time alone where you would take the massive, roiling ocean of college possibilities out there and reduce that ocean to the size of a nice, big swimming pool.

You now have crystal clear ideas about what specific kinds of colleges, universities, or technical schools might be fantastic options for getting your child through college debt-free and into a job he or she is going to love afterward. Now let's invite your child to leap into the pool.

This strategy will give your son plenty of college possibilities to explore and choose from—just not so many that he gets lost or drowns.

Find a time to talk to your son when you're both well fed, well rested, unlikely to be interrupted, and getting along well.

Have a conversation something like this: "Hey, Jack—I was looking at that career goal work you did in January and thinking a little bit about what sorts of colleges might help you get to that goal completely debt-free. Can I share some thoughts I came up with?"

If your son agrees, explain to him a few of the principles I explained to you in this chapter. Just hit a few of the high points from this month's list:

» Big state universities near home aren't always the best option.

» Nice private colleges far from home can actually end up being great places to get through college debt-free.

» A whole bunch of colleges have something called co-op college programs that sound absolutely awesome.

YOU NOW HAVE CRYSTAL CLEAR IDEAS ABOUT WHAT SPECIFIC KINDS OF COLLEGES, UNIVERSITIES, OR TECHNICAL SCHOOLS MIGHT BE FANTASTIC OPTIONS FOR GETTING YOUR CHILD THROUGH COLLEGE DEBT-FREE AND INTO A JOB HE OR SHE IS GOING TO LOVE AFTERWARD.

Then, show him your list of colleges, complete with your bullet-point reasons for liking them. Say something like this: "I was thinking maybe we could visit a few of these and see what you think of them. Maybe on the next weekday you have off of school? Why don't you look at some of these schools' websites, take a few virtual video tours, and see which ones you like?"

[9] *Parent, put steel in your backbone, and remember that it is absolutely, completely OK for you to guide your child in this way.*

As I close this section on using a clever strategy to choose which colleges to apply to, I can hear some parents asking me, "But shouldn't my child get to pick where he goes to college? If he really wants to go to a certain place, isn't it our duty as loving parents to just take out the necessary loans and send him there?"

My answer to this question is emphatic.

There are hundreds of colleges where your child can have a great college experience. It's not necessary for your daughter to attend a "dream school" if the debt incurred from doing so could lead to a nightmare life.

Here's my reply to one student who wrote me, wailing that she just had to attend an impractical, expensive college because it was "her dream since forever to do so."

> I understand about dreams, but when it comes to college and career, we need to get extremely practical. What you need is the shortest, fastest, least-expensive route to get to a career that *will support you financially.* When you get to your career goal and you're working and earning your own money, *then* you can get started on fulfilling your dreams. College is not the time to fulfill your dreams. College is the time to get busy, get practical, get it done, and get out.

THERE ARE HUNDREDS OF COLLEGES WHERE YOUR CHILD CAN HAVE A GREAT COLLEGE EXPERIENCE. IT'S NOT NECESSARY FOR YOUR DAUGHTER TO ATTEND A "DREAM SCHOOL" IF THE DEBT INCURRED FROM DOING SO COULD LEAD TO A NIGHTMARE LIFE.

Parent, if you are paying even one penny for this college education—if you are paying for even one set of dorm sheets, a thrift store desk lamp, or gas to drive to campus for the freshman move-in day—then your money is invested in this decision, and that means you get to have a voice in it. You don't have to be a coldhearted dictator inflexibly laying down the law to your 16-year-old, but I encourage you to have a number of kind, respectful, listening conversations that guide your child through the logic and strategy I've laid out for you. When your son is 20–22 years old, completely debt-free, and heading off to a great job that he excels at and loves, he'll thank you.

CHECKLIST

March–April of 10th Grade

1. Understand the *first* rule of choosing colleges: your local, four-year state university may not be your bargain choice.

2. Understand the *second* rule of choosing colleges: community colleges can be fantastic bargain options.

3. Understand the *third* rule of choosing colleges: an honors program at a public or private college or university can be a truly outstanding bargain choice.

4. Understand how financial aid actually works, and think about balancing FAFSA and CSS/profile schools accordingly.

5. Work by yourself to come up with a large list of maybe colleges using the strategies I provide. Then ruthlessly knock some of those maybe options off of the list based on criteria I suggest.

6. Look over the college list you've created.

7. Now that you've done your legwork, find a good time to gently and respectfully pull your child into the choosing colleges discussion.

8. Put steel in your backbone, and remember that it is absolutely, *completely* OK for you to guide your child in this way. When your son is 20–22 years old, completely debt-free, and heading off to a great job that he excels at and loves, he'll thank you.

9. Remember to read and share the free online bonus content I have provided on this subject at JeannieBurlowski.com/LAUNCH.

10. Check my book updates page at JeannieBurlowski.com/LAUNCH to see if I have made any recent updates to this chapter.

11. Always consult your financial planning professional before making any big financial decisions.

12. Make a note in your calendar to come back and read the next chapter of this book when your child is in May of 10th grade.

Be the first to hear about updates to the material in this book by reading my free weekly email newsletter every week. Anyone can subscribe to it at any time at JeannieBurlowski.com.

15 | *May of 10th Grade*

Once you've completed the tasks suggested in the previous two chapters of this book, it's time to start planning college visits to take place during the sophomore and junior years of high school.

Visiting schools online is OK in the early days of college exploration, when you as a parent/child team are just trying to quickly whittle down a long list of potential schools. Keep in mind, though, that the sunny professional photos, grassy 360-degree views, and high-definition videos you see on college websites, on CampusTours.com, and on ECampusTours.com are all designed to show colleges in their best possible light. So, take what you see there with a substantial grain of salt.

HOW TO USE THIS CHAPTER

Start by just reading through this chapter. As you read, don't worry about committing to any of it. Decision time will come at the very end of this chapter, when I give you a clear, at-a-glance checklist of every task I'm suggesting you consider right now.

Remember, you won't have to use every strategy I suggest; you'll just choose the ones you think will work for your family and either modify or discard the rest.

COLLEGE VISITS

For the colleges you and your child are genuinely interested in, nothing beats the in-person college visit. I strongly recommend that parents and students make these visits together during the sophomore and junior years of high school.

When choosing schools to visit, choose colleges in a range of sizes. Be sure to visit at least one midsized private college that doesn't require the CSS/Profile, at least one smaller private college that doesn't require the CSS/Profile, and at least one large state university. Visit other colleges as you become interested in them.

As much as possible, plan these visits for weekdays when your child is out of school but the college's classes are in session. This will allow your prospective college student to attend a live college class taught by a real college professor, and it'll also allow the student to get a sense of what the campus feels like when it's bustling with people and activity.

If you're considering a college located in a very hot or a very cold climate, purposely visit that campus when the weather there is likely to be at its worst. (If your daughter is going to have to endure 40-below-zero wind chills and walk through thigh-high snowdrifts to get to class most days, she might as well find out what that's like now.)

Carefully choose which college your child visits first.

Mom and Dad, here's a caution. Be very, very selective about which college your child visits first. Before you schedule a visit to any college or university, have a list drawn up of all the schools that you, your child, and your consultant think might be good fits—and then you, the parent, pick the college on the list that looks like the best option to you based on the criteria I stated above. Make sure your family visits *that* college first.

All you have to do to accomplish this is say something like, "Hey, why don't we go visit a bunch of schools in the Chicago area next month?"

Why am I so emphatic about this? Quite often, high school students will fall madly in love with the first college they visit.

"This is it! This is where I want to go!" might

be all you hear on the car ride home. The whole process of launching into college is stressful for your teen (whether he shows it or not), and it can feel stabilizing and freeing to him to have the decision finally made.

> **IF YOU'RE CONSIDERING A COLLEGE LOCATED IN A VERY HOT OR A VERY COLD CLIMATE, PURPOSELY VISIT THAT CAMPUS WHEN THE WEATHER THERE IS LIKELY TO BE AT ITS WORST.**

Sometimes it seems as though these students are like little geese just emerging from their shells, imprinting on the first thing they see and thinking it's their mother.

If that's going to happen, Mom and Dad, let's have it happen at the college you believe is potentially the best choice for your child academically, socially, and financially. There will be more colleges to tour later, of course, and you might all change your minds. I just want to set you up for the greatest possibility of success, starting out with this first college visit.

Note potential school-year, college visit days on a special paper calendar.

To make it easy for your family to figure out when you might have some fall, winter, and spring weekdays available for college visits, I suggest you print out a blank paper calendar and mark on it all the weekdays that your child's high school is not in session during the school year. You don't have to plan college visits for all of these days, of course, but do try to schedule some college visits on days when your high school is not in session but the prospective college is.

To keep your college visit expenses as low as possible, try to schedule multiple college visits on one trip. Organize a van-load of high school or church friends and their parents to travel to these campus visits together. And whatever you do, be sure to call the college admissions office ahead of time to schedule your visit. They will welcome you with open arms, many times even providing you with free overnight accommodations in dorm rooms with current students, free college cafeteria meals, informative campus tours, visits with potential sports coaches, access to classes in the student's area of interest, opportunity to participate in a chapel service, and free tickets to fun evening events. The admissions office can do a lot for you on these visits, so be sure to let them know in advance that you're coming.

Will your child be officially interviewed on this campus visit?

Some colleges require official interviews as part of the college application process. Will your child's official interview be held on this college visit day? If so, purposely schedule the interview to be held at the end of the campus visit day. This way, your son will have many thoughts and observations to talk about and good questions to ask.

Remember, though, that even if an official interview isn't scheduled, the admissions staff your child interacts with on these trips will be noticing and gathering impressions about his interest and enthusiasm, his warmth and personality, and his potential to be a great addition to their campus. These things can

significantly affect merit aid later on. For this reason, my advice to students is, "Dress neatly, bring comfortable walking shoes, greet adults you meet on campus and introduce them to your parents, and consider every campus interaction to be an 'interview' even if it's not officially so."

WHAT TO DO ON CAMPUS VISITS

When you visit a college, do three things. First, allow plenty of extra time to find the campus and locate a legal parking place. (On some campuses, this can be a real challenge.) Second, appoint one person in your group to take about 8–10 photos so you can remember this particular campus visit a year later. Third, print out copies of the questions I will provide and bring them along with you. I will want you to ask many questions of the admissions staff, the financial aid staff, the career center staff, and the student who provides your walking tour of campus. If your child is hoping to play a sport in college, visit the coach's office and ask questions there too. Write down anything interesting that you hear or notice on small 4" x 5" notecards. I'll explain why the 4" x 5" notecards are important at the end of this chapter.

APPOINT ONE PERSON IN YOUR GROUP TO TAKE ABOUT 8–10 PHOTOS SO YOU CAN REMEMBER THIS PARTICULAR CAMPUS VISIT A YEAR LATER.

What are some important questions to ask during campus visits?

I want to give you a detailed list of questions to ask on each of your campus visits. I've divided this list into questions that parents and students can ask in the admissions office, the financial aid office, the career center, and during the student-led campus tour. To make it easy for you to print out these questions (and to share them with friends who will also be visiting colleges this year), access the free online content below.

Print out one set for each parent and student going on the campus visit.

BONUS ONLINE CONTENT:
Download the article, "The Effective College Visit: Questions to Get Answered Before the Day Is Over" at JeannieBurlowski.com/LAUNCH.

Before you leave, drive around the campus one last time.

Be sure to include driving around the outskirts of the campus, noting what the neighborhoods are like in all four directions. Is this a place your daughter could see herself living for four years?

For practical reasons, create an informal scrapbook about your college visits.

The day after you return home from this visit, use a cheap spiral notebook to make an informal scrapbook about what you saw and experienced on this trip.

This isn't for sentimental reasons; it's for

practical reasons. I know you're thinking that this college you've visited is so distinctive and so special that you'll never forget it, but believe me—all those ivy-covered brick buildings, college classrooms, dorms, exciting major opportunities, and enthusiastic admissions counselors are all going to blur together after a while.

Paste or tape into the scrapbook printouts of the photos you took and the 4" x 5" notecards where you took notes when asking questions on campus. Add some handwritten notes about what you saw, what you experienced, what you felt, and what you thought were the assets and liabilities of each school. Jot down some details about the clothing you saw the college students wearing, so that when your son goes to college, he can plan to dress well while maintaining a modest clothing budget.

Start a new page and add additional printed photos and 4" x 5" notecards to this notebook every time you visit a new college. When you decide against a certain school, tear that school's pages out and place them in the back of the notebook.

Share your scrapbook pages with others in your group.

If you're a part of a school-based club or church group where parents meet together to strategize about debt-free college, consider asking every parent in your group to make color copies of these informal scrapbook pages with their names and phone numbers written at the top. Put everyone's copies together into one large, three-ring binder, and pass the binder around from family to family. This will be a great way for you to get up-to-date information on colleges you haven't had a chance to visit—straight from people you know and trust.

There may be cooler, more sophisticated, and more expensive ways to keep track of this information, but this notebook method is the quickest and cheapest way I know of to keep all of your campus visit information in one place and easily accessible for the decision day that is coming.

CHECKLIST

May of 10th Grade

☐ 1. Plan college visits for during the sophomore and junior year of high school. When possible, schedule them on weekdays when your son doesn't have school, but college classes are still in session.

☐ 2. If you're considering a college in a very hot or a very cold climate, purposely visit when the weather is likely to be at its worst.

☐ 3. Carefully choose which college your child visits first.

☐ 4. Print out the questions I've provided in this chapter and bring them along with you. (Print out one set for each parent and student going on the campus visit.)

☐ 5. On each campus visit, appoint one person in your group to take about 8–10 photos. Record anything interesting you hear or notice on the visit on small 4" x 5" notecards.

☐ 6. When you get home, keep your memory of this visit sharp by pasting or taping printouts of your photos and your 4" x 5" notecards into an informal scrapbook made out of a cheap spiral notebook.

☐ 7. When you decide against a certain school, tear that school's pages out and place them in the back of your notebook.

☐ 8. If you're a part of a school-based club or church group where parents strategize together about debt-free college, put copies of every family's informal scrapbook pages together into one large, three-ring binder that you can pass around from family to family.

☐ 9. Print out the free online bonus content I've provided entitled "The Effective College Visit: Questions to Get Answered Before the Day Is Over" at JeannieBurlowski.com/LAUNCH. Share the link with other families you know.

☐ 10. Check my book updates page at JeannieBurlowski.com/LAUNCH to see if I have made any recent updates to this chapter.

☐ 11. Always consult your financial planning professional before making any big financial decisions.

☐ 12. Make a note in your calendar to come back and read the next chapter of this book this coming June, after your child finishes 10th grade.

Be the first to hear about updates to the material in this book by reading my free weekly email newsletter every week. Anyone can subscribe to it at any time at JeannieBurlowski.com.

16 | *Summer After 10th Grade*

This summer your teen will take a giant leap forward when it comes to career development. By the time 11th grade starts this fall, your teen will even be ahead of many college grads in preparing for career life after college.

Remember the excitement you felt this last winter as you completed the steps I laid out for you back in chapter 13? Those steps helped you to see and appreciate your child at a depth you'd never been able to before. You learned what a truly gifted individual your child is as you paged through assessment results, learned about your teen's top five strengths based on Gallup research, saw his or her greatest interests laid out visually on a chart, and saw the exciting career opportunities that beautifully fit his or her personality type in the book, *Do What You Are.*

When you went through this process, your child picked out some interesting careers to explore. This summer will be the time to start that exploration in a practical way: through *job shadowing.*

HOW TO USE THIS CHAPTER

Start by just reading through this chapter. As you read, don't worry about committing to any of it. Decision time will come at the very end of this chapter, when I give you a clear, at-a-glance checklist of every task I'm suggesting you consider right now.

> **BY THE TIME 11TH GRADE STARTS THIS FALL, YOUR TEEN WILL EVEN BE AHEAD OF MANY COLLEGE GRADS IN PREPARING FOR CAREER LIFE AFTER COLLEGE.**

Remember, you won't have to use every strategy I suggest; just choose the ones you think will work for your family and either modify or discard the rest.

[1] *Sit down as a parent/student team and look once again at the contract everyone signed in the summer after 8th grade.*

High school graduation is now less than 24 months away. This is a good time to refresh your child's mind on your expectations for high school graduates living with you (or off of you) after the age of 18.

Express excitement at how far your child has come in the past two years when it comes to fulfilling the terms of this contract.

[2] *Clarify who will be paying for summertime purchases and activities.*

Remind your daughter that you'll be expecting her to cover all of her own expenses throughout the summer months using the little bit of money you provide, just as you have since September of her 9th-grade year.

If you haven't yet set this system up, see chapter 11 for a reminder of how to make your child responsible for paying all of her own expenses with the money you provide. This is critical for helping her to become a frugal money manager in college and in adult life.

[3] *Help your son get going on earning money this summer.*

Check to be sure that your son is recording all of his earnings in Evernote, including photos of each check or stack of cash he receives. It's critical that he keep track of every dollar he earns for two reasons: (1) so he knows when he hits the cutoff where he might unwittingly reduce his financial aid eligibility and (2) so he can prove he has earned income to put into his Roth IRA.

[4] *Help your teen organize a small summer project that benefits the humanitarian cause he's adopted as his own.*

This does not need to take a lot of time. Be sure he records everything he does on LinkedIn.

[5] *Use the instructions in chapter 9 to have your son practice for and take as many CLEP and DSST exams as possible this summer.*

Every one he takes and passes could save him up to $5,000 in future college costs, so if he balks at doing this, you might offer to pay him to do it.

[6] *Encourage your daughter to use cut and paste to apply for 10 private scholarships this summer and every other summer all the way through college and graduate school.*

Pay your daughter $50 for each scholarship application she fills out in a quality manner if that's what's necessary to motivate her.

[7] *Log your son into his account on LinkedIn and help him update his profile there.*

Add to his LinkedIn profile any awards he won at the end of 10th grade, as well as any work experiences, job-shadowing experiences, and volunteer and service hours he's had so far. Help your son link to more of his parents' friends, his friends' parents, and other adults he knows on LinkedIn.

[8] *Parent, think seriously about whether you might be ready for a job change by the end of August this year.*

I recommended two years ago that you consider doing this during the summer after your child's 8th-grade year. If you weren't able to do it then, it may not be too late.

Many colleges provide free or reduced-price college tuition for the children of their employees—even if those employees have only been working at the college for just two years prior to their children enrolling.

> **HELP YOUR SON LINK TO MORE OF HIS PARENTS' FRIENDS, HIS FRIENDS' PARENTS, AND OTHER ADULTS HE KNOWS ON LINKEDIN.**

If you're an accountant, a food service professional, a salesperson, a marketing expert, a groundskeeper, a custodian, a receptionist, a career counselor, a professional events coordinator, or an administrative professional, you might consider leaving your present company and getting a job on a college campus near your home for the next six years. If you do, you could end up getting free college tuition for your children as one of your employee benefits, saving your son or daughter over $80,000 in eventual college debt. A generous employee benefit such as this is likely to be completely free, with no strings attached, and tax-free.

Think hard about whether this might be a possibility for you.

[9] *Help your son find job-shadowing opportunities in one or more of the career fields that looked exciting to him as he completed my career assessment suggestions back in chapter 13.*

Job shadowing is very simple. Your son finds a person who does the job he might like to do someday, and he asks if he can follow that person around at work and see what they do all day.

To maximize this experience and really get the most out of it, I recommend that your son do four things:

» At the end of each day he shadows, he should write up some notes reminding himself of what he saw and what he experienced that day. These details will be important for later, when he's looking for stories to use in scholarship essays and college and grad school applications.

» During downtime on job-shadowing days, your teen should ask, "What kind of education is necessary for this career? If I'll need a four-year college degree, what major would you suggest?" By asking these questions of several different professional people, many students are able to walk onto their college campuses their first day knowing what major they intend to declare.

» Get the names of the people he meets while shadowing so he can connect to them on LinkedIn.

» The entire time he's shadowing, have your son keep his eyes wide open for anything he might be able to do to be helpful in that workplace environment. He might walk through a pediatrician's waiting room and notice that the toys need to be cleaned. He could be shadowing in a special-ed summer program and notice that the teacher could use help coming up with a clever design for a blank bulletin board. He might see an administrative person overwhelmed with details related to planning an event. When he notices, he can ask if he could be allowed to come back once (or better yet, on a regular basis) and volunteer to do work in that environment for free.

This is sheer brilliance.

Someday this career-focused volunteer work may end up being your son's most impressive work experience, the one outstanding thing that sets him apart from all other applicants for a job in his field.

Job shadowing can be done for a day, for a week, for a few hours a week, or for months on end. It can occur right in your hometown, or it can occur far away in another state where your son *just happens* to have a relative he can stay with for free while he shadows.

> **SOMEDAY THIS CAREER-FOCUSED VOLUNTEER WORK MAY END UP BEING YOUR SON'S MOST IMPRESSIVE WORK EXPERIENCE, THE ONE OUTSTANDING THING THAT SETS HIM APART FROM ALL OTHER APPLICANTS FOR A JOB IN HIS FIELD.**

Your high school son will need help finding people to shadow. Start by thinking of friends, family members, and acquaintances who do the job he'd love to do someday. Put out a request to all of Mom and Dad's Facebook friends. Parent, look among your own connections on LinkedIn. If you can't find anyone this way, then use Google to find people who do this job in your local community. Have your son or daughter call the person and say:

> I'm Garrett Erickson and I'm a high school student hoping to become a _____ after college. I'm wondering if I might be able to come in and shadow you on the job for a day. I'm available on a number of different weekdays this summer. Do you have any days when I could come in?

In certain sensitive professions, such as medicine, special education, or counseling, some professionals might tell your son that it's not possible for him to shadow because of privacy laws. If he gets this objection, here's a reply he can use:

> I have heard of that before. But from what I understand, if I promise in writing to keep everything I see and hear confidential, and if you—before the session begins—ask the (patient/parent/client)'s verbal permission to have a student present, that keeps us in compliance with privacy laws. Do you think we might be able to try that?

If the professional says no at this point, have your son just thank the person graciously and move on. Don't be discouraged, though.

There are people who will allow students to shadow in every profession, even neurosurgery. Just keep asking.

When your son finishes his shadowing day or shadowing week, encourage him to ask if there's anything he could do to come back to that same workplace as a volunteer. Here are my words to your child on this subject:

Tell them that you'll do anything, right down to scrubbing blood off of the emergency room floor, reading to first graders, helping with an office move, or cleaning up conference rooms after lunch meetings. Constantly express interest in learning more and doing additional tasks. Do all the shadowing and volunteering you can in this environment, bit by bit over long stretches of time. Connect with the professionals you get to know in this environment on LinkedIn, and remember to keep track of every minute of this valuable activity on your own LinkedIn profile.

Later, when you write about your career goal in scholarship essays and college applications, talk about this targeted, specific shadowing and volunteering. Include details about what you did, what you saw (with names of patients and clients omitted, of course), the length of time you were there, and what insights you gained from the experience.

This will turn out to be fantastically impressive to everyone who matters.

Parent, every time your son does job shadowing or volunteering, supervise him as he records the date, the place, and the number of hours on his LinkedIn profile. (He will not remember to do this himself until he is 24 years old.)

And if his shadowing experience shows him that he doesn't really like this profession much after all? That is completely OK. Better to find out now, rather than seven years from now when he has spent $80,000 and four years of his life in classrooms getting ready to do this job.

> **AND IF YOUR SON'S SHADOWING EXPERIENCE SHOWS THAT HE DOESN'T LIKE THIS PROFESSION AFTER ALL? THAT'S COMPLETELY OK. BETTER TO FIND OUT NOW, RATHER THAN SEVEN YEARS FROM NOW WHEN HE HAS SPENT $80,000 AND FOUR YEARS OF HIS LIFE IN CLASSROOMS GETTING READY TO DO THIS JOB.**

If your son does find out after job shadowing that he doesn't like the profession after all, cheerfully reassure him that it's no problem. Get out the folder where you carefully put away the results of the three assessments I prescribed in chapter 13. Get the *Do What You Are* book down off of the shelf again. Perhaps call your son's educational consultant and set up a time for another session. Decide on a different good-fit career to explore. That's what life is all about, isn't it? The difference for your son is that he's doing this career exploration at age 16, not at age 46 after making a long series of expensive, regrettable mistakes.

LAUNCH

[10] *Ask your daughter about her plan for organizing her 11th-grade academics.*

This is especially important if she'll be taking dual enrollment college classes in place of regular high school classes this fall.

Check in with her about what organizational system she'll be using for getting academic work done in a quality manner and turned in on time. A reminder of the six questions to ask her can be found in chapter 3.

If your daughter will be taking college-level courses this coming fall, I strongly suggest that she prepare herself by learning college study skills from a professional this summer. The 2.5-hour college study skills class I teach is called *The Strategic College Student: How to Get Higher Grades Than Anyone Else by Studying Less Than Most Other People*, and you can find out how to access it live or in recorded form by reading my free weekly email newsletter.

[11] *If your financial situation is complex, consider making an appointment with a certified public accountant or certified financial planner who specializes in financial planning for college.*

You're going to be making some very important family financial decisions between now and September 30 of your child's senior year of high school. Consider making an appointment now with a trained financial professional who is known to help families with college financing decisions. Show the person the checklists in this book and tell him or her which strategies you've used so far.

Your own personal financial planner may

have the specific, targeted expertise to be able to do this, or you can seek specialized help from one of the thousands of certified public accountants and certified financial planners who are members of the National College Advocacy Group (NCAG) at Ncagonline.org. If your income is very high or your financial situation very complicated, get help from highly respected Forbes contributor Troy Onink by signing up for one of the very valuable one-hour consultations he offers at Stratagee.com. Whichever option you choose, take steps now to find the person who will guide you through tax and financial planning both before and during college.

> **IF YOUR INCOME IS VERY HIGH OR YOUR FINANCIAL SITUATION VERY COMPLICATED, GET HELP FROM HIGHLY RESPECTED FORBES CONTRIBUTOR TROY ONINK BY SIGNING UP FOR ONE OF THE VERY VALUABLE ONE-HOUR CONSULTATIONS HE OFFERS AT STRATAGEE.COM.**

[12] *If divorce is a part of your family story, you might consider making a change to your daughter's living situation by September 30 of her junior year of high school.*

You already understand that on October 1 of your daughter's *senior* year of high school, her eligibility for need-based financial aid is going to be determined by a close examination of the income and assets of her parents. When divorce and remarriage make family life complicated, though, who exactly qualifies as your daughter's "parent" on financial aid applications? If you understand the rules now, you may be able to help your daughter get thousands extra in free money financial aid for college.

Who is the parent?

When a student's parents are divorced, FAFSA financial aid calculations are made using only the income and assets of the parent the student *lived with the most* during the 12 months before the date of the FAFSA form submission.

This can be a stunning revelation for families.

The person who counts as the parent for FAFSA financial aid calculations does not necessarily have to be the custodial parent as named in the divorce decree. The rules are stated this way at the FinAid website:

> The custodial parent for federal student aid purposes is the parent with whom you (the student) lived the most during the past 12 months. (The twelve month period is the twelve month period ending on the FAFSA application date, not the previous calendar year.) Note that this is not necessarily the same as the parent who has legal custody. If you did not live with one parent more than the other, the parent who provided you with the most financial support during the past twelve months should fill out the FAFSA. This is probably the parent who claimed you as a dependent on their tax return. If

you have not received any support from either parent during the past 12 months, use the most recent calendar year for which you received some support from a parent. These rules are based on section 475(f)(1) of the Higher Education Act of 1965 (20 USC 108700(f)(1)).[27]

Realizing this, some divorced parents will discover just in time that the parent the child does not typically live with has a far lower total household income than the parent the child usually lives with. (Household income includes this lower-income parent's new spouse, though, so be sure to figure that in.)

If it's feasible (and safe and healthy for the child), the divorced parents and the child might agree to have the child live with the lower-income parent for a minimum of 183 days during the 12-month period of time before submitting the FAFSA form. (If you're cutting it this close to the line, keep track of where the student is sleeping each night on a special paper calendar.)

Families who do this are able to have the lower-income parent serve as the official parent for FAFSA financial aid calculation purposes. Doing so means that the higher-income parent's household wealth (including the income of his or her new spouse) won't figure into those calculations at all. The higher-income parent's household assets will still count for the CSS/Profile financial aid application, of course—but that's OK. There are thousands of excellent, high-quality public and private colleges that don't even look at the CSS/Profile financial aid form.

---

27 "Divorce and Financial Aid," FinAid, accessed October 14, 2016, http://www.finaid.org/questions/divorce.phtml.

You might be thinking, "But is it really fair for this lower-income parent to have to take on the responsibility of paying for all the food and personal expenses of this child, leaving the wealthier parent to get off scot-free?" Good question.

Some divorced parents who've set up this kind of arrangement will create a written agreement where the wealthier parent agrees to be especially and specifically generous toward this lower-income household while these living arrangements are in place (likely through October 1 of the student's junior year of college). Cash payments will have to be reported on future FAFSA forms—so be careful about those—but the FAFSA form doesn't track physical gifts, even when they're necessities such as bedroom furniture, hockey equipment, clothing, shoes, school supplies, or bags of groceries left on the doorstep.

One divorced couple who did this chose to have the lower-income mother order her groceries online from her local grocery delivery service, and then the higher-income father simply used his debit card to pay the bill she owed to the grocery delivery company. This allowed the divorced father to "leave groceries on the doorstep" every week, even though he lived hundreds of miles away.

With these thoughts in mind and a written agreement created, the wealthier parent can agree to be generous without handing cash over to anyone. This can make the new living arrangement more equitable.

Note that biological parents who never married are treated the same as parents who are divorced, so these strategies apply to never-married parents as well.

IF YOU ARE A DIVORCED OR NEVER-MARRIED PARENT, BE SURE TO CAREFULLY READ THE ONE-PAGE DOCUMENT ON THIS SUBJECT LOCATED ON THE FINAID.ORG WEBSITE.

The financial aid rules concerning divorced or never-married parents can get complicated in some cases. If you are a divorced or never-married parent, be sure to carefully read the one-page document on this subject located on the Finaid.org website. You can get directly to the page you need by typing this shortcut into your web browser: Mnstr.me/2fGElMk.

CHECKLIST

Summer After 10th Grade

1. Sit down as a parent/student team and look once again at the contract everyone signed after 8th grade.

2. Reinforce once again that you'll be expecting your daughter to cover all of her own expenses this summer using the little bit of money you provide her every two weeks.

3. Help your son get going on earning summer income. Be sure he's keeping track of everything he earns in Evernote.

4. Help your teen organize a small summer project that benefits the humanitarian cause he's adopted as his own.

5. Use the instructions in chapter 9 to have your daughter practice for and take as many CLEP and DSST exams as possible this summer. Are there any additional ones she's now closer to passing because she studied that subject during her 10th-grade year?

6. Encourage your son to use cut and paste to apply for 10 private scholarships this summer.

7. Log your daughter into her account on LinkedIn and help her update her profile there.

8. Parent, think seriously about whether you might be ready for a job change by the end of August this year.

9. Help your son find summer job-shadowing opportunities using the instructions I've provided.

10. If your son job shadows in his potential career field and finds that he doesn't like the job after all, that's OK. Use the tools in chapter 13 to help him select a different career to explore.

11. Ask your daughter about her plan for organizing her 11th-grade academics. If she'll be taking college classes this coming fall, help her find a way to learn quality college study skills this summer before fall classes start.

12. Consider making an appointment with a certified public accountant or certified financial planner who specializes in financial planning for college.

13. If divorce is a part of your family story, carefully consider what your child's living arrangements will be starting September 30 of her junior year of high school.

14. Check my book updates page at JeannieBurlowski.com/LAUNCH to see if I have made any recent updates to this chapter.

☐ 15. Always consult your financial planning professional before making any big financial decisions.

☐ 16. Make a note in your calendar to come back and read the next chapter of this book when your child is in September of 11th grade.

Be the first to hear about updates to the material in this book by reading my free weekly email newsletter every week. Anyone can subscribe to it at any time at JeannieBurlowski.com.

17 | *September–January of 11th Grade*

There's a lot to accomplish in this chapter, but most of it is going to be fairly easy for you. If you've been following the instructions in this book since your child finished 8th grade, you're going to find yourself repeatedly nodding and saying, "Yep, I understand that. No problem, we're already doing that. Got it; we're acing that." This will be a great feeling.

Since this is an easier chapter, perhaps you could take some time in the next few weeks to go back through the checklists at the ends of chapters 3–16. Were there some instructions in those chapters you weren't able to carry out at the time? Maybe you could add a few of those to your to-do list for between now and January. Remember, nobody does *everything* suggested in this book. Just pick the strategies that make sense for your family and either modify or discard the rest.

HOW TO USE THIS CHAPTER

Start by just reading through this chapter. As you read, don't worry about committing to any of it. Decision time will come at the very end of this chapter, when I give you a clear, at-a-glance checklist of every task I'm suggesting you consider right now.

[1] *Have your son continue with that one special extracurricular activity he's going to stick with through all four years of high school.*

This year, have him think about how he can expand or enrich that activity for others.

How can he move into more leadership within it? Is there a way he and the other students in it with him could somehow find a way to serve the community? Encourage your son to propose that. Arrange it. Execute it. Enter the details on his LinkedIn profile.

Remember, someday this committed, long-term extracurricular activity might be what gets your child a lucrative merit-based scholarship or a preferential financial aid package at a college you could never otherwise afford.

REMEMBER, SOMEDAY THIS COMMITTED, LONG-TERM EXTRACURRICULAR ACTIVITY MIGHT BE WHAT GETS YOUR CHILD A LUCRATIVE MERIT-BASED SCHOLARSHIP OR A PREFERENTIAL FINANCIAL AID PACKAGE AT A COLLEGE YOU COULD NEVER OTHERWISE AFFORD.

[2] *Help your daughter think through how she will earn money during this school year.*

Check with her to be sure she's keeping track of everything she earns in Evernote and everything she does on LinkedIn. Remember that she can probably earn somewhere between $6,000 and $7,000 during this calendar year without impacting her future financial aid eligibility.

[3] *Continue having your daughter manage all of her own expenses using the little bit of money you provide for her.*

If you haven't started this yet, now is an excellent time to do so. The instructions for how to do this are located in chapter 11.

[4] *Continue planning college visits. Keep expenses low by taking your child's friends and their parents along to share expenses, and by visiting multiple college campuses on each trip.*

Try to schedule as many college visits as possible during this school year, during times when the college your son is looking at *does* have regular classes going on, but his high school *does not*.

Be sure to download and print my bonus online article "The Effective College Visit: Questions to Get Answered Before the Day Is Over" at JeannieBurlowski.com/LAUNCH before you go.

See chapter 15 for information on how to maximize college visits.

[5] *Brainstorm with your child about what she will do this year to help the humanitarian cause she's adopted as her own.*

This school year will be her last chance to complete a humanitarian project that will make a dramatic splash in her college applications. So if she can, this is the year to do it up big.

Make a plan and schedule it. If she needs an inspiring idea for a project to do, google "Eagle Scout Service Projects" and modify one of those to fit her humanitarian cause. Remember, if she pulls friends or school organizations in to help her, she gets points for leadership, as well as for service. Be sure to keep track of everything she does in her profile on LinkedIn.

[6] *Have your daughter do increasing amounts of job shadowing where she observes people working in her future career field.*

As she does this, have her constantly look for ways to turn those shadowing experiences into ongoing volunteer opportunities. Volunteering to help (with even the most menial tasks) will give her an opportunity to work with and learn from people doing the exact job she'll be doing someday.

For a reminder of how to set up job shadowing that leads to volunteering, see chapter 16. For a review of how students can get a strong sense of career direction and purpose as young as 10th grade, see chapter 13.

[7] *Register your daughter to take the SAT and/or the ACT for the first time. Work with her to register for a test date that occurs in the winter of her junior year of high school.*

What's the difference between the SAT and the ACT? They're two different products made by two different companies. Think: McDonald's and Burger King. Years ago the ACT was more popular in the Midwest, probably because it was created in Iowa. Now, though, both tests are widely (though not universally) accepted.

It wouldn't hurt for your daughter to take both, see which she does better on, and use that score for college admissions. If your daughter takes one of these standardized tests once and thinks she needs a higher score, she can do some extra preparation and take one or both tests again in the spring of her junior year and again in the fall of her senior year of high school. Colleges will see all the scores from all the times she's taken these tests, but they will make their decisions about her, using only the highest score she's received on each test.

» SAT registration information can be found here: Sat.collegeboard.org/register

» ACT registration can be found here: Actstudent.org

If your child struggles with standardized test performance, don't worry too much. As you've learned in this book, there's actually far more to college admission and attracting free money scholarships and merit aid than just grades and test scores. Plus, if you go to Fairtest.org, you'll find a list of over 800 colleges and universities that greatly de-emphasize or completely ignore SAT and ACT standardized test scores. More four-year colleges join the list every year.

[8] *When it's time for your teen to register for 12th-grade high school classes, suggest he register for as many dual enrollment college courses as possible.*

Even if your son didn't take dual enrollment courses in 11th grade, he may still be able to do it in 12th grade.

Before registration, check with a high school guidance counselor to make sure your son is fulfilling all the requirements for his high school graduation, and be sure he's had a professional college study skills class before he begins any dual enrollment courses.

For a review of what dual enrollment classes are and why they're so extraordinarily valuable for getting students through college debt-free, reread chapter 9, "February–April of 9th Grade."

> **FOR A REVIEW OF WHAT DUAL ENROLLMENT CLASSES ARE AND WHY THEY'RE SO EXTRAORDINARILY VALUABLE FOR GETTING STUDENTS THROUGH COLLEGE DEBT-FREE, REREAD CHAPTER 9, "FEBRUARY–APRIL OF 9TH GRADE."**

[9] *Register your teen for summer camp if he or she is willing to go.*

Experience at summer camp helps students suffer less from homesickness in the first year of college. Some camps even welcome high school students to volunteer at camp for weeks or months at a time during the summer, developing leadership ability in invaluable ways.

I'm a huge fan of the camps for all ages offered at Trout Lake Camps in Pine River, Minnesota. You can find out information about Trout Lake Camps at TroutLakeCamps.org.

Remember, senior high camps fill quickly, so register early.

[10] *Consider having your daughter register for a discounted community college course that she can take during the summer after 11th grade.*

Every community college course she gets credit for at her eventual four-year college is likely to result in thousands of dollars in savings for her.

[11] *Have your son start thinking about what kind of job he'd like to work at to earn money during the summer after 11th grade.*

Your son will not jeopardize his future financial aid eligibility if he keeps his earnings within these boundaries: earning up to somewhere between $6,000 and $7,000 each calendar year during the time frame stretching from January 1 of his sophomore year of high school to January 1 of his sophomore year of college.

CHECKLIST

September–January of 11th Grade

1. Consider going back through the checklists at the ends of chapters 3–16. Were there some instructions in those chapters you weren't able to carry out at the time? Add a few of those to your to-do list for between now and January.

2. Have your son continue with that one special extracurricular activity he's going to stick with through all four years of high school.

3. Help your daughter think through how she will earn money during this school year.

4. Continue having your daughter manage all of her own expenses using the little bit of money you provide for her.

5. Continue planning college visits. Be sure to download and print my free bonus online article "The Effective College Visit: Questions to Get Answered Before the Day Is Over" at JeannieBurlowski.com/LAUNCH before you go.

6. Brainstorm with your daughter about what she will do this year to help the humanitarian cause she's adopted as her own. This school year will be her last chance to complete a humanitarian project that will make a dramatic splash in her college applications.

7. Have your son do increasing amounts of job shadowing where he observes and volunteers to assist people who are working in his prospective career field.

8. Register your daughter to take the SAT and/or the ACT for the first time in the winter of her junior year of high school.

9. When it's time to register for 12th-grade high school classes, register your son for as many dual enrollment college courses as possible. Have him take a professional college study skills class beforehand.

10. Register your child for an upcoming summer camp if she's willing to go. Spots fill up quickly, so don't delay.

11. Consider having your son register to take a discounted community college course during the summer after 11th grade.

12. Have your son start thinking ahead to what kind of job he'd like to work at to earn money during the summer after 11th grade.

13. Check my book updates page at JeannieBurlowski.com/LAUNCH to see if I have made any recent updates to this chapter.

☐ 14. Always consult your financial planning professional before making any big financial decisions.

☐ 15. Make a note in your calendar to come back and read the next chapter of this book when your child is in April of 11th grade.

Be the first to hear about updates to the material in this book by reading my free weekly email newsletter every week. Anyone can subscribe to it at any time at JeannieBurlowski.com.

18 | *April—May of 11th Grade*

During this two-month period, your son or daughter is going to pull far ahead of others when it comes to high-quality college applications.

By the time school's out this coming May or June, your teen will have all of his or her letters of recommendation completed, and a stunning, high-quality college application essay in the bag and ready to go. This is going to put your teen on the fast track to getting all of his or her college applications completed *before* school starts this coming fall.

How does jumping ahead on these tasks help?

Well, even though I'm not in favor of "binding early decision" college application programs (which can wreak havoc with future financial aid opportunities), there is some advantage to getting college applications in early.

First, no one will admit this, but college admissions committees are at their fresh-

est when they first begin reviewing college applications in the late summer and early fall each year. Second, early applying students can make strong impressions simply on the basis of being sharp, on-the-ball, early-bird go-getters. Third, students who apply early are vying for the greatest number of available seats and the largest pool of free money merit aid. These students are less likely to get caught in situations where the admissions committee says, "Well, this is a great kid, but we already have so many students in our 'accept' pile. Let's come back to him later if we have some leftover space." Finally, your son will experience far less personal stress if he steps into his busy senior year of high school with his college applications all done and turned in.

> **STUDENTS WHO APPLY EARLY ARE VYING FOR THE GREATEST NUMBER OF AVAILABLE SEATS AND THE LARGEST POOL OF FREE MONEY MERIT AID.**

Let's get going on some steps that will put your child far ahead of the regular college application crowd.

HOW TO USE THIS CHAPTER

Start by just reading through this chapter. As you read, don't worry about committing to any of it. Decision time will come at the very end of this chapter, when I give you a clear, at-a-glance checklist of every task I'm suggesting you consider right now.

Remember, you won't have to use every strategy I suggest; just choose the ones you think will work for your family and either modify or discard the rest.

DID YOUR SON WRITE A *SCHOLARSHIP* **APPLICATION ESSAY WITH MY HELP MONTHS AGO? THAT ESSAY CAN BE UPDATED JUST A BIT AND MADE INTO A FANTASTIC COLLEGE APPLICATION ESSAY IN RELATIVELY LITTLE TIME.**

[1] *Have your son write one good, strong, college application essay two months before the end of 11th grade.*

I know it seems early to be thinking about this, but as you'll see in this chapter, April of 11th grade is the most strategic time for students to create strong college application essays.

Did your son write a *scholarship* application essay with my help months ago? That

essay can be updated just a bit and made into a fantastic college application essay in relatively little time.

If you'd like specialized instruction from me on how to create powerful college and scholarship application essays, watch my free weekly email newsletter for information on how to access my *Make Them Say Wow* class in either live or recorded form.

[2] *Have your son take his completed college application essay to a high school teacher or other mentor for editing and revision suggestions.*

If possible, have him do this six weeks or more before the end of the school year. Do not, under any circumstances, wait until the tail end of the school year to ask teachers for editing and revision help. If you're close to the end of the school year as you read this, ask friends or relatives to help instead.

[3] *Have your daughter write down the names of three or four adults she could ask to write letters of recommendation for the college and scholarship applications she'll be submitting this summer.*

For college applications, it's recommended that students ask two teachers who taught them tough classes in 10th or 11th grade. Your daughter can also ask employers, volunteer work supervisors, extracurricular activity advisors, youth pastors, people she's job shadowed, or others who've seen her at her best over the past three years.

[4] *Have your son call his high school guidance counselor's office and ask about the school's preferred method for sending high school transcripts and letters of recommendation out to colleges.*

The answer might be, "You give us a list of the colleges you're applying to, teachers give their letters to us, then we pack up your letter(s) along with your high school transcripts and send them all off together."

Or the answer might be, "You fill out this form asking us to send your transcripts, and your recommenders send their letters through the mail directly to colleges you're applying to. You supply all the necessary stamped, addressed envelopes, OK?"

Or the answer might be, "We want you to follow the recommender instructions you'll find at CommonApp.org. Read those instructions and proceed accordingly." If you get this answer, ask what you should do about colleges that don't accept the Common App. (Only 700 colleges in the U.S. do.)

Carefully write down the guidance office's answer to this question. You'll need the information later, when requesting letters of recommendation.

WAIVING RIGHTS TO INSPECT RECORDS

As part of the recommendation process, your son will be asked to sign a document waiving his legal right to inspect his letters of recommendation before they're sent off to colleges. I encourage him to sign this document. With everything he's done to be a top student in high school, his recommendations are likely

to be very positive. And if they are? A positive letter he hasn't seen weighs more than a positive letter he might have selected out of 10 he asked to have written and then inspected before sending.

If you are a homeschooling parent wondering how you are supposed to come up with high school transcripts, you can get excellent help from the Home School Legal Defense Association at Hslda.org. To get directly to the page you need, type this shortcut into your web browser: Bit.ly/2g6Ol2o.

[5] *Have your daughter type up a "dream sheet" of details she would love to have mentioned in each of her letters of recommendation.*

The more specific these details are, the better. Your daughter might write down that she'd like recommenders to talk about specific good grades in difficult subjects, all the college-level work she's done in high school, details about her job-shadowing and volunteer work, her long hours of work to earn money to pay for her own college education, her commitment and work on behalf of one great humanitarian cause all the way through high school, her leadership in high school extracurricular activities, and additional things that your daughter has been carefully noting all this time on her LinkedIn profile.

Remember, it's completely acceptable for recommenders to write about things they haven't actually seen firsthand, as long as all the details are true. I cannot emphasize strongly enough how truly worthwhile it is to put time and effort into creating this dream sheet. The detailed, enthusiastic letters of recommendation that your child's teachers and others will be able to write as a result of having this information may one day lead to your daughter being offered a stunning, generous amount of merit aid to help pay for her college education.

> **REMEMBER, IT'S COMPLETELY ACCEPTABLE FOR RECOMMENDERS TO WRITE ABOUT THINGS THEY HAVEN'T ACTUALLY SEEN FIRSTHAND, AS LONG AS ALL THE DETAILS ARE TRUE.**

[6] A full month or more before the end of the school year, have your daughter make in-person visits to potential recommenders.

This is the visit where she asks, "Would you be willing to write me a great letter of recommendation to go with my college applications?"

When your daughter asks for these letters of recommendation, she can hand her prospective recommender (a) her polished college application essay, (b) her dream sheet, (c) a written request that the letter be completed by June 15, (d) any forms the recommender is being asked to fill out, (e) a sheet of instructions on what to do with the letter when it's finished (this will vary depending on the policies of your high school's guidance office), (f) any stamped addressed envelopes necessary for mailing letters to colleges, and (g) a

stamped postcard addressed to the student, so that recommenders can let your daughter know the date her letter was completed and sent off.

Most recommenders will write a letter for your daughter, photocopy it, and send the same letter to every college she's applying to. This is completely OK. If a college appears to be asking a recommender to simply fill out a form, I suggest that the recommender fill out the form and then attach the written letter to it. A written letter will make a stronger argument in your daughter's behalf than a form ever could.

"Our son can't visit one of his recommenders in person."

If it's not possible to visit one or more of these recommenders in person, a phone call is your child's next best option. Your daughter can set up a phone call in advance by emailing the recommender, providing a reminder of who she is, and saying, "I'd like to talk to you on the phone for five minutes if I could. Here are three dates and times I'm available. What works for you?" An email request for a quick phone call can be effective, but because email can be easily ignored, email requests for letters of recommendation tend not to work very well.

It's very important for students to take care of these recommendation requests well before the end of the school year, when high school teachers and other school staff disappear for the summer.

[7] *Have your daughter visit her high school guidance counselor's office and ask (a) "Can you check to be sure that I'm completely set to graduate from high school on time?" and (b) "Can you give me a list of every scholarship you know of that I qualify for based on my age?"*

If your child needs an adjustment to her senior year fall class schedule in order to graduate from high school on time, now is the time to find that out.

When it comes to scholarships, create a plan for applying for every one of the suggested scholarships well in advance of deadlines. The wonderful college application essay your daughter has put together can be tweaked and modified to answer almost every one of the necessary scholarship application essay questions.

[8] *Have your son send handwritten thank-you notes to all of his essay editors and recommenders.*

Include a $10 or $25 gift card to a store that sells practical items along with each thank-you note. Revising these essays and writing these letters are hard work, and these people are worthy of the sincerest thanks.

> **THE WONDERFUL COLLEGE APPLICATION ESSAY YOUR DAUGHTER HAS PUT TOGETHER CAN BE TWEAKED AND MODIFIED TO ANSWER ALMOST EVERY ONE OF THE NECESSARY SCHOLARSHIP APPLICATION ESSAY QUESTIONS.**

MORE POWER, MORE CONFIDENCE

Students who take these steps in April and May of their junior year of high school go into their college application summer with an empowered sense of self-confidence. They have an edge over all other college applicants. Why? They have the best essays and the strongest possible letters of recommendation, so they've already got all the hardest parts of their college applications done!

CHECKLIST

April–May of 11th Grade

1. Have your son write one good, strong, college application essay two months before the end of 11th grade.

2. Have your daughter take her completed college application essay to a high school teacher or other mentor for editing and revision suggestions.

3. Have your son write down the names of four adults he could ask to write letters of recommendation for the college and scholarship applications he'll be submitting this summer.

4. Have your son call his high school guidance office and ask about the school's preferred method for sending high school transcripts and letters of recommendation out to colleges.

5. Have your daughter type up a dream sheet of details she would love to have mentioned in her letters of recommendation.

6. A full month before the end of the school year, have your son make in-person visits to potential recommenders.

7. Have your daughter visit her high school guidance counselor's office and ask (a) "Can you check to be sure that I'm completely set to graduate from high school on time?" and (b) "Can you give me a list of every local scholarship that I qualify for based on my age?"

8. Have your son send handwritten thank-you notes with enclosed gift cards to all of his essay editors and recommenders.

9. Watch your child go into the college application summer with an empowered sense of self-confidence and with an edge over all other college applicants.

10. Check my book updates page at JeannieBurlowski.com/LAUNCH to see if I have made any recent updates to this chapter.

11. Always consult your financial planning professional before making any big financial decisions.

12. Make a note in your calendar to come back and read the next chapter of this book in June after your child has finished 11th grade.

Be the first to hear about updates to the material in this book by reading my free weekly email newsletter every week. Anyone can subscribe to it at any time at JeannieBurlowski.com.

19 | *Summer After 11th Grade*

The summer after 11th grade is the biggest summer of all when it comes to a student's college preparation. There's a lot to do. If you start to feel overwhelmed, just jump to the checklist at the end of this chapter and I'll tell you which items can wait until this fall if necessary.

HOW TO USE THIS CHAPTER

Start by just reading through this chapter. As you read, don't worry about committing to any of it. Decision time will come at the very end of this chapter, when I give you a clear, at-a-glance checklist of every task I'm suggesting you consider right now.

Remember, you won't have to use every strategy I suggest; just choose the ones you think will work for your family and either modify or discard the rest.

[1] Go out to dinner with your son and look again at the contract you signed with him in June after he finished 8th grade.

You still have this contract hanging on the inside of a cupboard door, right? Celebrate how far you've all come in making progress toward the goals listed on that contract. Marvel that his high school graduation date is now less than 12 months away.

[2] If your daughter registered last spring to take a discounted community college course without you this summer, she'll be commuting from your home to those classes starting this month. Be sure she's had a professional college study skills class before she starts.

If she hasn't yet had a professional college study skills class, the 2.5-hour class I teach is called *The Strategic College Student: How to Get Higher Grades Than Anyone Else by Studying Less Than Most Other People*, and you can find out how to access it either live or in recorded form by reading my free weekly email newsletter.

[3] *Clarify who will be paying for summertime purchases and activities.*

Remind your son that you'll be expecting him to use the little bit of money you provide to cover all of his own expenses throughout the summer months, just as you have since September of his 10th-grade year.

See chapter 11 if you haven't set this system up yet. It's an ideal way to teach students to be frugal money managers all through college.

[4] *Help your daughter think through how she'll earn money this summer.*

She's currently working on earning the maximum $6,000–$7,000 she can earn this calendar year without compromising her financial aid eligibility. You as a parent may be choosing to match any funds she puts in savings to buy herself a car, though I won't be recommending that she take a car with her to college.

[5] *Check to be sure that your son is continuing to record all of his earnings in Evernote, including photos of each check and stack of cash he receives.*

This is important *not only* for proving that your son has earned income to put into his Roth IRA in a few months, but also for keeping track of income totals that will go on next year's financial aid applications.

[6] *Search for a list of CLEP and DSST exams, and see if there are any your son is now close to passing because he studied that subject during his 11th-grade year.*

If time allows, use the instructions in chapter 9 to have him practice for and take as many CLEP and DSST exams as he can this summer. Every one that he takes and passes could save him thousands of dollars in future college costs, so if he balks at doing this, you might offer to pay him to do it.

[7] *Help your son find summer job-shadowing and resulting volunteer opportunities in the career field he's exploring.*

My strategies for successful job shadowing can be found in chapter 16.

[8] *Log your daughter into her account on LinkedIn and help her to update her profile there.*

Include in her LinkedIn profile any awards she won at the end of 11th grade, as well as any work experiences, job-shadowing experiences, and volunteer and service hours she's had since her last LinkedIn update. Help her to link to more of her parents' friends, her friends' parents, her employers, and others on LinkedIn.

Remind your daughter that her scholarship applications and college applications are going to be a piece of cake because she's got all the necessary information right at her fingertips on her LinkedIn profile.

> **HELP HER TO LINK TO MORE OF HER PARENTS' FRIENDS, HER FRIENDS' PARENTS, AND OTHERS ON LINKEDIN.**

[9] *Encourage your daughter to use cut and paste to apply for 10 private scholarships this summer and every other summer, all the way through college and graduate school.*

Pay your daughter $50 for every scholarship application she fills out in a quality manner if that's what's necessary to motivate her.

[10] *If your son hasn't yet done the career work I suggested in chapter 13, it's critically important that you have him do that early this summer, before he chooses the colleges he'll apply to.*

The danger is that he could end up attending a college that doesn't even *have* preparation for the career he's going to do some day. Career clarification work, done very early on, can head off expensive and heartbreaking missteps on the way to getting an actual job after college.

[11] *Before you sit down with your daughter to finalize the list of colleges she'll be applying to this summer, reread the suggestions I provided in chapter 14.*

This will help you to bring a kind, empathetic voice of logic and reason to what may be an emotional topic for your teen.

[12] *Work alongside your son to choose the colleges he'll apply to. Start by going over the informal scrapbook pages you created after each of your college visits.*

If your son's career goal (based on the career clarification strategies I recommended in chapter 13) means that he's definitely going to need a four-year college degree, suggest that he apply to at least two "stretch" schools that seem like they may be hard to get into, at least two "safe" schools that seem like they'd be fairly easy to get into, and at least two colleges that fall somewhere in the middle. Spread these schools out across these categories:

» Two to four good-fit CSS/Profile schools

» One or two good-fit, four-year state schools that look only at the FAFSA form

» One community college located near your home

» Five to six good-fit private schools that look only at the FAFSA form

If the three career assessments I prescribed in chapter 13 indicate that your daughter is a good fit for a career that requires only a two-year technical college degree, that is excellent. Have her apply only to technical schools that (a) have the degree program she's looking for and (b) are located in an area where she'd like to attend college after high school. Remember that if your daughter lives at home or with a relative while taking technical school classes, she can save a bundle on college costs.

Remember, when you need information about colleges quickly, visit CollegeData.com. Just be sure to avoid the ad for the credit card at the top of the page. Credit cards can greatly endanger your child's possibilities of getting through college debt-free.

[13] *If summer is an expensive time for you and you're worried about money, call the admissions office at every college your daughter is applying to and ask them if they'd be willing to waive their college application fees for you.*

Many will. All you'll need is a code from the college to enter on their online college application.

[14] *Use CollegeData.com to determine which college application each college requires, and then have your son fill them out this summer. (The information you've been patiently compiling on your son's LinkedIn profile will help greatly with this.)*

The required application might be

» the Common Application located at CommonApp.org,

» the Common Application located at CommonApp.org with supplemental forms required,

» the Universal College Application located at Universalcollegeapp.com, or

» some other type of specialized application.

As your son fills out college applications, he might encounter a question that asks, "Are you planning to apply for financial aid?" Always answer yes. In most cases, doing so will not diminish his chances of admission. If answering yes does diminish his chances

of admission, it's a college you didn't want your child attending anyway.

[15] *If your daughter has filled out the Common Application located at CommonApp.org, make sure she's signed the signature page at the very end of the form.*

On the Common Application, the "submit" and "final" buttons are related to payment only. The student must complete the signature page in order to actually submit the application.

If any additional supplementary forms are required by any of the colleges your daughter is applying to, make sure she completes those as well.

[16] *Encourage your son to consider applying to honors programs at each of the colleges he's applying to.*

Honors programs can include exciting opportunities, such as interdisciplinary seminars, collaborative research projects, faculty-directed independent study, special advising and mentoring, exclusive lectures, interdisciplinary fulfillment of the college's general education requirements, and special extracurricular activities, social events, and community service projects—plus, generous scholarship awards. (At Emerson College in Boston, for instance, 50 incoming honors students each year are awarded half-tuition merit scholarships that are renewable for four years.)

Applying to an honors program usually

requires a few extra steps, including writing an additional essay beyond what is required for the college's regular online application. Contact each college's office of admissions to find out what is required.

[17] *If your son or daughter has decided to apply for an ROTC scholarship, complete that application next.*

For a reminder of the benefits and responsibilities of an ROTC scholarship, see chapter 14.

[18] *Beware: resist the urge to apply to a college by way of any kind of a "binding early decision" program.*

If your daughter is tempted to apply to a college via a "binding early decision" program in hopes of having a better shot at being admitted, call the admissions office right away and ask exactly what "binding early decision" means at that college.

This is important, because applying "binding early decision" can mean that your daughter is promising that if this school accepts her, she will withdraw all the applications she's submitted to every other school and accept this school's offer of admission, no questions asked. *Do not do this.* Your child may end up obligating herself to a college that will give her zero financial aid and merit aid, and then require her to take on massive amounts of student loan debt in order to pay for the privilege of attending. *There is no college that is worth this.*

It would be better for your daughter to keep her options wide open and decide where to attend based on which college entices her with the most attractive financial aid and merit aid package.

Can a college actually force a student to enroll and attend if he or she doesn't want to go there? No—but your daughter's promise to withdraw her applications from all other colleges will leave her high and dry with no financial aid or merit aid from any other college if she does try to enroll somewhere else during that same application cycle.

Some students who've naively applied to college under "binding early decision" programs have found their eventual financial aid packages stuffed with so many student loans that they've chosen to sit out of college for an entire year and start the application process over again the following year. This is an option no student wants to take when her primary goal is to finish college efficiently and get out into the workforce quickly.

[19] *Jump ahead in this book and glance through chapter 20, "Early September of 12th grade."*

There are strategies in that chapter that will help you to increase your child's financial aid eligibility right before you fill out the FAFSA form on October 1. If you know what those strategies are now, you'll have extra time to plan for them.

CHECKLIST

Summer After 11th Grade

☐ 1. Go out to dinner with your daughter and look again at the contract you signed with her after she finished 8th grade.

☐ 2. If your daughter registered last spring to take a discounted community college course without you this summer, she'll be commuting from your home to those classes starting this month. Be sure she's had a professional college study skills class before she starts.

☐ 3. Remind your daughter that you'll be expecting her to cover all of her own summer expenses using the little bit of money you give her every two weeks.

☐ 4. Help your son get going on the clever, fun way he'll be earning money this summer.

☐ 5. Be sure your daughter is continuing to record all of her earnings in Evernote, including photos of each check and stack of cash she receives.

☐ 6. Search for a list of CLEP and DSST exams, and see if there are any that your son is now close to passing because he studied that subject during 11th grade.

☐ 7. Help your son find summer job-shadowing and resulting volunteer opportunities in the career field he's exploring.

☐ 8. Log your daughter into her account on LinkedIn and help her update her profile there.

☐ 9. Encourage your daughter to use cut and paste to apply for 10 private scholarships this summer.

☐ 10. If your son hasn't yet done the career work I suggested in chapter 13, it's critically important that you have him do that early this summer, before he chooses the colleges he'll apply to.

The following steps can technically wait until this coming fall, but your child will experience far less stress if he or she completes them during the summer after 11th grade.

☐ 11. Before you sit down with your daughter to finalize the list of colleges she'll be applying to, reread the college selection guidelines I provided in chapter 14.

☐ 12. Work alongside your teen to choose the colleges he'll apply to. Start by going over the informal scrapbook pages you created after each of your college visits.

☐ 13. If money is tight for your family, call the admissions office at every college your daughter is applying to and ask them if they'd be willing to waive their college application fees for your family.

☐ 14. Use CollegeData.com to determine which college application each college requires, and then have your son fill them out.

☐ 15. If your daughter has filled out the Common Application located at CommonApp.org, make sure she's signed the signature page at the very end of the form.

☐ 16. Encourage your son to consider applying to honors programs at each of the colleges he's applying to.

☐ 17. If your son or daughter has decided to apply for an ROTC scholarship, complete that application next.

☐ 18. Say a firm no to applying to college under binding early decision programs.

☐ 19. Jump ahead in this book and take a quick glance through chapter 20. You'll get a sneak peek at (and more time to plan ahead for) strategies that can increase your child's financial aid eligibility for this coming October 1.

☐ 20. Check my book updates page at JeannieBurlowski.com/LAUNCH to see if I have made any recent updates to this chapter.

☐ 21. Always consult your financial planning professional before making any big financial decisions.

☐ 22. Make a note in your calendar to come back and read the next chapter of this book when your child is in early September of 12th grade.

Be the first to hear about updates to the material in this book by reading my free weekly email newsletter every week. Anyone can subscribe to it at any time at JeannieBurlowski.com.

20 | *Early September of 12th Grade*

If you've followed even a fraction of the suggestions in this book, you're now entering your child's senior year of high school far, far ahead of the game.

You've thought of and planned for things that never cross most parents' minds, and you've done so at the most strategic times possible.

Congratulate yourself on this. And let your achievement so far give you energy to move full force into this next very important month—so you can finish strong.

HOW TO USE THIS CHAPTER

Start by just reading through this chapter. As you read, don't worry about committing to any of it. Decision time will come at the very end of this chapter, when I give you a clear, at-a-glance checklist of every task I'm suggesting you consider right now.

Remember, you won't have to use every strategy I suggest; just choose the ones you think will work for your family and either modify or discard the rest.

[1] *Ask your daughter about her plan for organizing her 12th-grade academics.*

This is especially important if she's taking dual enrollment college classes now in place of regular high school curriculum. Check in with her about what organizational system she'll be using for getting academic work done in a quality manner and turned in on time. (A reminder of the six questions to ask her can be found in chapter 3.)

[2] *Continue having your daughter pay all of her own expenses using the little bit of money you provide for her every two weeks.*

This strategy will help you to raise a teen who goes on to be frugal and smart with money as an adult. If you haven't yet set this system up, see my suggestions for doing this in chapter 11.

227

[3] *Have a talk with your son where you carefully head off "senioritis."*

Some 12th graders figure, "Hey, my college applications are all in; why should I study hard or serve my community or keep up my focused extracurricular activity at this point? Nobody's going to notice or be impressed." This is absolutely untrue for two reasons.

First, in about four months, we're going to have your son send an update letter to each of the colleges he's applied to. This update letter will list specific details that will let the college know (right before they make their admissions and merit aid decisions!) that your son has continued to be a superstar all the way into January of 12th grade.

Second, your son is going to be applying for 10 scholarships each summer all the way through college and grad school. Committees reading those scholarship applications will also be impressed that he's continued to do great things throughout his senior year.

[4] *Counsel your daughter to remain committed to the special extracurricular activity she's sticking with through all four years of high school. This year, could she mobilize the students in that organization to do something big to serve the community?*

It doesn't matter if the extracurricular she's committed to all these years is the Accounting Club, the Drama Club, the high school robotics team, the student council, the speech team, or the choir. *Any* school-based group can plan activities that benefit the community. Could your daughter step up and lead this?

If your daughter and her friends lead a service project for their organization, they show focus, commitment, leadership, personal initiative, and hearts that want to serve. All great things to write about in the update letter she'll be sending to all the colleges she's applied to in about four months from now.

> **IF YOUR DAUGHTER AND HER FRIENDS LEAD A SERVICE PROJECT FOR THEIR ORGANIZATION, THEY SHOW FOCUS, COMMITMENT, LEADERSHIP, PERSONAL INITIATIVE, AND HEARTS THAT WANT TO SERVE.**

[5] *If your son has applied to any of the special co-op college programs I marked with an asterisk in chapter 14, have him apply for a WACE scholarship now.*

Remember, the WACE scholarship application requires only a 3.5 GPA and a 300-word essay on why you desire cooperative education. No letters of recommendation are required.

You can find WACE online at Waceinc.org.

[6] *Set aside time this coming October 1 (or soon after) to fill out the FAFSA form. Your child probably hasn't been accepted to any colleges yet, but that doesn't matter.*

Fill out the FAFSA form even though you

don't yet know which colleges are going to accept your child. When you're asked for a list of colleges your child might be attending, put down every college your child has applied to.

You aren't required to submit the FAFSA on the exact date of October 1, of course, but it's important that you file it as close to that date as possible each year you have a child in college the following fall. Doing so will put your daughter first in line for financial aid money to help her pay for college.

There are some very large financial awards that are handed out exclusively according to who gets their FAFSA form in first. Filling out the FAFSA either on or just after October 1 increases the possibility that your son or daughter could be awarded some of this money.

If you're reading this for the first time in December or January of your child's senior year of high school (or later) and you have not yet filled out the FAFSA form—don't despair. Your child still has a chance of receiving financial aid. But because the pool of financial aid money is limited, earlier applications are always preferable.

You will likely be able to fill out financial aid forms all by yourself using the official FAFSA directions and the detailed instructions I provide in chapter 22. If you'd like extra help, seek specialized help from one of the thousands of certified public accountants and certified financial planners who are members of the National College Advocacy Group (NCAG) at Ncagonline.org. If your income is very high or your financial situation very complicated, get help from highly respected

Forbes contributor Troy Onink by signing up for one of the very valuable one-hour consultations he offers at Stratagee.com.

[7] Apply now for an FSA ID for yourself. Have your child apply for a separate one that will be unique to him or her.

You and your child will each need a unique FSA ID (linked to each of your individual unique names and email addresses) when you sit down to apply for financial aid this coming October 1. If you don't have your FSA IDs by that date, you may have to wait three days to have them assigned, and that could delay your child's financial aid application.

TO AVOID POTENTIAL IDENTITY THEFT, DO NOT SHARE YOUR FSA ID WITH YOUR CHILD OR WITH ANYONE ELSE—NOT EVEN WITH A PROFESSIONAL PERSON HELPING YOU WITH FINANCIAL AID APPLICATIONS.

"What is an FSA ID?"

The FSA ID is a secure username and password system that keeps your family's personal information safe—while still allowing the system to properly identify your child's information as belonging to him. As a parent, you will need your own FSA ID, which will allow you to access and then sign your child's FAFSA form electronically. If you have more than one child attending college in a given year, you can use the same FSA ID to sign all of your children's financial aid applications.

It's very important that you keep your FSA ID strictly confidential. Allow your teen to keep his FSA ID confidential too. Because the FSA ID is used to sign legally binding documents electronically, it has the same legal status as a written signature. To avoid potential identity theft, do not share your FSA ID with your child or with anyone else—not even with a professional person helping you with financial aid applications.

"What happened to the old PIN number system?"

If you have an older child and have applied for financial aid in the past, you might wonder what happened to the old FAFSA PIN number system. It was changed on May 10, 2015, to increase usability and security. As the Federal Student Aid website of the U.S. Department of Education explains, "The modernized experience available with the FSA ID includes features such as resetting forgotten passwords with e-mail, using an e-mail address instead of a username to log in, and compatibility with more browsers and devices."[28]

"I already have a PIN. What should I do with it?"

If you already have a PIN, you'll be able to enter it during the registration process for the FSA ID. Doing so will instantly link your PIN information to your new FSA ID, saving you time. If you have a PIN but you've forgotten it, no problem. You'll be invited to enter the answer to your PIN "challenge question"

during the FSA ID registration process. Or you can just create an FSA ID from scratch.

HOW TO CREATE AN FSA ID

1. If you have any reason to believe that the Social Security Administration (SSA) might have a wrong name or a wrong birthdate on file for you or for your child, go to Ssa.gov now. There you'll find all the information you need to correct any errors. To avoid delays or problems with FSA IDs, legal names must be presented and spelled exactly the same way on Social Security cards, on federal income tax returns, and on FSA IDs.

2. You and your child will create your own individual unique FSA IDs at Fsaid.ed.gov. To do so, you will each be required to provide your name, mailing address, telephone number, date of birth, Social Security Number, language preference, unique email address, and a unique username and password. When it comes to FSA IDs, it's important that your parental email address, username, and password be *completely different from your child's.* If your child doesn't have his or her own separate email account, set up a free one for him or her at Gmail.com or Hotmail.com. Carefully and securely record these email addresses, usernames, and passwords in a safe place where other people won't be able to find them, but where you'll know exactly where they are a year from now. You will also be asked to provide answers to five challenge questions that

---

28   "What Happened to the Federal Student Aid PIN?," Federal Student Aid, accessed November 19, 2016, https://studentaid.ed.gov/sa/fafsa/filling-out/fsaid#pin-replacement.

may be used later for security purposes, and you will be asked to verify that you are at least 13 years old. If for any reason one or both of you do not have a Social Security Number, that's OK. Just enter 000-00-0000 when asked for your Social Security Number.

3. Your final step in creating your FSA ID will be agreeing to the terms and conditions of the Fsaid.ed.gov website and verifying your email address. Verifying your email address is optional, but I encourage you to do it. According to the website, if you verify your email address, you'll be able to "use your e-mail address as your username when logging into certain ED websites. This verification also allows you to retrieve your username or reset your password without answering challenge questions."[29]

4. Take great care to record which FSA ID information is yours, and which is your child's. If you accidentally mix up FSA ID information, you will face no end of headaches.

5. If you have low vision, the FSA website may be hard for you to read due to the colors used in the design of the page. You could ask someone to read it to you, or you may be able to change the colors on the page by using Select All (Ctrl-A) to invert the color of the text and make the page more readable.

6. If at any point you have problems creating or using your FSA ID, call 1-800-557-7394 (TTY 1-800-730-8913).

"Will my FSA ID expire?"

Your FSA ID *password* will expire and have to be reset every 18 months. Your FSA ID username will not expire.

"What should I do once I have my FSA ID?"

Once you've created your FSA ID, keep your username, password, and the answers to your challenge questions in a safe, secure place where they won't be found by others or forgotten. If you lose your FSA ID log-in information, you could lose access to your account and find yourself unable to log in to federal student aid websites.

For more information on FSA IDs, including what to do if you forget your username or password, go to the federal student aid web page that covers FSA IDs. You can get directly to it by typing this shortcut into your web browser: Bit.ly/2fKOd8f.

[8] *Take significant time before October 1 to consider adjusting 12 things about your family finances, so you don't accidentally appear wealthier than you are on this year's FAFSA form.*

Even if your household income is $200,000 per year, please try the following strategies.

29 "How Do I Get an FSA ID?," Federal Student Aid, accessed September 24, 2016, https://studentaid. ed.gov/sa/fafsa/filling-out/fsaid. Also, for more information about FSA IDs, read the article "Frustrations with the FAFSA's FSA ID" by Mark Kantrowitz at https://www.cappex.com/hq/articles-and-advice/paying-for-college/Frustrations-with-the-FAFSAs-FSA-ID.

You may still be eligible for more help paying for college than you ever thought possible.

If you've been reading the step-by-step instructions in this book, you already understand that the FAFSA form will be gathering information about *income* that you and your current high school senior son earned during this particular window of time: January 1 of his sophomore year of high school to December 31 of his junior year of high school. (As a reader of this book, you carefully thought through strategies for minimizing this income *over two years ago*.)

> **EVEN IF YOUR HOUSEHOLD INCOME IS $200,000 PER YEAR, PLEASE TRY THE FOLLOWING STRATEGIES. YOU MAY STILL BE ELIGIBLE FOR MORE HELP PAYING FOR COLLEGE THAN YOU EVER THOUGHT POSSIBLE.**

This income information isn't *all* that the FAFSA is going to ask you to report, however.

The FAFSA is also going to ask you to report what your bank accounts and other assets look like on the exact day you complete, sign, and file your FAFSA.

Here's just one example. If, on the day you fill out your FAFSA, you've just deposited a large paycheck, but you have not yet purchased groceries or paid your bills, you are going to look wealthier than if you fill the form out on a day when your bank account just happens to be more depleted.

With this thought in mind, I want you to take some time this month (right before you fill out the FAFSA) to look carefully at all of your family financial assets (including student assets).

Make a careful accounting of every dollar you and your senior in high school have in savings accounts, checking accounts, money market accounts, brokerage accounts, certificates of deposit, stocks, bonds, other securities, mutual funds, commodities, and elsewhere, and then consider strategically moving (or, as financial planners like to say, "repositioning") some of that money before you have to report it on FAFSA.

12 STRATEGIES FOR REPOSITIONING ASSETS RIGHT BEFORE YOU FILL OUT THE FAFSA FORM

As you consider using the following strategies, do two things. First, be sure to preserve an emergency fund as a safety net just in case you encounter unexpected expenses over the next three to six months.

> **SHOW YOUR FINANCIAL ADVISING PROFESSIONAL THIS BOOK. TELL HIM OR HER THAT YOU'LL BE FILLING OUT THE FAFSA THIS COMING OCTOBER, AND ASK IF YOU SHOULD BE DOING ANY OF THESE 12 THINGS.**

Second, I strongly suggest that you visit a certified public accountant, certified financial planner, or other qualified investment advisor, show him or her this section of this book, and get professional help applying the following strategies to your family's particular individual situation. If you hesitate to do this because you don't know which professionals in your community are trustworthy, consider one of the carefully vetted investing professionals that best-selling author Dave Ramsey recommends on the SmartVestor section of his website. You can get directly to Dave Ramsey's SmartVestor search page by typing this shortcut into your web browser: Bit.ly/2fKKjw6.

Show your financial advising professional this book. Tell him or her that you will be filling out the FAFSA form this coming October, and you are wondering if you should do the following:

1. Consider using your available extra cash to pay down your family's high-interest consumer debt, such as car loans, credit cards, and even your home mortgage.

2. Think about squirreling extra cash away in retirement accounts, since every penny in retirement accounts is tucked safely away from the prying eyes of every financial aid application process.

3. Pay in advance for a needed home remodel, such as a new roof or more energy-efficient windows, or purchase a necessary appliance, such as a more energy-efficient furnace, air conditioner, or refrigerator. Why? Because the FAFSA won't ask you to reveal anything about the value of the home you live in or the value of anything inside it.

4. Use your extra cash to pre-pay for advertising, buy new equipment, update your computer network, or build a new warehouse for your family business that has 100 or fewer employees. Or put extra money into the farm that you and your family live on. Why? Because these capital expenditures lower your income in the year that you purchase them, and then (as icing on the cake) the FAFSA won't ask you to reveal the value of these items when it evaluates your assets as part of the financial aid application process.

5. Make all your usual monthly purchases right before you fill out the FAFSA form. Pay all your usual monthly bills, and as you do, pay as much extra on your high-interest car loans and credit cards as you possibly can. If you don't have car loans or credit cards, go to the store and get the largest haul of groceries you've ever bought in your life, and spend a whole Saturday preparing meals for your freezer. Make an extra payment (or more) on your home mortgage if possible. With the exception of your emergency fund, do whatever you can to reduce the available cash sitting around in your savings accounts, checking accounts, money market accounts, brokerage accounts, certificates of deposit, stocks, bonds, other securities, mutual funds, commodities, and other accounts.

6. Just be sure that if you're going to buy anything, you don't rely on credit to do so. Your objective will be to drain your cash down, not incur more debt for your family. Having additional family debt does not help you in any way in any financial aid calculation process. Your family debt will

actually make it *harder* for you to get your kids through college debt-free.

7. If you own a family business, set aside time to look carefully at your company's human resources. Does your family-owned company currently have 101 full-time employees? If so, you may decide to quickly offer one employee early retirement, bringing your total number of full-time employees down to just 100. Why? Because if a family business has 101 full-time employees or more, the assets of that business will be included in certain financial aid calculations. Family businesses with only 100 full-time employees or fewer, however, are excluded from those financial aid calculations—even if they bring in $1 million a year in profits.

8. If your child has substantial assets such as an UGMA (Uniform Gift to Minors Act) or UTMA (Uniform Transfers to Minors Act) account in his name, his assets could take a direct hit when need-based financial aid is calculated. Ask your financial advisor if it might be a good idea for you to purposely drain down these UGMA and UTMA accounts before filling out the FAFSA form. It's not possible to simply cash out an UGMA or UTMA account or transfer ownership of it to another person, so don't try that. However, since the law says that the money in an UGMA or UTMA account must be used for the benefit of the beneficiary, it's possible to use those funds to buy the child the computer and printer he'll need for college, or transfer those funds into a 529 college savings plan where the child is named as beneficiary. This works well, because as we've discussed previously, 529 college savings accounts are scrutinized at the lower parent rate and so have minimal impact on financial aid eligibility. If you're going to do this, though, note that there may be certain tax implications in your situation. For this reason, be sure to consult your financial or tax advisor before making any final decisions.

9. Before filling out the FAFSA form, check to see how much money your son has in accounts in his name. (I'm not talking about 529 plans where your son is named as beneficiary—those are safe. I'm talking about other types of accounts.) Here's why. On the day you fill out the FAFSA form, the financial aid calculation process is going to look at all the money in your son's name (not including 529 and retirement plans), and automatically reduce his need-based financial aid by 20 percent of that amount. If your son has $10,000 in the bank in his own name on the day you fill out the FAFSA form, his future financial aid award may be instantly reduced by as much as $2,000. Oh no. Where can your son stash his money to keep it from prying eyes at this point?

10. The first place your teen should consider stashing that money is on deposit with you, the parent. Remember the contract you all signed as a family during the summer after your son's 8th-grade year? (See chapter 4 for a reminder.) In that contract your son agreed to this:

My parents have set aside some money to help me pay for college or another type of job-training program. Here's what I will be required to do to get that money: I will pay my parents a $1,000 deposit out of my own money for each semester that they help me with college costs. At the end of each of my college semesters, I will log my parents into the computer and show them the official record of the grades I earned. If my college grades are mostly A's with maybe one B, my parents will return that $1,000 deposit to me, and I can use it to get them to help pay for my next semester. If I play my cards right, I'll be able to make it all the way through four years of college on this one deposit and get my $1,000 back permanently once I graduate. But if I have a few bad semesters and have to fork over three or four $1,000 deposits to my parents, that won't be so bad. Four thousand dollars of my own money is a small price to pay for a $160,000 college education!

11. This month will be a great time for this teen to pay that first $1,000 deposit to his parents. But then—what about the child's remaining savings? Some teens with a lot of extra money in savings will say to their parents, "Dad, here's my $10,000. Could you put the whole thing into that 529 plan you have for me?" This may be a good idea, since every $10,000 in a 529 plan reduces future financial aid awards by only about $564.

12. Other teens strike a deal with their parents. "Tell you what, Dad," a son might say. "I've got $10,000 here. How about if I lend you this money to pay off your highest-interest credit card debt, and then you note how much your monthly credit card bills are reduced as a result—and put that amount of money into my 529 plan each month?" Most parents are overjoyed at the thought that they could spend years paying money into their child's college fund instead of to a credit card company. Students, if you do use this strategy, just be sure to clarify with your parents that this is a *loan*, and have them sign a promissory note so that they eventually repay your loan to them in full. The optimal time for them to repay you? Sometime after your family has filled out your last FAFSA form (on October 1 of your junior year of college).

> **MOST PARENTS ARE OVERJOYED AT THE THOUGHT THAT THEY COULD SPEND YEARS PAYING MONEY INTO THEIR CHILD'S COLLEGE FUND INSTEAD OF TO A CREDIT CARD COMPANY.**

"How does 'repositioning' money in this way help us?"

Moving money around in this way can accomplish two things. First, it keeps the money from sitting around in parent or student accounts where it will be noticed as a wealth asset in financial aid calculation processes. Second (in the case of paying down the parent's consumer debt and home mortgage), it can free parents financially so they are in a better position to help students with college costs when the time comes.

Some families at this point will ask, "What about trust funds? Do they count as family assets in the financial aid application process?" The answer is yes. Trust funds must be reported on financial aid application forms, even if those funds are not currently available to either the parents or the child.

There's no hiding trust fund money. When it comes to the FAFSA form, if only interest or principal will be available, then the trust officer should calculate the present value and report that.

"Oh, my goodness. Is it really OK for us to strategize to this extent?"

We talked about this two years ago, when I gave you strategies for keeping your income low for this FAFSA form you are about to fill out. The gentle reassurance I gave you then is worth repeating here:

As you read these strategies, do you find yourself huffing in disapproval that anyone would try to "play the system" by making their financial situation look dire on the FAFSA form?

Do you think that the most ethical thing is to have families make all their financial decisions blindly throughout this important time, be stunned and shocked at how little aid they qualify for, and then sign their children up for indentured servitude to student loan payments through age 50?

Let me be clear about this. The financial aid rules and policies in the U.S. are set up to reward families who take the steps I've outlined in this chapter. Wealthy families already know about these strategies; they have specialized lawyers and consultants and accountants to help them figure these things out. If we keep these strategies secret, we will only disadvantage the middle class and low-income families who need them most.

Use the strategies. Your kid's future financial life is at stake.

[9] *Make a recurring note in your calendar that reminds you to read through the strategies in this chapter again every September that you have a child in college the following fall.*

This will help you as the years go by to be sure that you are positioning yourself as effectively as possible in every FAFSA form you fill out.

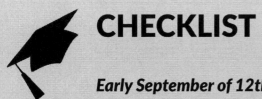

CHECKLIST

Early September of 12th Grade

1. Ask your daughter about her plan for organizing her 12th-grade academics.

2. Continue having your daughter pay all of her own expenses using the little bit of money you provide for her every two weeks.

3. Have a talk with your son where you carefully head off "senioritis."

4. Counsel your daughter to remain committed to the special extracurricular activity she's sticking with through all four years of high school. This year, could she mobilize the students in that organization to do something big to serve the community?

5. If your child has applied to any of the co-op college programs described in chapter 14, have him or her apply for a WACE scholarship now.

6. Get out your calendar and set aside time on this coming October 1 (or as soon as possible after that) to fill out the FAFSA form.

7. Apply now for an FSA ID for yourself. Have your child apply for a separate one that will be unique to him or her.

8. Take significant time before October 1 to consider possibly adjusting 12 things about your family finances, so you don't accidentally appear wealthier than you are on this year's FAFSA form. Consider getting a professional financial advisor to help you.

9. Make a recurring note in your calendar that reminds you to reread the 12 asset repositioning strategies in this chapter again every September that you have a child in college the following fall.

10. Because this chapter's information on repositioning assets before filling out the FAFSA is so important, please use Facebook to tell other parents about this book.

11. Check my book updates page at JeannieBurlowski.com/LAUNCH to see if I have made any recent updates to this chapter.

12. If you know of any students whose parents are refusing to help them with their FAFSA forms, please help those students out by showing them the next chapter of this book.

13. Always consult your financial planning professional before making any big financial decisions.

14. Make a note in your calendar to come back and read chapter 22 of this book on October 1 when your child is in 12th grade.

Be the first to hear about updates to the material in this book by reading my free weekly email newsletter every week. Anyone can subscribe to it at any time at JeannieBurlowski.com.

21 | *Special Notes for Students Whose Parents Won't Help*

This book is mainly for parents, but if you're a student who's reading it because your parents are refusing to help you, please accept my deepest sympathy.

Your parents may mistakenly believe that if they refuse to help you, then the government will be forced to pay for your college. This is absolutely not true. If your parents refuse to help you, the government will not step in and pay for your education.

If you are facing this circumstance, carefully read the section of the FinAid website entitled, "What Can You Do If Your Parents Refuse to Help?" You can get directly to that page by typing this shortcut into your web browser: Mnstr.me/2gvcH6D.

If your parents want to flatly refuse to give you one penny to pay for your education, they have the right to do that, but you as a student should still do everything you can to coax them to at least fill out financial aid forms for you every October 1, starting in your senior year of high school and ending in your junior year of college.

> **YOUR PARENTS MAY MISTAKENLY BELIEVE THAT IF THEY REFUSE TO HELP YOU, THEN THE GOVERNMENT WILL BE FORCED TO PAY FOR YOUR COLLEGE.**

Assure your parents that the data they enter

on financial aid forms will, by law, be kept confidential from you, from any ex-spouses, and from others in accordance with the Family Educational Rights and Privacy Act (FERPA). Filling out financial aid forms will not obligate your parents to give you any money for college. Doing so may, however, help you get some free money government aid or college merit aid that will help you pay for college yourself. Besides that, parental completion of these financial aid forms is absolutely necessary if you as a student are going to be able to get the lowest-interest, best-term loans to pay for college on your own.

Can't I just declare independence from my parents and be done with it?

Prior to 1992 a student could claim independence from his or her parents if (a) "the parents didn't claim the student as an exemption on their tax returns for two years" and (b) "the student provided evidence that he or she was self-supporting."[30] The laws have changed since 1992, though, so this definition of independent student is no longer valid.

Under the current rules, you would have to satisfy at least one of the following criteria in order to be considered independent for financial aid application purposes:

» You are an orphan or ward of the court (or you *were* a ward of the court until you reached age 18).

» You are a veteran of the Armed Forces of the United States.

» You are a graduate or professional student.

» You are married.

» You have one or more legal dependents other than a spouse. (A dependent is some person who receives more than 50 percent of his or her support from you. This could be a child you've given birth to or legally adopted, or it could be an elderly relative or some other person.)

» You will be 24 years of age or older by December 31 of the award year. This means that if you are 23 years old now or will turn 23 by this coming December 31 and you hope to enter college 11 months from now, then you *will* be 24 by December 31 of your award year. Go ahead and fill out financial aid forms as an independent student. If you're younger, though, you automatically qualify as a dependent student for financial aid application purposes.[31]

If you don't meet any of these requirements, then you automatically qualify as a dependent student.

It is possible for you to hire an attorney to petition the court to have your parents' parental rights terminated on the grounds of abandonment. In order for the court to grant

---

30 "What Can You Do If Your Parents Can't Help Pay for School?," FinAid, accessed September 24, 2016, http://www.finaid.org/otheraid/parentsrefuse.phtml.

31 Ibid.

this petition, though, you will likely need to provide evidence that your parents have ceased all support for and contact with you for at least one year.

If your parents still refuse to fill out financial aid applications for you even after your respectful, understanding requests, I encourage you to call the financial aid office of a college you may want to attend, and request a "professional judgment review." A professional judgment review gives you the opportunity to have a phone or in-person appointment with a college financial aid staff person where you get to explain your unique difficult circumstances. Sometimes financial aid officers are able to talk to parents and convince them that it's safe for them to at least fill out the financial aid forms—even if the parents are firmly set against paying any money for education. In some very rare instances, the college's financial aid office may even be able to grant you independence from your parents by providing you with what is called a "dependency override." Dependency overrides are very difficult to get, though, and are usually reserved for unusual circumstances:

» Parents are incarcerated or presumed dead.

» The student was sexually or physically abused by the parents or can document a hostile or neglectful relationship with his or her parents. The student will need to provide copies of protection from abuse orders, court documents, social worker reports, doctor reports, police records, and letters from clergy, as appropriate.

» Parents cannot be located. For example, a student who emigrated to the U.S. without his or her parents, became a U.S. citizen, and has not been able to contact his or her parents (or even know whether they are still alive).

» The student was legally adopted by his or her current guardian.

» The student is Amish and has been shunned or banished because of his or her desire to seek an education and, as a result, no longer has any contact with family.[32]

> **IN SOME VERY RARE INSTANCES, THE COLLEGE'S FINANCIAL AID OFFICE MAY EVEN BE ABLE TO GRANT YOU INDEPENDENCE FROM YOUR PARENTS BY PROVIDING YOU WITH WHAT IS CALLED A "DEPENDENCY OVERRIDE."**

Whatever you do, student, don't be tempted to forge financial aid application forms and sign your parents' names to them. The penalties are severe, and you will most certainly be caught when the FAFSA form you fill out doesn't perfectly match your parents' tax returns.[33]

---

32 Ibid.

33 Ibid.

"Maybe I should just get married then!"

If you're considering getting around parental dependency rules by getting married, be careful of two things:

First, what matters is your marital status as of the date you submit your FAFSA form, the first of which will be in early October, 11 months before you begin college classes following high school. If you submit your FAFSA form on October 5 and you get married on October 6, you will be considered dependent on your parents for financial aid purposes for the entire upcoming year. Federal law specifically prohibits colleges from changing a student's marital status in the middle of a year.

Second, you may see some extra financial aid benefit if your married household income ends up to be less than your parents' income (especially if you and your spouse are both attending college at the same time). However, remember that your new spouse's income and assets will count as your income and assets in your financial aid application calculations. If your new spouse is wealthier than your parents are, that may negatively affect how much financial aid you'll be awarded for college.

"I'm worried that because of my parents' citizenship status, I won't be able to get any financial aid for college."

I have good news for you. Your parents' citizenship status doesn't affect your eligibility for financial aid for college one bit. FAFSA doesn't even *ask* about your parents' citizenship status. If one or both of your parents don't have Social Security Numbers, you can enter "000-00-0000" where the form asks for that information.

22 | *October 1 of 12th Grade (Filling Out FAFSA)*

This is one of the most important chapters in this book. This time, don't just choose the strategies you think will work for your family and either modify or discard the rest as I've suggested before. This time the stakes are very high. Read these instructions carefully and follow them as closely as you can.

[1] *Fill out the FAFSA form on October 1, or as soon as possible after that. This will allow your child to get first in line for financial aid money.*

Always, *always* fill out the FAFSA every October 1 that you will have a child in college the following fall. Some of your smartest parent friends are going to blow off filling out the FAFSA form because they think, "Oh, our family makes too much to qualify for any Pell grants. It's not worth our time to fill out these forms."

Don't make this mistake.

Your child could receive financial assistance to help pay for college even if you earn $200,000 per year and have significant assets. The FAFSA form isn't *just* used to apply for Pell grants, remember. It's also the gateway to nine separate federal student aid programs, over 600 state aid programs, and most of the college-based (institutional) aid available in the United States. Besides that—if your child *does* some day need to take out a student loan (even just temporarily to get through a tight spot), the best, least-expensive student loans are *only* available to students whose parents have filled out FAFSA forms the previous October.

Massive amounts of free money are left on the table every year by parents who mistakenly assume, "Oh, we're not going to qualify for anything anyway."

> **MASSIVE AMOUNTS OF FREE MONEY ARE LEFT ON THE TABLE EVERY YEAR BY PARENTS WHO MISTAKENLY ASSUME, "OH, WE'RE NOT GOING TO QUALIFY FOR ANYTHING ANYWAY."**

The FAFSA form is not that difficult to fill out. I'll give you specific, written help as you go through it, and I'll answer all the most common questions that parents have about FAFSA.

Let's do this together and just see what great things might happen.

[2] *When filling out the FAFSA form, follow the stated directions exactly.*

Every year there are students who don't receive the student aid money they deserve because their parents made careless errors on the FAFSA form.

Even PhDs and lawyers mess up the FAFSA form, usually due to not following the *plainly stated directions*. Don't let this scare you; just let it inspire you to read the directions and follow them carefully.

[3] *Know and carefully avoid more than 30 errors parents commonly make on FAFSA forms.*

Even when you *are* carefully reading and following directions exactly, it's still normal to come upon certain instructions that make you wonder, "Oh, boy. What do they mean by *that*?" This doesn't just happen on the FAFSA form; it happens anywhere people

are expected to read and follow written instructions.

When you're filling out the FAFSA form, I want you to have absolutely *zero* confusion over "what they mean by that." I want you to feel confidence and clarity that you are filling out this form with the best possible answer in every blank.

To help you, I'd like to give you a list of more than 30 errors parents commonly make on FAFSA forms. This list will answer many of the questions that are going to pop into your head when you're deciding what your answers should be.

To access this list, download and print out the bonus online content I'm providing next. Use this material to save yourself time and increase your confidence in filling out the FAFSA form. Then, share this bonus online resource with friends who also want to get their kids as much free money for college as possible.

BONUS ONLINE CONTENT:
Download the list
"30+ Common FAFSA Mistakes
and How to Avoid Them" at
JeannieBurlowski.com/LAUNCH.

You have my permission to share this link online, on social media, in school newsletters, on personal, business, and school websites, and from the auditorium stage on high school financial aid night. It's my goal to help as many families and students as possible with this information; we never know when access to a simple resource like this might empower a family to send a kid to college when they'd never be able to otherwise.

[4] *Every September, consider, "Is there a possibility I could have a child in college or technical school next year at this time?" If the answer is yes, download a fresh copy of this bonus online content. (Note this in your personal calendar now.)*

The federal government can change financial aid policies anytime, as happened on September 13, 2015, when the White House abruptly announced sweeping, deeply confusing changes to the federal financial aid application process. If something like this ever happens again, I'll be able to keep you updated by promptly changing this bonus online content.

[5] *Don't feel frightened or stressed about filling out the FAFSA form.*

If you make a mistake, you can always make corrections to the form later. I'll remind you of the best time to do this, and I'll explain exactly how to make those corrections.

[6] *As soon as you're ready to start filling out official financial aid forms, go to Fafsa.ed.gov to fill out the FAFSA form.*

As of this writing, it's still acceptable to submit paper versions of official financial aid applications, but I suggest that you always fill out financial aid forms online, clicking "save"

every second page or so. Online versions of financial aid forms will catch obvious mistakes you've made and notify you immediately of what you need to change. Mistakes made on pencil and paper financial aid forms can take weeks to correct and cause costly financial aid delays.

[7] *Stay away from FAFSA-related scam websites.*

Be sure you don't accidentally try to fill out the FAFSA at phishing sites such as "Fafsa. com" or "Freefafsagov.com." These are scam sites that purport to collect your information from you and then use it to fill out the FAFSA form for you (for a fee of course). Don't use them.

Remember, the true FAFSA application is found only at Fafsa.ed.gov. When you get there, check for the notice on the banner that says, "An Office of the U.S. Department of Education."

> **BE SURE YOU DON'T ACCIDENTALLY TRY TO FILL OUT THE FAFSA AT PHISHING SITES SUCH AS "FAFSA.COM" OR "FREEFAFSAGOV.COM."**

[8] *Use the FAFSA's "IRS Data Retrieval Tool." It'll be a big help.*

The IRS Data Retrieval Tool will automatically fill in certain sections of your FAFSA form for you, using information you've already entered on income tax returns.

This will be very helpful. It'll save you from having to print out old tax returns and then comb through them looking for numbers to enter on the FAFSA, and it'll greatly reduce errors that could delay your child's financial aid application.

When you see the opportunity to use the IRS Data Retrieval Tool, I suggest you accept it. You'll answer a few screening questions designed to make sure you're eligible to use the tool, and then you'll be temporarily transferred over to the IRS website. Once on the IRS website, you'll answer a few questions proving that you are who you say you are, and then the IRS website will show you the details that are about to be transferred straight to your FAFSA form.

At this point, with the details in front of you, you'll be able to, (a) transfer the data as is, or (b) update the data if you believe that's necessary. Note that if you transfer the data *as is* without changing it, you will greatly reduce the possibility that your child's FAFSA will be "selected for verification."

You'll then be transferred back to the FAFSA website where you will continue filling out the rest of the FAFSA form.

"What's the problem with being selected for verification?"

Being selected for verification isn't a problem per se, but it can be a hassle, and it will delay your child's financial aid application. If your child's FAFSA is selected for verification, you'll be required to take several additional steps, including completing IRS Form 4506-T, which you can request by calling

1-800-908-9946.

"My daughter files her own separate tax returns. Will she use the IRS Data Retrieval Tool too?"

Yes. She can also use the IRS Data Retrieval Tool to report information she entered on her separate income tax return.

"Can anyone use the IRS Data Retrieval Tool?"

Certain people with certain special circumstances can't use the IRS Data Retrieval Tool. You can find out who *can't* use the tool by going to the Finaid.org website. To get directly to the page you need, type this shortcut into your web browser: Mnstr. me/2fseMjB.

[9] If you want help filling out financial aid forms, here are good places to get help:

» See a list of frequently asked FAFSA questions at Fafsa.ed.gov/help.htm.

» Access the help that the federal government provides through Student Financial Aid Services, Inc. at 1-866-514-8938.

» Call the Federal Student Aid Information Center at 1-800-4-FED-AID (1-800-433-3243).

» In the case of especially difficult individual family questions, call the financial aid office at one of the colleges your child applied to. Most of the people who staff financial aid offices at colleges consider it their mission to help students and families.

» You can also contact one of the thousands of certified public accountants and financial planners who are members of the National College Advocacy Group, located at Ncagonline.org.

[10] *Fill out the CSS/Profile form if necessary.*

If your child has applied to any colleges that require the CSS/Profile form in addition to the FAFSA form, I suggest that you fill out the FAFSA form *first*. Then, when you've finished, complete the online registration process for filling out the CSS/Profile form. You can get directly to the page you need for this by typing this shortcut into your web browser: Bit.ly/2fsd9CH.

Remember, of the over 7,250 colleges and universities in the U.S., fewer than 400 require the CSS/Profile form. There's a chance you will not be filling the CSS/Profile form out at all.

You can find out whether one or more of the colleges your child has applied to requires the CSS/Profile form by typing this shortcut into your web browser: Bit.ly/2fFGKXD.

[11] *Fill out any additional financial aid forms that may be required by individual colleges your child has applied to.*

If a college financial aid office ever asks you for additional information, always reply

promptly and completely. You'll put yourself far ahead of families who delay and forget to respond to these requests.

These additional financial aid forms could come to your *home postal address* or to your *email inbox* at any time, so be sure to watch for them. Be sure to carefully watch your email spam and promotions folders from now until next May just in case an important financial aid email accidentally ends up there.

[12] *Print out copies of all of the financial aid forms you've filled out and keep them in a safe place.*

You might need these documents later.

[13] *Be encouraged. You are doing great!*

I understand that filling out a government form while being careful to follow a large set of rules isn't the most fun way to spend an afternoon. It's kind of like doing your taxes, except the stakes are higher and accidental errors can end up being costly for someone you dearly love. Even so, *be encouraged.* You are doing far more than many parents ever do to ensure you're filling out financial aid forms in the best possible, most precise way, and that's going to pay off for your child over and over again.

CHECKLIST

October 1 of 12th Grade (Filling Out FAFSA)

☐ 1. Fill out the FAFSA form on October 1 (or as soon as possible after that).

☐ 2. When filling out the FAFSA form, follow the stated directions exactly.

☐ 3. Know and carefully avoid the most common FAFSA errors. To learn what they are, download my bonus online content on this subject at JeannieBurlowski.com/LAUNCH.

☐ 4. Put a reminder in your calendar that you'll need to return to the link above and download a fresh copy of this bonus online content every September that you'll have a child in college the following fall. (Note this in your personal calendar now.)

☐ 5. Don't feel frightened or stressed about filling out the FAFSA; you'll be able to make corrections to it later.

☐ 6. As soon as you're ready to start filling out the FAFSA, go to: Fafsa.ed.gov.

☐ 7. Stay away from FAFSA-related scam websites.

☐ 8. Use the FAFSA's "IRS Data Retrieval Tool." It'll be a big help.

☐ 9. If you need help while you're filling out the FAFSA, access one of the five useful resources I've provided in this chapter.

☐ 10. Fill out the CSS/Profile form if necessary.

☐ 11. Fill out any additional financial aid forms that may be required by individual colleges your child has applied to. Carefully watch your email spam and promotions folders from now until next May just in case an important financial aid email ends up there.

☐ 12. Print out copies of all of the financial aid forms you've filled out. Keep them in a safe place.

☐ 13. Be encouraged. You are doing *great!*

☐ 14. Check my book updates page at JeannieBurlowski.com/LAUNCH to see if I have made any recent updates to this chapter.

☐ 15. Always consult your financial planning professional before making any big financial decisions.

☐ 16. Make a note in your calendar to come back and read the next chapter of this book on or about October 15 when your child is in 12th grade (approximately two weeks from now).

Be the first to hear about updates to the material in this book by reading my free weekly email newsletter every week. Anyone can subscribe to it at any time at JeannieBurlowski.com.

23 | *October 15–30 of 12th Grade*

This is a very important chapter. This time, don't just choose the strategies you think will work for your family and either modify or discard the rest as I've suggested before. This time the stakes are very high. Read these instructions carefully and follow them as closely as you can.

[1] *Check to be sure you've received your copy of your child's Student Aid Report (SAR).*

The Student Aid Report usually arrives via email or postal mail within two weeks of the date that you filed the FAFSA. The Student Aid Report will give you some idea of your child's eligibility for federal student aid, and it will list the answers you entered on your most recent FAFSA form.

If two weeks have passed since you filed your FAFSA and you haven't yet received a Student Aid Report, there may have been some problem with your FAFSA submission. Check your FAFSA status by going to

Fafsa.ed.gov. Log in there with your FSA ID, and then go to the "My FAFSA" page. Select "View" or "Print Your Student Aid Report (SAR)" and you'll have immediate access to it.

If your Student Aid Report is not there, I suggest calling the Federal Student Aid Information Center at 1-800-4-FED-AID (1-800-433-3243). Ask them what could be the problem.

[2] *Carefully check your Student Aid Report for possible errors.*

Do all the figures you submitted look accurate? Could a figure have been put in the wrong box? Does your Expected Family Contribution (EFC) look accurate?

[3] *If your Student Aid Report contains errors, correct those errors right away.*

To correct errors, go to the FAFSA homepage at Fafsa.ed.gov and use your FSA ID to log into "FAFSA on the Web." Then click "Make FAFSA Corrections."

You'll be allowed to correct any field on your FAFSA form other than your Social Security Number.

> **MORE THAN 750,000 STUDENTS A YEAR WHO ARE NOTIFIED THAT THEY HAVE FAFSA ERRORS FAIL TO REVISE THEIR AID APPLICATIONS. THIS SMALL OVERSIGHT COSTS STUDENTS MILLIONS IN FINANCIAL AID MONEY EACH YEAR.**

Making these corrections is tremendously important. The U.S. Department of Education reports that more than 750,000 students a year who are notified that they have FAFSA errors *fail to revise their aid applications*. This seemingly small oversight costs students millions of dollars in financial aid money each year.

When you've finished all your corrections, be sure that all the correct people have signed the online correction. Signatures may be provided electronically using FSA IDs. Remember, you must complete all the required steps and receive the official FAFSA confirmation stamp in order for your changes to be effective.

If you need any help with completing your FAFSA, making corrections to it, or understanding your Student Aid Report, reach out to one of the helpful resources I've provided in chapter 22 of this book.

If you've made a correction to your FAFSA, you will receive a new Student Aid Report that reflects all the changes you've made. If these corrections in any way affected your Expected Family Contribution (EFC), you'll see that change on your new Student Aid Report. Each college's financial aid administrators will see the changes too and will adjust your financial aid package(s) accordingly.

[4] *If you submitted the CSS/Profile financial aid form and you'd like to make changes to it, do that now as well.*

As of this writing, you cannot make changes to your CSS/Profile financial aid application online.

Print out the CSS/Profile Acknowledgment Report, make your changes on the paper form, and send paper copies of that report to all the financial aid offices at all the CSS/Profile colleges your child has applied to. As of this writing, this is the only way to notify CSS/Profile colleges that you have corrections to your CSS/Profile form.

[5] *After you receive your Student Aid Report, your FAFSA may be one of the 30 percent of FAFSA forms selected for "verification."*

If your form is selected for verification, it's critically important that you return the requested verification paperwork as quickly as possible, or you may risk delaying your financial aid award letter. This could cause your child to get less financial aid for college.

[6] *Students may retake SAT and ACT tests (if necessary) through December of the senior year of high school, but you'll need to register soon.*

Colleges will see all the scores from all the times your daughter has ever taken these tests, but their decisions about her will take into consideration only the highest score she's received on each test.

» SAT registration information can be found here: Sat.collegeboard.org/register.

» ACT registration can be found here: Actstudent.org.

If your daughter's college applications have already been submitted and she'd like the schools to look at this new, stronger standardized test score, she can contact individual college admissions offices and ask them to consider her new score.

"Help! We are stressing out about standardized test scores!"

If standardized tests are causing you or your child extraordinary stress, do two things. First, reread chapter 2 of this book. You'll immediately feel that stress and anxiety being replaced by reason, good sense, and hope.

Second, remember that it's not too late to apply to one of over 870 "test optional" colleges and universities. Test optional schools believe that standardized test scores aren't strong predictors of success in college, so they evaluate students based on grades, accomplishments, and other non-quantitative factors.

A test optional school may still ask your daughter for a standardized test score if she's from out of state, is applying for a certain major or scholarship, or falls into a particular applicant category (you can find out details on the college's website), but in general, test optional schools can be good bets for students whose scores tend to be their Achilles heel.

> **TEST OPTIONAL SCHOOLS BELIEVE THAT STANDARDIZED TEST SCORES AREN'T STRONG PREDICTORS OF SUCCESS IN COLLEGE, SO THEY EVALUATE STUDENTS BASED ON GRADES, ACCOMPLISHMENTS, AND OTHER NON-QUANTITATIVE FACTORS.**

The Niche college search website provides an excellent list of test optional colleges and universities that are thought to be especially high quality. You can get directly to that list by typing this shortcut into your web browser: Bit.ly/2g8Xold.

You can find Fairtest.org's complete (alphabetized) list of all colleges and universities in the U.S. known to be test optional by typing this shortcut into your web browser: Bit.ly/2fIRyEv.

CHECKLIST

October 15–30 of 12th Grade

☐ 1. Check to be sure that you've received your copy of your child's Student Aid Report (SAR). If you haven't, follow the steps I suggest to find out what's wrong.

☐ 2. Carefully check your Student Aid Report (SAR) for possible errors.

☐ 3. If your Student Aid Report contains errors, correct them right away. Have all the correct people sign the revisions, and then carefully examine your new Student Aid Report when it arrives.

☐ 4. If you submitted the CSS/Profile financial aid form and you'd like to make changes to it, do that now as well.

☐ 5. If your FAFSA is selected for verification, return the requested verification paperwork right away. Don't delay.

☐ 6. If you'd like to have your child retake SAT or ACT tests, register to do that now.

☐ 7. If standardized tests are a sore spot for your child, consider "test optional" schools.

☐ 8. Check my book updates page at JeannieBurlowski.com/LAUNCH to see if I have made any recent updates to this chapter.

☐ 9. Always consult your financial planning professional before making any big financial decisions.

☐ 10. Make a note in your calendar to come back and read the next chapter of this book when your child is in early November of 12th grade.

Be the first to hear about updates to the material in this book by reading my free weekly email newsletter every week. Anyone can subscribe to it at any time at JeannieBurlowski.com.

24 | *November— December of 12th Grade*

This chapter is a lighter one with less for you to do. (Whew! After what you've been through since September 1, you could use a break.)

All I'll be asking you to do during these two months will be some easy check-ins, just to make sure things are proceeding as we've been planning.

You might want to put a little extra time into planning memorable holidays for your family during this two-month period. Close, warm family memories will help provide your teen a stable platform from which to launch into adult life.

HOW TO USE THIS CHAPTER

Start by just reading through this chapter. As you read, don't worry about committing to any of it. Decision time will come at the very end of this chapter, when I give you a clear, at-a-glance checklist of every task I'm suggesting you consider right now.

Remember, you won't have to use every strategy I suggest; just choose the ones you think will work for your family and either modify or discard the rest.

[1] *Check to be sure that all of the letters of recommendation your son requested to accompany his college applications were actually sent in as expected.*

Your son gave his recommenders postcards to mail back to him when they finished his letters of recommendation. Did all of those postcards come back?

[2] *Touch base with your daughter about how she's doing with organizing a project to help the humanitarian cause she's adopted as her own.*

Remember, if she pulls in friends to help her, she gets points for leadership as well as for service. Be sure to keep track of everything she does in her profile on LinkedIn.

Her service will continue to be helpful for future scholarship applications, and it will also impress the colleges she's applied to when she sends them an update letter in the winter of her senior year of high school. (I'll remind you.)

[3] *Have your son continue with that one special extracurricular activity he's going to stick with throughout all four years of high school.*

If he moves into additional leadership within the activity or creates additional ways for the group to serve the community, that will be very helpful for him to include on future scholarship applications and in the update letter he'll be sending to colleges soon.

[4] *Have your daughter do increasing amounts of job shadowing where she observes people at work in her future career field.*

As she does this, have her constantly look for ways to turn those shadowing experiences into ongoing volunteer opportunities. Volunteering to help (with even the most menial tasks) will give her opportunity to work with and learn from people doing the exact job she might be doing some day. This can give her a tremendous edge when it comes to future scholarship applications, college internship applications, and even job applications after college. For a reminder of how to set up job shadowing that leads to volunteering, see chapter 16 of this book.

[5] *If your son has applied to any colleges he's not yet visited, choose dates to visit those colleges soon.*

Try to schedule these college visits on days when the college he's looking at *does* have regular classes going on, but your son's high school doesn't.

Remember, it's foolish for your son to enroll at a college he's not yet visited. Transferring from one college to another is always expensive, so we want to be as certain as possible that he will love the first college he enrolls at and want to stay there straight through college graduation. An in-person college visit greatly enhances this possibility.

> **REMEMBER, IT'S FOOLISH FOR YOUR SON TO ENROLL AT A COLLEGE HE'S NOT YET VISITED.**

For a reminder on what to do, look for, and ask on college visits, see chapter 15 of this book.

[6] *Parent, if you haven't done so yet, get the Evernote app on your smartphone. Start using it to keep track of every penny you pay for college-related expenses.*

I suggest that each parent and stepparent set up a dedicated Evernote notebook just for recording college-related expenses. If you have multiple children, create a separate college expense notebook in Evernote for each of them.

If you write a check to cover a college-related expense, make an entry in this notebook that includes a photo of the check. If you buy something online, make an entry in this notebook that includes a screenshot of the payment screen. If you get a paper receipt from Walgreens or Target, circle the college-related expenses on it and attach a photo of that receipt to an Evernote entry. Ask your high school senior daughter to do the same.

It's especially important to keep careful records of the college-related expenses you pay starting January 1 of your child's senior year of high school. Continue doing this until your youngest child graduates from college. This is for two reasons. First, money you withdraw from a 529 savings plan can only be used for college-related expenses. This strategy provides proof of where that money went. Second, there are tax advantages available to parents who pay certain college expenses. A good tax preparer can help you make sure you're benefitting from all of these tax advantages, but only if you have good records on everything you've spent.

[7] *Your child may receive some college acceptances and financial aid packages during this time period. If this happens, jump ahead and take a sneak peek at chapter 26.*

Once you've read chapter 26, set these acceptances and financial aid packages aside. Make a firm commitment that your family won't make any college decisions until you can carefully examine the financial aid packages from all of the colleges that have accepted your child. Only then will you be able to examine the packages side-by-side and make the best possible financial decisions for your child's future.

CHECKLIST

November–December of 12th Grade

☐ 1. Check to be sure that all letters of recommendation were actually sent in as expected.

☐ 2. Touch base with your daughter about how she's doing with organizing a project to help the humanitarian cause she's adopted as her own.

☐ 3. Encourage your son to continue with that one special extracurricular activity he's going to stick with throughout all four years of high school.

☐ 4. Encourage your daughter to do increasing amounts of job shadowing where she observes people at work in her future career field.

☐ 5. If your son has applied to any colleges he's not yet visited, choose dates to visit those colleges soon.

☐ 6. If you haven't done so already, get the Evernote app and start using it to keep track of every penny you pay for college-related expenses.

☐ 7. Your child may receive some college acceptances and financial aid packages during this time period. If this happens, jump ahead and take a sneak peek at chapter 26, and then set this acceptance paperwork aside.

☐ 8. Check my book updates page at JeannieBurlowski.com/LAUNCH to see if I have made any recent updates to this chapter.

☐ 9. Always consult your financial planning professional before making any big financial decisions.

☐ 10. Make a note in your calendar to come back and read the next chapter of this book when your child is in early January of 12th grade.

Be the first to hear about updates to the material in this book by reading my free weekly email newsletter every week. Anyone can subscribe to it at any time at JeannieBurlowski.com.

25 | *Early January of 12th Grade*

In the beginning of January this year, you might hear some people mentioning books or websites that talk about filling out the FAFSA form on or soon after January 1.

"What?" you'll think. "We did that already. Did we do it too early?"

Don't worry. The people, books, and websites you find talking about January 1 FAFSA submission dates are using outdated information. On September 13, 2015, President Obama changed the earliest FAFSA submission date to October 1. If you've been following the step-by-step instructions in this book, you used exactly the right FAFSA timing and exactly the right FAFSA strategy. You're in good shape.

This chapter is another lightweight one. Only three things to do this month. Let's get these three tasks out of the way now, before the real excitement starts to hit your family in February.

HOW TO USE THIS CHAPTER

Start by just reading through this chapter. As you read, don't worry about committing to any of it. Decision time will come at the very end of this chapter, when I give you a clear, at-a-glance checklist of every task I'm suggesting you consider right now.

Remember, you won't have to use every strategy I suggest; just choose the ones you think will work for your family and either modify or discard the rest.

[1] *Once he knows his first semester senior-year grades, have your son type up a businesslike update letter and send it to the admissions office at each college he's applied to.*

If your son hasn't written a business letter in a while, he can use Google or YouTube to find business letter writing instructions. It will be perfectly OK for him to write just one update letter and then simply change the inside address for each school.

In this letter, your son can let the colleges know about any noteworthy academic achievements he's had recently, as well as all the continued volunteer work, job shadowing, and focused extracurricular involvement he's completed since the last time they heard from him three to seven months ago. This letter will likely arrive at the college just as important admissions and financial aid decisions are being made—and could potentially tip important decisions in your son's favor.

Only a tiny fraction of college applicants are going to think to do this, so it has the potential to give your son or daughter a significant edge.

When the letter is complete, it should be printed, signed, folded into a business-sized envelope, and sent straight to the director of admissions (you can get his or her name off of the college's website) in care of the college's admissions office.

Is there a chance that the director of admissions may never see this letter? Yes. Somebody, though, will see it, read it, tuck it into your son's file, and possibly mention it to others. Can you imagine the meeting of the admissions committee where your son's name is on the table, and one of the committee members says, "Oh, the Banks kid? We got a letter from him yesterday. He and six of his friends ran a half marathon in November and raised $5,000 for clean water in Haiti."

> **ONLY A TINY FRACTION OF COLLEGE APPLICANTS ARE GOING TO THINK TO DO THIS, SO IT HAS THE POTENTIAL TO GIVE YOUR SON OR DAUGHTER A SIGNIFICANT EDGE.**

Here's our ultimate goal: we want to make the admissions committee at this college so excited to have your son that they call up the financial aid office in the next building over and say, "Hey. Guys. Do *whatever you have to do* to get this kid here." This kind of thing happens all the time. And it can happen to your child.

[2] *If your child has applied for an ROTC scholarship, be aware that all required ROTC paperwork must be properly signed and submitted by February 28, six months before the start of college.*

This is a good time to make sure that every ROTC scholarship requirement has been met and every necessary paper properly turned in.

[3] *Start now to plan a special family vacation for the summer after your child graduates from high school.*

This doesn't have to be expensive. A huge life change is coming for all of you; be intentional now about building beautiful family memories of this time of life while you still can. Close, warm family memories will give your high school graduate a stable platform from which to launch into adult life.

CHECKLIST

Early January of 12th Grade

1. Have your child write and send an update letter to the admissions office at each college she's applied to.

2. If your child has applied for an ROTC scholarship, be aware that all required ROTC paperwork must be properly signed and submitted by February 28, six months before the start of college.

3. Plan a special family vacation to take place during the summer after high school graduation.

4. Check my book updates page at JeannieBurlowski.com/LAUNCH to see if I have made any recent updates to this chapter.

5. Always consult your financial planning professional before making any big financial decisions.

6. Make a note in your calendar to come back and read the next chapter of this book on February 1 when your child is in 12th grade.

Be the first to hear about updates to the material in this book by reading my free weekly email newsletter every week. Anyone can subscribe to it at any time at JeannieBurlowski.com.

26 | *February 1 to Early April of 12th Grade*

Hold on tight; this is the two-month period where the big financial decisions are made.

HOW TO USE THIS CHAPTER

Plan to read this chapter *twice.* Your first time through, don't worry about committing to any of it. Your second time through, complete the steps I suggest *as you read the content below.* I will still include a checklist at the end of this chapter, but I hope that by the time you get to the checklist, you will have already completed nearly everything on it.

And if you don't want to complete all the steps I suggest below? That's OK. As always, just choose the strategies you think will work for your family and either modify or discard the rest.

[1] *College acceptance letters will start arriving any time now, but don't let anyone publicly announce where your child is going until all the financial aid award letters have also arrived.*

Colleges vary as to when they send out offers of admission. Some send out offers as early as February 1; others send them out in late March or early April. The season of receiving college acceptance letters can be a scary time for parents because three things are happening all at the same time: the child is jumping up and down with excitement and calling everyone with the news, colleges are asking for a nonrefundable deposit to save the child's spot, and you as a parent have no idea what specific financial aid package each school is offering or how they all compare.

I understand that getting an acceptance

letter from a dream school is unbelievably exciting, but I strongly recommend that you and your daughter agree to keep acceptances confidential and quiet until final decisions have been made about where she's actually going.

Why do I say this? It can be emotionally difficult for your daughter if she's already called her grandparents, told all her friends at school, and plastered social media with the news that she's going to a certain college, only to find out a few weeks later that the college's financial aid package was so disappointing that she's not able to go there after all. Some parents have felt so terrible saying, "No way, Honey; that college isn't practical" to a teen after the news has gotten out that they've gone ahead and said yes to a college they couldn't afford, resulting in years of heartbreaking student loan debt for their child. *Don't let this happen to your child.*

When final college decisions have been made, *then* your daughter can feel free to tell everyone: "I got into ____, ____, ____, and _____, but I've decided to go to ____ because _____. I'm really excited for next fall!"

In most cases, a financial aid award letter will arrive shortly after each offer of admission. I strongly suggest that your family not make any final college decisions until you've received financial aid award letters from *all* of your child's accepting colleges and carefully examined them both individually *and* side by side.

Your family has until about May 1 to decide which colleges are coming in at the lowest net price, make the big decision on which college your child will actually attend, and send in the required deposit.

> **I STRONGLY RECOMMEND THAT YOU AND YOUR DAUGHTER AGREE TO KEEP ACCEPTANCES CONFIDENTIAL AND QUIET UNTIL FINAL DECISIONS HAVE BEEN MADE ABOUT WHERE SHE'S ACTUALLY GOING.**

WHAT TO DO ABOUT BEING "WAIT-LISTED"

Your daughter may be notified that she has been wait-listed at one or more of the colleges she applied to. Wait-listed means that the college would love to have her, but they only have so many available seats, and all those seats have been offered to others. If one of the students who has been officially accepted to that college declines to attend, that will open up a seat and make room for a student who's been sitting on the waiting list.

According to the National Association for College Admission Counseling (NACAC), approximately 30 percent of wait-listed students do end up being accepted to colleges that have wait-listed them.[34] The *problem* with being admitted to a college from a waiting list, though, is that the admission usually includes little to no need-based financial aid

---

34 "Waitlisted? Now What!," CollegeData, accessed November 19, 2016, http://www.collegedata.com/cs/content/content_getinarticle_tmpl.jhtml?articleId=10140.

or merit aid. Why is this? Because the college had a limited pool of financial aid and merit aid money to hand out, and all that money was offered to students who were accepted right off the bat.

If your daughter has been placed on a college's waiting list, I suggest she set that college aside temporarily. Help her use the strategies in this chapter to compare all the financial aid awards from all the colleges that *have* accepted her, and have her choose one of those colleges to attend. (If you need a reminder of why choosing one of these colleges won't hurt her future one bit, reread chapter 2 of this book.) Once your daughter has settled on one of these accepting schools, she can come back to the colleges that have wait-listed her and ask herself, "If I were to suddenly get notice this coming July that I have been admitted to this college from its waiting list but would get *zero* financial aid or merit aid to attend, would I accept that offer?"

If her answer is no—she would not attend after being accepted from the waiting list—I recommend that your daughter ask to have her name removed from that college's waiting list in order to make room for other students.

If, however, her answer is, "*Yes*, I would definitely accept admission at this college that's wait-listed me, even if I received zero financial aid or merit aid to help me pay for it," have her read chapter 27 of this book carefully. I will have additional waiting list strategies for her there.

In sum, for now, set the wait-listing schools aside. Concentrate on analyzing the financial aid packages of the colleges that *have* accepted her as I suggest in this chapter.

[2] *When exciting college acceptance letters start to come in, use the leverage you have right then to get your daughter to read a whole book on how to succeed in college.*

The day after your child opens that first college acceptance letter, when she's still very excited, casually ask her, "They want a $475 deposit to hold your spot at Emory. It's due on May 1, which is about __ weeks from now. Who are you thinking is going to pay that deposit?"

Your daughter will stand there, stricken, scrambling to think of a way to make you think that it's your duty as a parent to pay that $475 deposit.

> **HERE'S MY OFFER TO YOU, HONEY. IF YOU'LL READ AN ENTIRE BOOK ON HOW TO SUCCEED IN COLLEGE AND THEN ACE THE ORAL QUIZ I'LL GIVE YOU ON THE MATERIAL, I'LL PAY THAT $475 DEPOSIT FOR YOU ON MAY 1.**

Let her squirm and think about this for as long as you can stand it, and then casually say, "Tell you what. I'm glad to chip in for a few college expenses if I know you're really driven and serious about succeeding at it. Here's my offer to you, Honey. If you'll read an entire book on how to succeed in college and then ace the oral quiz I'll give you on the material, I'll pay that $475 deposit for you on

May 1. You've got ___ weeks to finish the book and take my oral quiz. How does this sound to you?"

(Parents, my book for students is entitled *FLY: The 6 Things You Absolutely Must Do to Be Brilliant in College and Get a Job You Love Afterward.* You can find more information on it in my free weekly email newsletter.)

[3] *Go over each financial aid award letter very carefully.*

Colleges use financial aid award letters to notify students and their families about the types, amounts, and sources of financial aid that they are willing to make available to a particular student. This collection of financial aid is often referred to as a "financial aid package."

Read each award letter carefully. Award letters may also include an estimation of the college's Cost of Attendance (COA), your Expected Family Contribution (EFC), how much of your need the award will cover, and other information about your financial need as determined by the college. Each award letter will also likely include information on the deadline for accepting the aid, requests for additional documentation that you will be required to submit, an explanation of when and how the money will be disbursed, the academic period the award will cover, and the process for declining or accepting the aid.

When you receive each financial aid award letter, check to see whether you are required to return a signed copy of it to the college's financial aid office. Some colleges will require you to sign and return the letter

within a specified time. For colleges requiring that, sign the award letter and turn in any additional requested materials by the deadline. Completing this step does not commit your child to attending this college, but neglecting to do so could jeopardize him receiving the financial aid if he does decide to attend there.

Some colleges use secure online portals for delivering financial aid award letters instead of sending them by mail. Log-in information may have been sent to your family in your child's acceptance letter packet.

If you have not received a financial aid award letter by mid-April, call the college's financial aid office and ask about it.

[4] *Use the following strategies to figure out which college is offering your son the best deal.*

I wish that evaluating financial aid packages were easy, but the process is tricky because financial aid packages aren't standardized. In some cases, a college may offer your child what looks like a sweet deal—thousands of dollars in free money financial aid to help pay for college—but when you look closely at the figures, you realize that even with that large amount of financial aid, you're still left with thousands of dollars coming out of your family pocketbook in the form of cash payments and student loans.

Your goal is to calculate what attending each college is *actually* going to cost in the long run. In the rest of this chapter, I'm going to help you to figure that out.

The first step is for you to determine, "What would be the *total cost* for my kid to attend this college for one year?"

START WITH THE STICKER PRICE

The college makes a stab at providing you a sticker price by coming up with an average Cost of Attendance (COA) figure that supposedly applies to the majority of students enrolling. The *problem* is that this figure may not accurately reflect your child's individual situation.

Your child's Cost of Attendance (COA) may be higher than the college has estimated if

» your child will be living and eating on campus, but the college has not included room and board costs;

» your child will need to buy plane tickets to get home for Christmas and summer breaks, but the college has only calculated local area bus fares into its transportation allowance;

» your child is required to pay certain extra fees or make certain extra purchases for being involved in a certain major, art, or sport, but the college has not allowed for these expenses;

» your child has been using a family computer throughout high school and will need to buy a computer and printer to take to college. This cost may or may not have been included in the "other expenses" that the college calculates; or

» your child has extra costs related to a disability, and those costs have not been included.

If you have reason to believe that your child's cost to attend this particular college will exceed the Cost of Attendance (COA) listed in her award letter, contact the financial aid office to politely explain and discuss a possible adjustment. The financial aid office has the authority to increase the Cost of Attendance (COA) for your particular situation, which will increase your family's financial need. If your family's financial need turns out to be higher than first thought, and if the college has some additional financial aid available, this could increase your aid package and make the college more affordable.

Once you know your child's actual Cost of Attendance (COA) for this school, do the math so that you are looking at your child's total cost *per year*. (You'll need this figure for later.) Don't worry if your child's total cost per year looks astronomically high. The figure provided to you by the college only tells *part* of the cost story. In the next few pages, I'm going to help you to bring this number way, way down.

[5] *To figure out the true cost of a college for your particular family, reach out to its financial aid office and find out the answers to the following questions.*

Some financial aid award letters contain a "frequently asked questions" section or link that will answer these questions before you even ask them. If this college doesn't offer that, then call and ask the following questions of a financial aid office staff member.

Write down the answers you receive and the name of the person you speak to on a sheet of paper, and then attach that sheet of paper to your copy of the college's financial aid award letter.

> **DON'T WORRY IF YOUR CHILD'S TOTAL COST PER YEAR LOOKS ASTRONOMICALLY HIGH. THE FIGURE PROVIDED TO YOU BY THE COLLEGE ONLY TELLS** *PART* **OF THE COST STORY.**

Question #1 for the financial aid office: "I see that you're recommending that our son take out $8,000 in student loans each year. If he applies for and wins private scholarships while he's in college, will those scholarships decrease this loan amount, or will you use that scholarship money to reduce the free money financial aid you've offered him?"

You may have asked this question of this college before, but ask again now, just in case the college's policy has changed. If this financial aid office *does* use private scholarship money to reduce its free money gift aid rather than to decrease students' future debt burdens, that may be enough to knock this college off of your list of prospects.

Question #2 for the financial aid office: "The financial aid I'm seeing on this award letter—that's renewable for all four years, right? My daughter isn't going to get these grants only just this year, and then be surprised by doubled college costs when she's a

sophomore, correct?"

Question #3 for the financial aid office: "How much do college costs usually increase per year? I know that we reapply for financial aid every year. If our income and assets stay the same, will our free money gift aid increase each year to cover these extra costs? Will I need to call you each year and ask about that?"

Question #4 for the financial aid office: "One of our daughter's financial aid awards is a work-study grant. How many hours will she be required to work each semester in order to earn the full work-study award she's been offered? How much money will she be paid per hour when she does this work? Does she give her paycheck to the college, or can she keep the money to pay for things like tape and printer ink? Are work-study jobs readily available, or are they hard to get? Do you have a web address where we could go to look at the types of work-study jobs available at your college? How soon can our daughter apply for a work-study job that looks good to her?"

I suggest that students apply for their college work-study jobs as soon after deciding on a college as that college will allow. A student who does this has the best chance of getting the work-study job he or she most wants. In the best possible scenario, this would be a work-study job that somehow connects to his or her *future career goal.* (Want to be a librarian some day? Try to get a work-study job in the college library. Want to run a food service company someday? Try to get a work-study job in the college cafeteria.) That's not always possible, but it's worth thinking about.

For a review of how high school students can start to zero in on career goal before ever starting college, see chapter 13 of this book.

Question #5 for the financial aid office: "What will my daughter be required to do to keep the grants and scholarships you're awarding her? Does she need to maintain a certain minimum GPA? Does she need to take a particular number of credits per semester? Does she need to complete any certain tasks, such as community service? How does she report that when she completes it?"

Question #6 for the financial aid office: "We are trying to pay cash for college. Is there a way that I can apply for a budget plan that will allow me to stretch out our family's share of the college costs over the 10 months of each academic year, so I won't have to pay the cash we owe all in one lump sum on the first day of each school year?"

Question #7 for the financial aid office at an out-of-state state university: "You're a state-funded institution, and we're from outside your state. Are there any additional reciprocity, consortium, or other programs we could apply to that would bring our son's tuition down further at your school? Are there special steps we would need to take each year to stay in one of those programs? If we were to consider moving to your state, what residency requirements would we need to meet in order to qualify for reduced-cost, in-state tuition at your university?"

> **WANT TO BE A LIBRARIAN SOME DAY? TRY TO GET A WORK-STUDY JOB IN THE COLLEGE LIBRARY. WANT TO RUN A FOOD SERVICE COMPANY SOMEDAY? TRY TO GET A WORK-STUDY JOB IN THE COLLEGE CAFETERIA.**

Question #8 for the financial aid office: "Are there any Parent PLUS Loans included in my child's financial aid package?" Wait for the answer. If the response is yes, then say, "I am not willing to take out any Parent PLUS Loans. What alternatives does my child have?"

Mom and Dad, a Parent PLUS Loan is a student loan that you, the parent, are expected to pay back in full, with interest. Even if your child does not succeed in college, refuses to finish her degree, and does not ever find a job in her field, you will still be liable for full Parent PLUS Loan amounts, including all interest and penalties, whether you can afford the payments or not.

Your child may earnestly promise to help you with your future Parent PLUS Loan payments, and she *may* actually come through on that promise, but don't plan on ever being able to officially transfer a Parent PLUS Loan into your child's name. If you do so, you'll forever forfeit the few special protections that a Parent PLUS

Loan can provide (such as possible lower payment options, public service loan forgiveness, and deferments).

Friends of mine in the student loan servicing industry have asked me to warn you: be extremely careful when it comes to Parent PLUS Loans. They've led some parents into heartbreaking financial disaster, right at a time when they were hoping to (or worse, needing to) retire.

Be especially wary if you hear anyone say to you, "Oh, just go ahead and accept this bundle of loans. Yes, there's a Parent PLUS Loan in the package, but you probably won't qualify for that one. So don't worry." I suggest that you say a firm no to this, and ask that the bundle of loans be restructured without the Parent PLUS Loans in there.

> **FRIENDS OF MINE IN THE STUDENT LOAN SERVICING INDUSTRY HAVE ASKED ME TO WARN YOU: BE EXTREMELY WARY OF PARENT PLUS LOANS. THEY'VE LED SOME PARENTS INTO HEARTBREAKING FINANCIAL DISASTER.**

The truth is that unless you have some enormous red flags on your credit record, you probably *will* qualify for Parent PLUS Loans even if you have no income to pay them back. Why is this? Because, astoundingly, your personal income is not even a consideration when the decision is made to give you Parent PLUS Loan money, and there are *no limits* to the amount of this loan money you can be given and asked

to pay back. This means you could be a poor widow barely getting by on $1,100 per month, and you could still be awarded Parent PLUS Loans that require you to make loan payments of $1,000 per month for *10 years*. And if you can't pay? If you default? You could be slammed with massive penalties that make the debt load even more unbearable.

This has happened to other people. Don't let it happen to you.

If you do decide, against all my pleading, to take out a Parent PLUS Loan, be sure to take it out in the name of your child's parent who has the highest annual income. There have been cases where a stay-at-home mom filled out the paperwork for the Parent PLUS Loan because she happened to have time in the afternoon on the day it was due. Her medical doctor husband subsequently died, and she was left with impossible-to-pay loan payments because all the paperwork was in her name.

> **YOU COULD BE A POOR WIDOW BARELY GETTING BY ON $1,100 PER MONTH, AND YOU COULD STILL BE AWARDED PARENT PLUS LOANS THAT REQUIRE YOU TO MAKE LOAN PAYMENTS OF $1,000 PER MONTH FOR** *10 YEARS.*

If you'd like to figure out whether your household budget will be able to handle the payments on the Parent PLUS Loans the financial aid package is suggesting for you, you can estimate that you'll be paying about

$120 a month for 10 years for every $10,000 you borrow. Multiply that by the number of years your child will likely be in college and by the number of children you have. If you borrow $10,000 per year and have two children interested in four-year degrees, you will likely be making loan payments of almost $1,000 per month for 10 years. How will you feel if you've done this and your child doesn't complete college, or doesn't get a decent job in his field after he graduates? How old will you be when that 10 years is up? How might this interfere with you saving for your retirement?

Do the math. You might decide that asking your child to take his first two years at a community college while living at home beats taking out Parent PLUS Loans hands down.

> **HOW WILL YOU FEEL IF YOU'VE DONE THIS AND YOUR CHILD DOESN'T COMPLETE COLLEGE, OR DOESN'T GET A DECENT JOB IN HIS FIELD AFTER HE GRADUATES? HOW OLD WILL YOU BE WHEN THAT 10 YEARS IS UP?**

If you're told that Parent PLUS Loans are absolutely unavoidable at this college, keep reading this chapter. There might still be a way for you to sidestep them.

[6] *If your daughter has completed any amount of college credit during high school, call each college's registrar's office and ask for an Articulation of Transfer Agreement.*

Pose your question this way: "Our daughter has already passed a few CLEP tests, done some AP work, and completed other actual college coursework in high school. Before she accepts your school's offer of admission, we need to know for sure how many of the college credits she's earned so far are going to transfer to your university. Can you provide us an Articulation of Transfer Agreement, along with a statement of how many more credits our daughter will need to complete at your college in order to earn a bachelor's degree? How soon could we get that from you?"

The Articulation of Transfer Agreement is an official written agreement that explains exactly which of the credits your child has already earned will transfer to this college. Taking this step is important, because if a college decides not to accept credits that your son has worked hard to earn, that action may instantly remove this college from the list of schools your son is seriously considering attending.

[7] *Take careful note of how much longer your son will need to attend each college in order to earn a bachelor's degree.*

Does the amount of college credit your son earned in high school knock an entire year off of the time it'll take him to earn a four-year degree at this college? If so, you'll only have to plan to cover *three* years of college when you take the next step I prescribe.

Does the amount of college credit your daughter earned in high school knock *two* entire years off of the time it'll take her to earn a four-year bachelor's degree? If so, you'll only have to plan to cover *two* years of college when you take the following step. Whoo-hoo!

[8] *Calculate how much this child's entire remaining bachelor's degree education is likely to cost you at each of the colleges she's been accepted to.*

You already have a clear idea of the total Cost of Attendance (COA) for *one year* at this college for your particular child. (You calculated it in task #4.) Multiply that number by the number of years your child will have to attend this particular college in order to receive a bachelor's degree.

The number you get when you do this is the best estimate we have of the total cost to get your child from where she is right now to her college graduation day at this particular college. Write this number down on the piece of paper you've attached to this college's financial aid award letter.

Now let's start reducing that number.

SUBTRACT ALL THE FREE MONEY THE COLLEGE IS OFFERING

Carefully write down the total cost you just arrived at, and then subtract from it all the free money financial aid, tuition waivers, housing waivers, grants, and merit aid your child is being offered to attend this particular college. If your child will only be attending this college for three years, be sure you're subtracting only three years' worth of this wonderful free gift aid. (For the time being, ignore all the student loans you're being offered.)

If you have any questions about which line items on the financial aid award letter are free money that never needs to be paid back and which line items are loans that must be paid back, call the financial aid office and ask.

The number you get after all this subtraction is the best estimate we have of the total amount that your family will *actually need to pay* (in cash or by taking out loans) to cover the cost of this college education.

Now let's reduce that number *further.*

NOW SUBTRACT EVEN MORE

Now subtract the total amount of all the private scholarships that your daughter has won since she first started applying for them when she was in 8th grade. (Did your daughter receive an ROTC scholarship? Subtract the amount of that scholarship too, unless it was already listed as one of the free money scholarships on your financial aid award letter.)

Now subtract the amount of money that Grandma has spent years squirreling away in a 529 plan in her own name with your child named as beneficiary, if Grandma is willing to share that figure with you. (Just remember not to start using Grandma's 529 money to pay college expenses until January 1 of your child's sophomore year of college. That's the point at which her generous gift can no longer hurt your child's financial aid eligibility.) See chapter 3 of this book if you need a reminder of how to have a great conversation with grandparents on this subject early in your child's life.

Now subtract all the money you've saved up over the past 18 years in your Upromise.com account. (For a reminder of how Upromise.com works, see chapter 3.)

Now subtract all the money you've saved for your daughter in a state-sponsored 529 plan or in other accounts.

The number that remains is the actual (net) out-of-pocket, bottom-line amount that your family must find, earn, or borrow to cover the cost for this child to attend this college.

Write this new number down on the piece of paper you've attached to this college's financial aid award letter. Label it: "*Here's what we still need to come up with.*"

[9] Think: "How much would it cost our family each month if we were to pay all the remaining costs for this college right out of our own pocket?"

To figure out how much this would be, divide your "*Here's what we still need to come up with*" number by the number of months between now and your child's projected college graduation date.

The figure you get as a result is how much you and your child (she's going to work part-time through her college years too) will have to cover *each month* in order for her to graduate from this particular college debt-free.

For families who've been following the instructions in this book since their child was in middle school, this number might be less than zero.

But even if you still have to pay $17,000 more in total to cover this child's college costs, let's look at what you could do about that. If she'll be graduating from college 39 months from now, you can still set a goal of somehow finding the cash to cover the approximately $436 per month you'll need to pay off that entire amount before she graduates from college. As you think about this, think beyond just the income you get from working. Could you manage this if you do something creative, like renting out your daughter's childhood bedroom to another student who's attending college near your house?

Whatever the monthly payment amount you've just come up with is, carefully write it down in two places: (1) on the piece of paper you've attached to this college's financial aid award letter and (2) on the informal scrapbook page you made for this college when you visited college campuses during 10th, 11th, and 12th grades. Write the number in thick red marker. Circle it. Label it: "*Here's what we'd need to pay each month to get Emily through debt-free.*" This is the best estimate we have of the actual (net) out-of-pocket amount you and your daughter will have to pay to get her through this college with zero student loan debt.

Does this amount still seem insurmountable to you? Does it look as though despite everything you've done, you're *still* going to have to take out loans to pay for college?

Maybe it's time to politely ask the college to give you some additional free money financial aid.

[10] *If there's a problem with the free money financial aid award your child has received at one or more colleges, use due process to politely ask them to reconsider.*

Every so often, there's a legitimate problem with the financial aid award that a student receives from one or more colleges. Sometimes a mistake was made by the parents when filling out a financial aid form. In other cases, families filled out final versions of their financial aid forms in October of their child's senior year of high school only to have their family fortunes turn suddenly for the worse due to

» the death of a family member,

» a marital separation or divorce,

» a sudden loss of job or lowered income,

» the onset of serious illness or disability,

» sudden overwhelming medical or dental bills,

» a mistake on a tax return that has now been corrected,

» the news of the impending birth of a sibling,

» the sudden need to provide care for an elderly parent or grandparent,

» the sale of a home and subsequent move,

» a sudden increase in child care expenses,

» a change to the number of dependents in a household, or

» siblings suddenly deciding to also attend college.

> **DOES THIS AMOUNT STILL SEEM INSURMOUNTABLE TO YOU? DOES IT LOOK AS THOUGH DESPITE EVERYTHING YOU'VE DONE, YOU'RE *STILL* GOING TO HAVE TO TAKE OUT LOANS TO PAY FOR COLLEGE? MAYBE IT'S TIME TO POLITELY ASK THE COLLEGE TO GIVE YOU SOME ADDITIONAL FREE MONEY FINANCIAL AID.**

Or it could simply be that the least-favorite college your son has been accepted to has given him a fabulous financial aid package, and his first-choice college has given him little or nothing.

In any of these circumstances, it's perfectly acceptable to call the college financial aid office and ask if it would be possible for you to appeal your financial aid award.

Make this call right away, as soon as you realize there's a problem. Almost all schools have a standard process they use for responding to requests like this, and the most favorable responses go to families who appeal early, while colleges still have additional financial aid money left to hand out.

Check for an official outline of the college's financial aid appeal process on its website before you call, and when you do, avoid being confrontational. Just open a conversation about how you and the financial aid office might work together to bring college within reach for your child.

SAMPLE QUESTIONS TO ASK WHEN APPEALING FINANCIAL AID AWARDS

Here are some questions that other parents have asked when appealing financial aid awards:

» "Your school's financial aid award leaves our family with approximately $_____ to pay out of pocket after gift aid and merit aid are subtracted from our daughter's Cost of Attendance. College B, though, has given us enough gift aid and merit aid to reduce that out-of-pocket number down to just $_____. Could I send you college B's award letter, and you see if there's anything you could possibly do to come closer to matching it? Maddi would really like to attend your college if we can find a way to make it financially feasible."

» "We've had some big changes to our family finances since we filed our financial aid forms five months ago. Could you and I talk about these changes, and would you perhaps consider an adjustment to our daughter's financial aid package?"

» "What are our options for receiving more aid?"

» "What can we do to find more scholarships to pay for college?"

» "Who at the college should my son talk to about finding more part-time work in addition to the work-study grant?"

» "Our income during our child's sophomore and junior years of high school looked abnormally high on our financial aid forms because of some unusual income surges that will not be repeated." (This may have been an insurance settlement, inheritance, sales commission, one-time employment bonus, or some other windfall.) "Could you adjust our financial aid award accordingly?"

Parent, if you decide to open an appeal process, be prepared to provide pay stubs, bank statements, medical and dental bills, and other documentation as proof of the change in your circumstances.

Is it worth it to try to appeal a financial aid award in the way I've described? Yes. According to one national study, approximately half of all financial aid appeals result in higher financial aid awards. One student used due process to appeal his financial aid award even though he felt sure he'd probably not get anything more, and he walked away with $30,000 in additional free money financial aid to help pay for college. If you feel you might have a case, definitely follow financial aid office procedure and appeal.

> **ACCORDING TO ONE NATIONAL STUDY, APPROXIMATELY HALF OF ALL FINANCIAL AID APPEALS RESULT IN HIGHER FINANCIAL AID AWARDS.**

[11] *Ask whether your son might get more free money financial aid for college if he were to sit out of college for a year, start over with a new financial aid application next October 1, and attend four-year college at the same time as a younger sibling.*

If you have children in consecutive grades in high school (a boy in 12th grade and a girl in 11th grade, for instance), your older child could tell a four-year college that's accepted him that he'd like to "defer his admission" for one year and begin his studies there 14 months after his high school graduation. Admissions staff will usually happily agree to this. If they want a student this year, they'll want him next year too.

If this older brother will live at home for the 14 months after high school and take as many inexpensive community college courses as possible during that time, he could start at his favorite, more expensive four-year institution the same fall his younger sister begins college. He would likely be able to transfer in enough community college credits to make him at least a college sophomore, and he and his sister could both reap significant financial benefits—since families with two or more children in college at the same time tend to receive far more free money financial aid for college. This is true even if the siblings attend completely different colleges.

Students who choose to do this plan should be careful to check with their future four-year college registrar before enrolling in any community college classes. This will ensure that every community college class taken

during that 14-month period will transfer to the desired four-year college.

[12] *If a college's costs are prohibitive, but your child really wants to attend there, consider having your son turn down the college's dormitory room and board package and instead spend his academic years living with roommates in an off-campus apartment or in a rented room in a private home.*

Before you suggest this, check out apartment, utility, and transportation costs near the campus, figure in the cost of groceries, and call the financial aid office to find out how much this decision might save your family overall.

The college housing office may even be able to direct you to large online listings of apartments and rooms to rent near the campus.

[13] *If you'd like additional help calculating how much college is actually going to cost you, you could try using one of these two online tools provided by the federal government.*

The following tools are designed to help families decode and compare financial aid awards.

The Simple Award Comparison Tool

This tool, available at Finaid.org, compares the financial aid packages of three different colleges, highlighting any significant differences. It also calculates out-of-pocket costs and estimates the lifetime cost of any educational loans. To get directly to the page where this tool is located, type this shortcut into your web browser: Mnstr.me/2ftrBdm.

The Advanced Award Comparison Tool

This tool, also available at Finaid.org, is somewhat like the Simple Award Letter Comparison Tool, except that it includes some nonfinancial criteria as well when comparing colleges. To get directly to the page where this tool is located, type this shortcut into your web browser: Mnstr.me/2fF5LPD.

[14] *If you feel that taking out student loans is truly the only option you have left, try very hard to take out only loans that allow the future possibility of public service loan forgiveness (PSLF).*

Forget private loans and other kinds of unsubsidized student loans. There's currently only one main loan that allows for PSLF: a Federal Direct Student Loan administered under the William D. Ford Federal Direct Loan (Direct Loan) Program.

This detail is critically important for you as a borrowing family, so let's get the facts on this straight from the authorities at Studentaid.ed.gov:

> A qualifying loan for PSLF is any loan you received under the William D. Ford Federal Direct Loan (Direct Loan) Program. You may have received loans under other federal student loan programs, such as the Federal Family Education Loan

(FFEL) Program or the Federal Perkins Loan (Perkins Loan) Program. Loans from these programs do not qualify for PSLF, but they may become eligible if you consolidate them into a Direct Consolidation Loan.[35]

An additional benefit of these Federal Direct Student Loans (and other federally subsidized student loans) is that these loans have lower interest rates, plus the federal government will pay the interest that accrues on the loan balances while the student is in college.

Note that the only way to get William D. Ford Federal Direct Loans (or any other federally subsidized student loans) is to properly fill out the FAFSA form each and every year.

[15] *Understand why preserving the possibility of future PSLF is so important.*

If your daughter takes out only Federal Direct Student Loans that qualify for PSLF, she'll have the option of having all of her student loans forgiven just 10 years after college—in exchange for making 120 modest, on-time student loan payments while working 30 hours a week or more in a profession that serves the community or the world.

This might mean that for 10 years after college, your daughter works as an EMT, a police officer, a firefighter, a military enlistee, a teacher in a public school, or a public librarian. It might mean that she works for a tax-exempt charity, takes a job on a military base as a

---

35 "Which Types of Federal Student Loans Qualify for PSLF?," Federal Student Aid, accessed September 24, 2016, https://studentaid.ed.gov/sa/repay-loans/forgiveness-cancellation/public-service.

civilian, works a government job at any level, or takes one of hundreds of other paying community service jobs that qualify for PSLF.

Your daughter won't be *obligated* to spend 10 years in one of these careers, mind you, but she'll have the *option* to if she suddenly decides at age 22 that she wants to do whatever is necessary to get a burdensome amount of student loan debt forgiven and off her back. This is the option that you as a parent are trying very hard to protect for her right now.

Honestly, I hope your daughter never needs PSLF. I hope that the help I've given your family makes it possible for her to graduate college completely debt-free and move directly into a career she excels at and loves. But just in case she makes any inadvisable decisions along the way, let's protect PSLF as a possible option for her.

[16] *Do not, under any circumstances, take out even one private student loan.*

I cannot begin to tell you how horrifically destructive private student loans can be to a student's financial future. If you feel convinced that there's absolutely no way for your child to attend college without borrowing, then borrow *only* under federally subsidized student loan programs.

If your son hits a ceiling where he isn't allowed to take out any more federal student loans, then the best plan for him is to stop attending college altogether or enroll in a less expensive college. Or do as my friend David did: he worked his way through college by working two and three jobs and saving money for an entire year, and then

working part-time while going to college for a year. He repeated this cycle four times over eight years until, at age 26, he had a college degree with no odious private loans to pay back.

> **IF YOU FEEL CONVINCED THAT THERE'S ABSOLUTELY NO WAY FOR YOUR CHILD TO ATTEND COLLEGE WITHOUT BORROWING, THEN BORROW** *ONLY* **UNDER FEDERALLY SUBSIDIZED STUDENT LOAN PROGRAMS.**

[17] *If your daughter does take out any student loans, encourage her to get rid of them all before her college graduation date by applying for more private scholarships.*

If your daughter feels that she absolutely *has* to take out student loans to pay for college, please remember that students can apply for additional private scholarships throughout their college years. Have her continue applying for 10 scholarships each summer, all the way through the completion of graduate school. In many cases, scholarship winnings can be used to pay off student loan balances if the student is still enrolled in college at the time she wins them.

Remind your daughter that my two-hour class on how to write brilliant scholarship application essays is called *Make Them Say Wow*. It'll help her write one main scholarship application essay that she can tweak and use over and over again. You can access this class (either live or in recorded form) by reading my free weekly email newsletter.

[18] *Instruct your son to carefully guard his student loan money, using it only for tuition.*

Warn your child over and over again that loan money is to be used *only* for college tuition and *never* for a fancier apartment, for spring break vacations, for buying cars, or for buying a celebratory round of beer for everyone in a bar.

> AND THE $4 COFFEE SHOP LATTE THAT'S A MUST-HAVE FOR STARTING EACH DAY? THAT'LL ADD UP TO $5,824 OVER FOUR YEARS (TIME TO SHOP AT A THRIFT STORE FOR A COFFEEMAKER).

Impress upon your son that every time he's tempted to whip out a credit card or spend student loan money on something other than college tuition, he should ask himself, "Would I buy this right now if it were twice the price?" Every $1 of credit card or student loan money spent will cost approximately $2 by the time the student pays back the loan, given typical interest rates and repayment terms. Emphasize to your child that spending just $20 extra a week on restaurant food, entertainment, or impulse items can cost a college student more than $3,000 by graduation. And the $4 coffee shop latte that's a must-have for starting each day? That'll add up to $5,824 over four years (time to shop at a thrift store for a coffeemaker).

[19] *Just so she's aware for the future, let your daughter know about the emergency grants (such as Scholarship America Dreamkeepers grants) that may be available to her through her college financial aid office.*

If your daughter someday faces an unforeseen financial emergency that threatens her being able to continue in college, a short-term grant may provide her with financial help to get through the emergency, as well as additional resources and student services such as financial literacy materials designed to help students develop long-term money management skills.

The financial aid office at your daughter's college or university can help her find and apply for short-term emergency grant money if necessary.

[20] *Look over the informal scrapbook you made of all the notes and photos you took on all your college visits. Look closely at the monthly costs you've circled with a thick red marker for each college.*

Let these things guide you as you and your child talk through final college decisions.

If you find your daughter insisting that she absolutely *must* attend the most exorbitantly expensive college she's been accepted to because "it's her dream school," consider using a strategy other parents have used with great success: place a cap on how much you as parents will pay for a bachelor's degree. "We'll give you $_____, Tiffany, that's it. It's your job to make that money stretch to cover all the years of college you have left. Why don't you take some time to think about this, and get back to us with your decision when you're ready?"

> **IF YOU FIND YOUR DAUGHTER INSISTING THAT SHE ABSOLUTELY *MUST* ATTEND THE MOST EXORBITANTLY EXPENSIVE COLLEGE SHE'S BEEN ACCEPTED TO BECAUSE "IT'S HER DREAM SCHOOL," CONSIDER USING A STRATEGY OTHER PARENTS HAVE USED WITH GREAT SUCCESS: PLACE A CAP ON HOW MUCH YOU AS PARENTS WILL PAY FOR A BACHELOR'S DEGREE.**

[21] *If your family truly can't afford four-year college without loans, I strongly suggest that your son start off in community college. It won't hurt his life one bit.*

I include the previous information about loans only very reluctantly. The far better strategy I recommend is this: if your family can't afford to pay the monthly payment on your son's four-year college costs without taking out loans, have your son choose the four-year college he'll eventually attend and then call that college's admission's office and say, "Thanks for admitting me, but with your permission, I'd like to defer my admission for a year or two. I'm going to complete all the community college courses I possibly can before I come." Most colleges will be glad to hold your son's spot until he can get there, so he won't have to go through the whole college application process all over again.

Then, for the next 18 months, your son can

live at home under your family's rules, work for money, and earn as many community college credits as possible—even attending community college classes straight through summer breaks. As he does this, be sure to have him check with his four-year college registrar each semester so he can be sure that every community college class he takes will fill a necessary spot on his degree plan at that institution.

If you need reassurance that community college will not damage your son's future professional life in any way—even if he is an elite, gifted high achiever—please reread chapter 2 of this book.

Your son can shorten his time in community college and get out even faster by preparing for and taking CLEP and DSST tests to earn credit-by-examination credit starting as soon as possible. (For a reminder of how to prepare for and take CLEP and DSST tests starting as early as 7th grade, see chapter 9 of this book.)

This community college strategy will work for students of any ability level, but it works *especially* well for a student who was an underachiever in high school. Many students are thrilled to find out that if they work hard in community college and do well there academically, their high school grades will be wiped from the record and forgotten. The four-year college your son is longing to attend may take one look at his great grades in community college and offer him a generous free money merit scholarship (one not dependent on financial need) to attend that four-year college as a junior and senior. After all, many (30 percent or more) of the eager young 18-year-olds who excitedly started at this four-year college as freshmen will have dropped out by then, so the admissions office will have spaces it's eager to fill with quality students who've proven themselves in community college.

If your son chooses this community college option, the only name that will appear on his bachelor's degree and on his résumé after he graduates from college will be the name of the four-year college he loves.

For a reminder of what block transferring is and exactly what steps your son should take if he's transferring from a community college to a four-year college, review chapter 14 of this book.

CHECKLIST

February 1 to Early April of 12th Grade

This chapter's checklist is a long one! Don't let it overwhelm you. Focus your efforts on going through the content in this chapter in a careful, step-by-step manner. When you finish, you'll be able to mark off every item on this checklist very quickly.

☐ 1. College acceptance letters will start arriving any time now, but *don't publicly announce where your child is going* until all of the financial aid award letters have also arrived.

☐ 2. If your child has been wait-listed at any college, use the suggestions in this chapter and in chapter 27 to decide what to do about that waiting list status.

☐ 3. When college acceptance letters start to come in, use the leverage you have right then to get your daughter to read a whole book on how to succeed in college.

☐ 4. Go over each financial aid award letter very carefully.

☐ 5. Use the step-by-step strategies in this chapter to figure out which college is offering your child the best deal.

☐ 6. To figure out the *true cost* of a particular college for your specific family, reach out to the college's financial aid office and ask the questions listed in this chapter. (Some financial aid award letters contain a "frequently asked questions" section or a link that will answer all or some of these questions for you.)

☐ 7. If your daughter has completed any college credit in high school, call each college's registrar's office and ask for an Articulation of Transfer Agreement. (You need to know now whether the college credits your daughter has already earned will transfer to this college or not.)

☐ 8. Take careful note of how much longer your daughter will need to attend each college in order to earn a bachelor's degree. The answer may be different for each college. (If you've played your cards right using the strategies in chapter 9 of this book, it may be just two or three years.)

☐ 9. For each college, take its *total cost* for your particular child, subtract the total amount of all the private scholarships your daughter's won, the amount Grandma's been squirreling away in a 529 plan in her own name with your child named as beneficiary, the amount in your Upromise.com account, and all the money you've saved for your daughter in a state-sponsored 529 plan or in other accounts, and watch the cost get lower and lower and lower.

10. Think, "How much would it cost our family each month if we were to pay all the remaining costs for this college right out of our own pocket?" If you've been following the suggestions in this book since your child was in middle school, your cost might be less than zero.

11. If there's a problem with the amount of free money financial aid your child is receiving from one or more colleges, use due process to politely ask those colleges to reconsider.

12. Ask the financial aid office whether your son might get more free money financial aid for college if he were to sit out of college for a year, start over with a new financial aid application next October 1, and attend college at the same time as a younger sibling.

13. If a college's costs are prohibitive, but your child *really* wants to attend there, consider having your son turn down the college's dormitory room and board package and instead spend his academic years living with roommates in an off-campus apartment or in a rented room in a private home. Check with the financial aid office to see if this would save money or not.

14. If you'd like additional help calculating how much college is actually going to cost your family, try using one of the two federal government online tools provided in this chapter.

15. If you believe that taking out student loans is truly the *only* option you have at this point, try very hard to take out *only* loans that allow the possibility of public service loan forgiveness (PSLF).

16. Understand why preserving the possibility of future PSLF is critically important.

17. Do *not* take out any private student loans. Not even one.

18. If your child takes out any student loans at all, encourage him or her to get rid of them all before college graduation by applying for more private scholarships.

19. Instruct your son to carefully guard his student loan money and use it *only for tuition*.

20. Just so she is aware for the future, let your daughter know that in an emergency, her college's financial aid office may be able to help her access a short-term emergency grant, such as the one mentioned in this chapter.

21. Look over the informal scrapbook you made of all the notes and photos you took on your college visits. Look closely at the monthly costs you've circled in thick red marker for each college. Let these things guide you as you talk through final college decisions.

22. If your daughter insists that she *must* attend an exorbitantly expensive college because "it's her dream school," consider placing a cap on how much you as parents will pay for her bachelor's degree.

23. If it turns out that your family truly can't afford four-year college without loans,

strongly consider having your child start out in community college. As I wrote in chapter 2 of this book, it won't hurt your child's life one bit.

☐ 24. Check my book updates page at JeannieBurlowski.com/LAUNCH to see if I have made any recent updates to this chapter.

☐ 25. Always consult your financial planning professional before making any big financial decisions.

☐ 26. Make a note in your calendar to come back and read the next chapter of this book when your child is in late April of 12th grade.

Be the first to hear about updates to the material in this book by reading my free weekly email newsletter every week. Anyone can subscribe to it at any time at JeannieBurlowski.com.

27 | *Late April of 12th Grade*

ime for a breather.

The chapter you just completed was one of the most complicated, but one of the most rewarding chapters in this entire book. The work you just finished is going to affect your child for decades into the future. It may even affect the lives of your grandchildren and your great-grandchildren. Stop for a moment to fully appreciate that. Give yourself credit. You are doing something truly great here.

Your teen doesn't yet know what a gift this is to him or her, but I do. I thank you wholeheartedly for all you're doing.

If you did not yet complete all the steps in chapter 26, please go back and do those as soon as possible. Your deadline is May 1. If you're ready for just a few more easy tasks right now, read on.

HOW TO USE THIS CHAPTER

Start by just reading through this chapter. As you read, don't worry about committing to any of it. Decision time will come at the very end of this chapter, when I give you a clear, at-a-glance checklist of every task I'm suggesting you consider right now.

Remember, you won't have to use every strategy I suggest; just choose the ones you think will work for your family and either modify or discard the rest.

[1] *Keeping cost factors in mind, have thoughtful family discussions where you as a team make a final decision on where your high school senior will attend college this coming fall.*

Remember, no pressure.

The tired old phrase, "If you don't get into a good college, you won't be able to get a good job when you graduate" is an absolute myth. (For a reminder of why this is true, reread chapter 2 of this book.) Whether your child is heading to community college or to an elite private college this coming fall, it doesn't matter. What matters is (a) the quality career direction he has before he starts, (b) the focused job shadowing and volunteering he does early on and with consistency related to his career field, (c) the paid internships he applies for and works at while he's in college, and (d) the other opportunities he jumps on that make his individual college experience great.

What we want is for your son to approach his future career like a craftsman, using his own personal reading, job shadowing, volunteering, interning, and other activities to *develop his own abilities in his future career field*—from 10th grade all the way through his college years.

> **WHAT WE WANT IS FOR YOUR SON TO APPROACH HIS FUTURE CAREER LIKE A CRAFTSMAN, USING HIS OWN PERSONAL READING, JOB SHADOWING, VOLUNTEERING, INTERNING, AND OTHER ACTIVITIES TO** *DEVELOP HIS OWN ABILITIES IN HIS FUTURE CAREER FIELD*—**FROM 10TH GRADE ALL THE WAY THROUGH HIS COLLEGE YEARS.**

If he does this, the college degree he eventually earns will simply add polish and credential to the greatness your son has been developing on his own for six years or more. Will this make him successful in career and in life regardless of what name is on his college diploma? *Yes.*

When you talk about your daughter's upcoming college experience, express enthusiasm and excitement that your family is doing everything possible to get her through college completely debt-free and then directly into a job she loves afterward. These are far more substantial things to be excited about than a college's fancy brand name, athletic teams, on-campus amenities, or U.S. News and World Report ranking.

[2] *If your son has been wait-listed at a college and still has interest in attending there, despite the probable scarcity of financial aid and merit aid, take the following steps now.*

As a family, make a firm decision on which college your son will attend if the wait-listing school never comes through with an admission offer. Plan to commit to this "Plan B" school on May 1 with its required paperwork and financial deposit. Yes, your son may end up losing this deposit if he's eventually accepted to his favorite school from its waiting list and decides to switch schools in July, but that's the gamble you're going to have to take. Sending the required deposit to an accepting school on May 1 will protect your son's interests by ensuring that he definitely has at least *one* college to attend this coming fall.

Have your son return the card or fill out the online form indicating his interest in remaining on the waiting list at the "Plan A" school.

If your son is hoping to get into a college from its waiting list, you may want to have your family stay quiet about his college decisions until the final verdict is in, later this summer. This will mean no spilling the news to grandparents or friends, and no posting college decisions on social media other than "I got into Skidmore. Not sure yet whether I'm going there or not." It can be embarrassing to a teen to announce one college decision in May and a completely different one in July.

If your son would like to enhance the possibility he'll be plucked from a waiting list and offered admission, have him write a businesslike letter to the school's dean of admissions.

> **IT'S NOT CONSIDERED OK TO SEND REPEATED BEGGING EMAILS, COOKIES, HANDMADE BLANKETS, OR QUIRKY YOUTUBE VIDEOS TO THE ADMISSIONS OFFICE IN HOPES OF BEING ACCEPTED FROM A WAITING LIST.**

This letter should highlight all of your son's most noteworthy achievements, even if they've been mentioned previously, and include details such as recent strong grades, improved standardized test scores if there are any, and any new achievements or interesting experiences. This letter should also express your son's avid interest in the school (including specific details on what he's eager to study there), and the assurance that your son *will definitely attend* if offered admission. "Will definitely attend" is a critically important factor in getting off of a waiting list, since the last thing the college wants to do in July is scramble to locate another student to take your son's seat if he declines an admission offer made

from the waiting list. Your son may also want to include one (and only one) fresh letter of recommendation from a teacher or other adult who can attest to his current levels of accomplishment and this school being an exceptionally good fit for him based on what he wants to study. He may also request an in-person interview with an admissions staff person if he hasn't yet had one.

These are the accepted ways for students to increase their odds of getting off of a college admission waiting list. It's not considered OK to send repeated begging emails, cookies, handmade blankets, or quirky YouTube videos to the admissions office in hopes of being accepted from a waiting list. These things will be seen as more annoying than helpful.

If your son decides at any point that he's no longer interested in a college where he's been wait-listed, have him call and ask to have his name removed from that college's waiting list. Your thoughtful son will be making room for other students who are genuinely eager to attend.

[3] *Have a thoughtful conversation with your child about what's going to happen with her high school graduation gift money.*

This discussion will not be about what your son or daughter "deserves." This discussion will be about what a mature and responsible person does with a windfall.

Explain to your daughter that when unexpected and unearned money comes to her, it's her responsibility to think strategically about how she can invest and use that money to get the greatest good out of it.

Some students, after having this discussion with their parents, decide to put this sign on the slotted box where friends and relatives slide greeting cards filled with money at the high school graduation party:

> *75% of any gift money I receive today is going to further my education.*
>
> *15% is going to the charity I've worked on behalf of for four years, Healing Haiti.*
>
> *10% of gift money I receive today is going to be blown on ice cream and iTunes.*
>
> *Thank you so much for being here today!*

[4] *Have a frank discussion with your child where you let him or her know clearly that you will not be helping anyone get a credit card for "emergencies."*

A national survey at Debt.org reports that the average credit card debt for college students on the day of their college graduation is $4,100. A huge number of students rack up credit card debt twice that or more.[36] The bulk of this money was charged on credit cards that parents got for students to use "in case of emergency."

Question of the day: how much of that $4,100 do you think was spent on actual emergen-cies, and how much of it was spent on beer and pizza?

It's all too easy for hungry college students to splurge on luxuries like restaurant food if they have a credit card handy to slide onto the little silver tray at the end of the meal. The main thought in your son's mind at that point is, "I'm hungry; I don't want to miss this time with my friends; I don't want to embarrass myself by ordering only french fries and water, and besides—I'm going to be making such massive sums of money with my French Literature degree after college that this little bit I'm putting on my credit card right now will be a breeze to pay off."

Don't let your child fall into this trap. Warn your daughter that for every $1 she puts on any credit card other than a debit card, she should plan on having to pay $2 back to a credit card company in the future. What we hope is that the $16 pizza doesn't look quite so enticing when she realizes it's going to eventually cost her $32.

Parents, I know you want your kids to be safe. You have nightmares about a car breaking down on a deserted highway at 2:00 a.m., and your beautiful daughter having to walk 10 miles for help while wearing gossamer and high heels. In a thunderstorm. I truly understand that you would take any risk to prevent that. But let me suggest a better and safer alternative than just giving her carte blanche to run up credit card debt.

---

36 "Student Loan Debt Statistics," Debt.org, accessed September 24, 2016, https://www.debt.org/students/debt/.

> **IT'S ALL TOO EASY FOR HUNGRY COLLEGE STUDENTS TO SPLURGE ON LUXURIES LIKE RESTAURANT FOOD IF THEY HAVE A CREDIT CARD HANDY TO SLIDE ONTO THE LITTLE SILVER TRAY AT THE END OF THE MEAL.**

Get your daughter a cell phone and a special debit card with $150 of your money loaded onto it. Instruct her that this particular debit card is to be used only for genuine emergencies. If her car breaks down on a deserted highway, she should lock her car doors, use her cell phone to call the police to come and get her, and when they do, ask them to take her to a safe hotel. She should check into this hotel using the debit card you've provided, go to her room, lock and chain the door, order room service for dinner, and then call you to make a plan for what to do next.

No need for a credit card.

> **GET YOUR DAUGHTER A CELL PHONE AND A SPECIAL DEBIT CARD WITH $150 OF YOUR MONEY LOADED ONTO IT. INSTRUCT HER THAT THIS PARTICULAR DEBIT CARD IS TO BE USED ONLY FOR GENUINE EMERGENCIES.**

Besides the $150 emergency debit card that you provide for her, your daughter should also have her own debit card preloaded with her own money (or a very modest amount of money you provide) for her own use. She can use this personal debit card to make purchases, rent cars, make hotel reservations, pay bills, make purchases at retail stores, or get cash at ATMs. The benefit of the debit card is that she will be spending only available funds and so will learn to strategize to make her cash stretch rather than relying on debt to get the things she wants.

Parent, close your eyes for a moment and imagine your eventual college graduate daughter (struggling to make ends meet as all young adults do) sitting down and writing checks for $400 each month to credit card companies so she can pay 18 percent interest on the $4,100 in credit card debt that she ran up during college.

Now imagine her not having to do that.

That's the freedom you buy for your daughter when you do not get her a credit card for "emergencies."

[5] *You may have dear friends or relatives who didn't strategize early on about debt-free college the way you have, and they may now be feeling sick at how much student loan debt their child is going to be taking on. Here's how you can help.*

I've put together a free bonus online resource for parents who find themselves looking at way too much future student loan debt. It very kindly explains several helpful things that families can try at the last minute to reduce future student loan debt. You can share this with friends individually or on social media by directing them to the link below.

BONUS ONLINE CONTENT:
Download the article "HERE'S HELP:
Last-Minute, Last-Ditch Strategies for
Reducing Future Student Loan Debt"
at JeannieBurlowski.com/LAUNCH.

CHECKLIST

Late April of 12th Grade

☐ 1. Have thoughtful family discussions where you as a team make a final decision on where this high school senior will attend college this coming fall.

☐ 2. If your son has been wait-listed at a college and still has interest in attending there despite the probable scarcity of financial aid and merit aid, take the steps prescribed in this chapter now.

☐ 3. Talk with your son this month about what's going to happen with the high school graduation gift money.

☐ 4. Explain to your daughter that you will not be helping her to get a credit card "for emergencies."

☐ 5. If you have friends who are feeling sick over how much student loan debt their child will be taking on, you can help by sharing the free bonus online article I've provided for them at JeannieBurlowski.com/LAUNCH.

☐ 6. Check my book updates page at JeannieBurlowski.com/LAUNCH to see if I have made any recent updates to this chapter.

☐ 7. Always consult your financial planning professional before making any big financial decisions.

☐ 8. Make a note in your calendar to come back and read the next chapter of this book on May 1 when your child is in 12th grade.

Be the first to hear about updates to the material in this book by reading my free weekly email newsletter every week. Anyone can subscribe to it at any time at JeannieBurlowski.com.

28 | *May 1 of 12th Grade*

May 1 of the senior year of high school is known by two names: the "common reply date" or the "national candidate's reply date." In either case, it's the deadline for accepting offers of admission at most colleges.

By this time, your son knows which colleges have accepted him and what all the final versions of his financial aid packages look like, so it's time to make a choice (considering all the important criteria I listed in chapter 26).

It's also time for *celebration*. Even if you've used only *a few* of the strategies in this book, your family is far, far ahead of most when it comes to setting your child up for a fulfilling, stable, and happy financial and career future. High fives to all of you!

HOW TO USE THIS CHAPTER

Start by just reading through this chapter. As you read, don't worry about committing to any of it. Decision time will come at the very end of this chapter, when I give you a clear, at-a-glance checklist of every task I'm suggesting you consider right now.

Remember, you won't have to use every strategy I suggest; just choose the ones you think will work for your family and either modify or discard the rest.

[1] *Tell the winning college yes.*

This will be your son's first official act as a college student, so make sure he does this *himself*.

Commitment paperwork and a financial deposit will be required. Today is the deadline, so don't delay.

Do not under any circumstances commit to two different schools to avoid having to make a final college choice. Doing so makes life very difficult for colleges. It's unethical, and it could result in your son's offers of admission being rescinded at both colleges where he's trying to keep his options open.

If your son has been wait-listed at a college and is still hoping to be admitted there, have him commit to the best "Plan B" school where he's actually been accepted, and then follow the instructions I provide in chapter 27 to increase his chances of being admitted to his first choice school from its waiting list.

[2] *If your daughter has not yet read an entire book on how to succeed in college (and passed a parent-administered oral quiz on it), be empathetic and kind as she digs into her savings and pays the required $400 college deposit out of her own money.*

This is a great time for your daughter to learn that people who work hard to come through on promises *on time* save money.

[3] *When looking at college housing options, pick the least-expensive option available.*

College students don't need elegant digs with granite countertops and on-site fitness facilities. Let them enjoy these things when they're older, when they've worked hard to earn them for themselves. The objective now is to save as much money as possible on college housing costs.

If it's going to be a struggle for you to get this child through college debt-free while paying for on-campus housing and cafeteria food, you might look into what it would cost to house this child with roommates in an off-campus apartment during the college years. Even considering rent, utilities, gro-

ceries, and increased transportation costs, it could save your family a bundle. (If your daughter has received need-based financial aid, though, check with the college's financial aid office to see whether reducing your child's Cost of Attendance [COA] in this way could reduce her financial aid award.)

> **COLLEGE STUDENTS DON'T NEED ELEGANT DIGS WITH GRANITE COUNTERTOPS AND ON-SITE FITNESS FACILITIES. LET THEM ENJOY THESE THINGS WHEN THEY'RE OLDER, WHEN THEY'VE WORKED HARD TO EARN THEM FOR THEMSELVES.**

[4] *If your son will be covered by your parental health insurance plan while he's in college, take official steps to let the college know that right now.*

Federal law requires that every college student be covered by health insurance. This makes sense. Problems arise, though, when students are automatically charged for health insurance even though they're already covered at home.

If your child is already covered, call the college's bursar's office and ask where you can find the college's *insurance waiver form* online. Fill it out and turn it in immediately.

If you don't do this early enough, you could find yourself slapped with a $2,000–$5,000 health insurance charge that will be very difficult to have removed from your bill. To keep yourself safe from unnecessary charges, complete the insurance waiver form as soon as you know where your child will be attending college.

TO KEEP YOURSELF SAFE FROM UNNECESSARY CHARGES, COMPLETE THE INSURANCE WAIVER FORM AS SOON AS YOU KNOW WHERE YOUR CHILD WILL BE ATTENDING COLLEGE.

[5] Send a copy of your best financial aid award letter to your financial planning professional. He or she will learn a lot from it.

Good financial planning professionals are always looking to get better at what they do. The more they're able to follow the debt-free college journeys of people like you, the more knowledge they gain for helping others.

Besides all that, your good news is going to make this person's day.

CHECKLIST

May 1 of 12th Grade

☐ 1. Tell the winning college yes.

☐ 2. If your daughter has not yet read an entire book on how to succeed in college (and passed a parent-administered oral quiz on it), be empathetic and kind as she digs into her savings and pays her $400 college deposit out of her own money.

☐ 3. When looking at college housing options, pick the least-expensive option.

☐ 4. If your son will be covered by your parental health insurance plan while he's in college, take official steps to let the college know that right now.

☐ 5. Send a copy of your best financial aid award letter to your financial planning professional. He or she will learn a lot from it.

☐ 6. Check my book updates page at JeannieBurlowski.com/LAUNCH to see if I have made any recent updates to this chapter.

☐ 7. Always consult your financial planning professional before making any big financial decisions.

☐ 8. Make a note in your calendar to come back and read the next chapter of this book soon after your child's high school graduation.

Be the first to hear about updates to the material in this book by reading my free weekly email newsletter every week. Anyone can subscribe to it at any time at JeannieBurlowski.com.

29 | *Soon After High School Graduation*

What a milestone! In just 18 short years, you've gotten your child from diapers to the high school graduation stage. And now you have him poised to launch into debt-free college and a career he'll excel at and love. This is an extraordinary accomplishment, and I congratulate you with all my heart.

The next three chapters of this book are just as important as the previous ones. They will help you to lower college costs even further and set your child up for a smooth and healthy transition through this summer and into college.

HOW TO USE THIS CHAPTER

Start by just reading through this chapter. As you read, don't worry about committing to any of it. Decision time will come at the very end of this chapter, when I give you a clear,

at-a-glance checklist of every task I'm suggesting you consider right now.

Remember, you won't have to use every strategy I suggest; just choose the ones you think will work for your family and either modify or discard the rest.

[1] *Mom and Dad, this is likely to be a very emotional summer for you. Please take good care of yourselves.*

You've spent 18 years bonding with this child, and it seems like only a moment ago she was a chubby baby in footy pajamas, a potty-training toddler, and an elementary schooler learning to ride a bike. At times the thought of her going out into this world without you may seem like more than you can bear. You may find yourself erupting into tears at odd moments. *This is completely OK.* It's to be expected. Be sure you're taking care of your own needs this summer by getting adequate rest, eating well, taking the time necessary to recharge your own batteries, keeping other life stressors down if possible, and sharing what you're feeling with other adults close to you who understand.

What you're going through this summer is temporary. It will get better. I promise.

WHAT YOU'RE GOING THROUGH THIS SUMMER IS TEMPORARY. IT WILL GET BETTER. I PROMISE.

[2] *Clarify who will be paying for summertime purchases and activities, and remind your daughter that her first $1,000 deposit is due to you this summer.*

Advise your daughter that you'll be expecting her to cover all of her own expenses throughout the summer months using money you provide—just as you have since September of her 9th-grade year. (If you haven't yet set this system up, see chapter 11 of this book.)

The most important fee your daughter will have to pay this summer is the $1,000 deposit you are asking her to pay to you each semester that you give her money for college.

Let's review that part of the contract you signed with her after she finished 8th grade. It said,

> My parents have set aside some money to help me pay for college or another type of job-training program. Here's what I will be required to do to get that money: I will pay my parents a $1,000 deposit out of my own

money for each semester that they help me with college costs. At the end of each of my college semesters, I will log my parents into the computer and show them the official record of the grades I earned. If my college grades are mostly A's with maybe one B, my parents will return that $1,000 deposit to me, and I can use it to get them to help pay for my next semester. If I play my cards right, I'll be able to make it all the way through four years of college on this one deposit and get my $1,000 back permanently once I graduate. But if I have a few bad semesters and have to fork over three or four $1,000 deposits to my parents, that won't be so bad. Four thousand dollars of my own money is a small price to pay for a $160,000 college education!

YOUR SON WILL BENEFIT FROM HAVING SOME "SKIN IN THE GAME."

I strongly suggest that you put a recurring entry in your calendar reminding you to ask your daughter for another $1,000 deposit every single semester, unless she logs you into the computer and shows you the official record of her excellent grades. No matter how good a kid she is, she will benefit from having some "skin in the game."

[3] *Call the financial aid office at your daughter's college and ask this question: "I have all of my financial aid award information here in front of me. Can you tell me which of the items on this list we received because of our family's financial need?"*

Financial aid information is notoriously

difficult to interpret, so it's a good idea to go straight to the financial aid office to get the answer to this very important question. As you listen to the answer, circle the items on the list that are there specifically because of your family's financial need.

Then ask this: "If our family income were to greatly increase in the next year or two, would we be in danger of losing these awards?"

If the answer is yes, then your family will want to continue with the income and asset-reducing strategies I've suggested in this book *all the way until January 1 of your youngest child's sophomore year of college.* That's the magic date when extra income can no longer hurt your family's eligibility for need-based financial aid.

But what if the financial aid office tells you, "No, your family income and assets were too high for you to get any need-based financial aid. None of the awards you're looking at came to you because of financial need."

If the financial aid office gives you *this* answer, then you've discovered something very significant.

You spent the past 29 months conducting a tremendously valuable experiment—and now you have your answer. Even after you employed every strategy you possibly could, your family income and assets are still too high for you to receive need-based financial aid for college.

This is an answer that no one could have given you with any certainty 29 months ago. Oh, someone in an office somewhere could have offhandedly and with very little information

tried to tell you, "Your income's too high; you won't get anything." However, I am here to tell you: financial aid calculations are interwoven, complex, and dependent on a vast number of constantly shifting factors—so much so that you never really know whether you might get need-based financial aid until you try.

> **HOWEVER, I AM HERE TO TELL YOU: FINANCIAL AID CALCULATIONS ARE INTERWOVEN, COMPLEX, AND DEPENDENT ON A VAST NUMBER OF CONSTANTLY SHIFTING FACTORS—SO MUCH SO THAT YOU NEVER REALLY KNOW WHETHER YOU MIGHT GET NEED-BASED FINANCIAL AID UNTIL YOU TRY.**

You tried; you didn't get it. So now you know. Now you really know.

This news—that you will likely never get need-based financial aid—is liberating for you, because it means you can now stop making financial decisions based on what's going to protect future financial aid eligibility.

You *will* keep on filling out the FAFSA every year, just in case your fortunes ever take a sudden downward turn, but you can now safely and confidently throw off all of the careful restrictions you've placed around your income and assets since December 31 of your child's 10th-grade year.

You can now freely

» take on extra jobs, increasing parent and student income as much as you want to.

» pull money out of Roth IRAs for educational expenses (as long as you've provided for retirement in some other way).

» hire new employees for your family business without concern that you'll go over 100 full-time employees and in doing so make your family business visible on the FAFSA.

» move off of the family farm. (If it becomes an "investment farm" where you don't personally reside, it doesn't matter anymore.)

» thank Grandma wholeheartedly for the money she's been saving in that 529 plan in her own name with your child named as beneficiary, and then take that money and freely spend it on this year's college expenses (rather than carefully waiting until your son reaches January 1 of his sophomore year of college).

» increase the balances in your bank accounts, portfolios, and other investments without concern that the money in them will sabotage your child's future financial aid awards.

Now you can turn to strategies that those who need to carefully guard financial aid eligibility are not able to use. Like this one.

[4] *If protecting financial aid eligibility is no longer a concern, suggest that your daughter find a full-time summer tuition reimbursement job.*

Wouldn't it be great if your daughter could work not only for a paycheck, but for the reimbursement of a portion of her college tuition as well? And what if she could work this job near home this summer, and then next fall, transfer within the company to a part-time job in the same city where her college campus is located?

If your daughter is no longer concerned about keeping her income in the $6,000–$7,000-per-year range to maintain financial aid eligibility, this might be an excellent possibility. Especially since the first $5,250 of the tuition your daughter's employer pays for her each year is given to her tax-free. According to FinAid,

» Your employer may provide you with up to $5,250 in employer education assistance benefits for undergraduate or graduate courses tax-free each year, per section 127 of the Internal Revenue Code. ... The benefits must have been paid for tuition, fees, books, supplies, and equipment. These expenses must have been incurred for the education of the employee and not for the employee's spouse or dependents.[37]

Some students set their sights so firmly on tuition reimbursement jobs that they actually move to their college town one to three months before college classes start in order to snap up jobs with companies that offer tuition reimbursement. If your son happens to have a grandma or an aunt living in his college town who's willing to have him as a congenial housemate for a few months, that

---

37 "Employer Tuition Assistance," FinAid, accessed September 24, 2016, http://www.finaid.org/otheraid/ employertuitionassistance.phtml.

may be exactly what he needs to make this plan work. (Just warn your son to remember to help Grandma or Aunt Jane with groceries, meal prep, household chores, and dishes.)

> **SOME STUDENTS SET THEIR SIGHTS SO FIRMLY ON TUITION REIMBURSEMENT JOBS THAT THEY ACTUALLY MOVE TO THEIR COLLEGE TOWN ONE TO THREE MONTHS BEFORE COLLEGE CLASSES START IN ORDER TO SNAP UP JOBS WITH COMPANIES THAT OFFER TUITION REIMBURSEMENT.**

When a student is shopping for a job that will continue during the college academic year, I suggest that she look for one that will allow her to work lots of evening hours, but relatively few daytime hours if possible. This is because daytime is the best time for completing academic work. (Some people even go so far as to say that one hour of studying done during daylight hours is equal to *two hours* of studying done after dark.)

And lest you worry that working at a job for pay might reduce your child's grades in college, let me reassure you: studies show that students who work part time for money during the academic year actually earn higher GPAs than students who don't. (Students who try to work *full time* while going to college, however, have graduation rates 50 percent lower than those of other students.) In my opinion, every college student should work for money during the academic year—

if possible for an employer who offers tuition reimbursement.

For a sample list of employers who might offer tuition reimbursement benefits to your son or daughter, review chapter 14 of this book.

[5] *If your son didn't qualify for any need-based financial aid and you don't have to protect his financial aid eligibility, you could consider buying a house near his college campus.*

This strategy isn't for families still in the process of trying to appear needy for financial aid applications, since rental properties count against families in financial aid calculations. But if you know with certainty that your family isn't receiving need-based aid anyway, you might benefit from buying a home (even an inexpensive mobile home) in the city where your son is going to attend college.

If your responsible, levelheaded son or daughter lives in this house for four years, that will *greatly* reduce the amount you'll be paying for dormitory room and board during the college years. The actual financial benefit, though, could go far beyond that. If your child fills this home with the maximum number of roommates and then lives there with them to screen rental applications, collect rents, coordinate cleaning schedules, manage maintenance issues, and see that the lawn gets mowed and the trash gets hauled to the curb, your family may be able to turn a handsome profit during the years your son is in college.

If you're going to try this buy-a-house strategy, I have a number of thoughts for you to keep carefully in mind as you do so.

You can access my recommendations on this subject by downloading the free bonus online content below. (You can also easily share this resource with other parents who tell you that their kid didn't get any need-based financial aid either.)

BONUS ONLINE CONTENT:
Download the article "BUYING A HOUSE: How to Use Real Estate to Reduce College Costs After Not Getting Any Financial Aid" at JeannieBurlowski.com/LAUNCH.

[6] *If your daughter is receiving need-based financial aid and therefore needs to keep her income on the low side throughout this year, remind her to track her earnings carefully so she'll be aware when she starts to approach cut-off points.*

If your daughter received need-based financial aid as a part of her financial aid award package, she'll want to keep her income below a certain ceiling each year until January 1 of her sophomore year of college so she remains eligible for that aid. The income amount she'll want to stay

under was $6,310 per year (after taxes) in 2015–16, but that amount increases by $60–$130 each year at a rate in keeping with inflation.

Note that this income amount does *not* include earnings from federal work-study jobs, assistantships, fellowships, or cooperative education programs. Your daughter can have unlimited income from those sources without diminishing her financial aid eligibility in any way.

[7] *Be sure that these two things are being regularly entered into Evernote: (1) your son's income (including photos of each check or stack of cash he receives) and (2) receipts documenting every dollar you and he spend on his college-related expenses.*

You'll need these records (a) for tax purposes, (b) for proving that you're justified in pulling money out of his 529 savings plan, (c) for making sure your son doesn't cross an income line into diminishing his financial aid eligibility, (d) for proving income that allows your son to make Roth IRA contributions, and (e) for entering on next year's financial aid applications.

Remember, your family fills out financial aid applications every year, even if you're sure you won't get anything. Filling out the forms every year allows your child to be in the pipeline to receive aid just in case your family fortunes suddenly go backward due to lost income or high medical bills.

REMEMBER, YOUR FAMILY FILLS OUT FINANCIAL AID APPLICATIONS EVERY YEAR, EVEN IF YOU'RE SURE YOU WON'T GET ANYTHING.

[8] *If your child has any money sitting around in UGMA or UTMA accounts, jump at the chance to use that money to pay as many of this year's college bills as you can.*

Using up UGMA and UTMA money now may make your child more eligible for financial aid the next time you fill out the FAFSA form.

 # CHECKLIST

Soon After High School Graduation

☐ 1. Mom and Dad, this is likely to be a very emotional summer for you. *Take good care of yourselves.*

☐ 2. Clarify who will be paying for summertime purchases and activities, and remind your daughter that her first $1,000 deposit is due to you this summer.

☐ 3. Call your daughter's financial aid office. Find out whether any part of her financial aid package was dependent on financial need.

☐ 4. If she's not receiving any need-based financial aid, you can now safely reverse all your income and asset-reducing efforts and instead try other, larger-scale strategies instead.

☐ 5. If you no longer need to keep your daughter's income low, encourage her to find a job that offers tuition reimbursement as an employee benefit. The first $5,250 of tuition reimbursement money she earns each year will be tax-free; the extra she earns over and above that will be helpful too.

☐ 6. If you no longer have to try to protect your son's financial aid eligibility because he didn't qualify for help anyway, you could consider buying a house near his college campus. Use the online resource provided in this chapter to do this wisely.

☐ 7. If your daughter *is* receiving need-based financial aid and therefore needs to keep her income on the low side throughout this year, remind her to track her earnings carefully so she'll be aware of when she starts to approach cut-off points.

☐ 8. Be sure that these two things are being regularly entered into Evernote: (1) your son's income, including photos of each check or stack of cash he receives; and (2) receipts documenting every dollar you and he spend on his college-related expenses.

☐ 9. If your child has any money sitting around in UGMA or UTMA accounts, jump at the chance to use that money to pay as many of this year's college bills as you can.

☐ 10. Check my book updates page at JeannieBurlowski.com/LAUNCH to see if I have made any recent updates to this chapter.

☐ 11. Always consult your financial planning professional before making any big financial decisions.

☐ 12. Make a note in your calendar to come back and read the next chapter of this book early in the summer after 12th grade.

Be the first to hear about updates to the material in this book by reading my free weekly email newsletter every week. Anyone can subscribe to it at any time at JeannieBurlowski.com.

30 | *Early Summer After 12th Grade*

This June and July are going to fly by in a blur.

Sometimes you'll feel like Dorothy in *The Wizard of Oz*, up in the tornado, looking out the bedroom window as miscellaneous pieces of your life fly by. Entire Saturdays will be lost when your daughter insists that there is no greater priority in this entire world than getting her a new dorm room comforter and matching pillow sham at IKEA. You may feel nagging worry that in all the turmoil, you're forgetting something.

This chapter's list is designed to keep you calm and on track. Remember, if you're able to use even *a few* of the strategies listed here, you'll be far ahead of the game when it comes to launching your teen into college and career life.

HOW TO USE THIS CHAPTER

Start by just reading through this chapter. As you read, don't worry about committing to any of it. Decision time will come at the very end of this chapter, when I give you a clear, at-a-glance checklist of every task I'm suggesting you consider right now.

Remember, you won't have to use every strategy I suggest; just choose the ones you think will work for your family and either modify or discard the rest.

[1] *Have your daughter create a printed thank-you letter with her picture on it and send it out.*

I strongly recommend that every student send out a one-page printed letter that thanks the people who've helped her get to college. A form letter with a graduation photo photocopied onto it is perfectly OK for this. In this form letter, your daughter can talk about the career she's aiming toward, tell everyone she's excited to have set a goal of getting through college debt-free in under four years with job offers at graduation, list the colleges she got into and which one she's chosen to attend, and relay any happy news about merit aid or scholarships she's received. On the bottom of the letter, she should leave a blank space to handwrite an individual thank you to anyone who gave her a high school graduation gift.

(I absolutely love to get these letters. My address is: Jeannie Burlowski, P.O. Box 702, Circle Pines, MN 55014.)

I recommend that your daughter send a copy of this letter to special teachers she's had over the past 12 years, as well as mentors, guidance counselors, youth pastors, volunteer job supervisors, people she job shadowed, close relatives, people who wrote her letters of recommendation for scholarship and college applications, and others who've given of themselves to help her.

I strongly suggest doing this for two reasons. First, it's always good manners to share our news and our profuse thanks with the people who've helped make our lives better. The second reason to send these letters, though, is that you want your daughter to remain memorable to these people. She may be applying for even bigger things in the future, and she may need these people's networks and their letters of recommendation again and again over the next six years or more.

For some very special mentors and contacts, your daughter may even want to send a newsy thank-you update letter *every single year.* Have her put a recurring reminder about this in her calendar.

> **FOR SOME VERY SPECIAL MENTORS AND CONTACTS, YOUR DAUGHTER MAY EVEN WANT TO SEND A NEWSY THANK-YOU UPDATE LETTER** *EVERY SINGLE YEAR.*

[2] *Research how the public transportation works on and near your son's college campus, so he won't have to bring a car with him to college.*

Does the public transportation system nearest your son's college consist of a city bus, a subway system, or light-rail? Find out whether the college furnishes free or reduced-price bus, subway, or light-rail passes.

Is there an app for bus and train schedules? Which bus or train stop is nearest to your daughter's future dormitory?

Could your son easily get by without a car if he uses an alternative low-cost ride service such as Uber or Lyft? When busses or trains won't do and your daughter and her friends absolutely need a car to get somewhere, can they split the cost of a car-share, using a company such as Zipcar, Connect, WeCar, or City CarShare—or low-cost, peer-to-peer, car-sharing services such as Turo and Getaround?

Figuring out how your son or daughter can get by without a car at college can save your family thousands in car payments, gas, oil, maintenance, and parking fees over four years of college.

Do you doubt that college students can actually get by without having cars of their own on campus? Call the college parking service and ask what percentage of students do not bring cars with them to college. The high number will surprise you.

> **FIGURING OUT HOW YOUR SON OR DAUGHTER CAN GET BY WITHOUT A CAR AT COLLEGE CAN SAVE YOUR FAMILY THOUSANDS IN CAR PAYMENTS, GAS, OIL, MAINTENANCE, AND PARKING FEES OVER FOUR YEARS OF COLLEGE.**

[3] *Even though your son won't have a car with him at college, keep him covered under your family auto policy.*

Your son will likely still drive your car during school breaks. He'll drive his friends' cars. And he will also need coverage if he uses a car-sharing service of any kind during the time he's away at college.

[4] *Start getting packed for that family vacation you planned last spring.*

Create some family memories that will be a stabilizing, centering force for your child throughout the transition ahead.

[5] *Check to be sure that every bit of the college credit your daughter earned in high school has been officially transferred to her college.*

It's important to do this before your daughter accidentally registers to take a college class she's already completed in high school. (Names of classes can change slightly from one institution to another, so this can happen more easily than you think.) Double-check to make sure that her college registrar's office is aware of every bit of her AP and CLEP credit, all of her dual enrollment credit, and any other college credit she earned in high school.

Make sure your daughter has a complete, written list of all college credit with her when she meets with her college advisor to discuss next fall's class registration. This will help ensure that she chooses the best possible set of classes to take next fall.

[6] *Have your son or daughter register for college courses at the earliest possible opportunity using the following four strategies.*

Have your daughter ask the college to help her to arrange an in-person or telephone appointment with a college academic advisor before she registers for fall college courses.

In this meeting, your daughter should tell the advisor,

> I'm planning to be a _____ major and I want to graduate in four years or less. I want to get all of my required prerequisite classes out of the way as fast as possible so I can jump right into my most interesting coursework and then start applying for internships as early as I can.

Here are all the college credits I have so far. Can you help me figure out what are some required prerequisite courses I should try to sign up for this fall?

(As I'll be telling your daughter later, her goal will be to get *quickly* to the classes that apply most directly to her future career field. It's these classes that will give her the knowledge and skill that will make her a great candidate for career-building internships early on—long before the last semester of her senior year of college.)

Emphasize to your daughter that it's very important for her to meet with her academic advisor in this way *every single semester*. Doing so may help her plan her academic track so well that she's able to double major and still graduate from college in record time.

Double majoring can be a brilliant strategy, especially for a student who desperately wants to take college classes in a field with lower future income potential (like art, music, humanities, or sociology). If your daughter will pair a major in one of these fields with a major in a better-paying field—for instance, combining a degree in music performance with a second degree that will give her a teaching credential, or pairing an art degree with a graphic design or web design credential—she will be more likely to find herself readily employable after college.

These advisor meetings are important. If your daughter balks at scheduling them because the advisor she's been assigned just doesn't seem helpful, she can ask the dean of her department to assign her a different one.

Encourage your daughter to take the lightest course load possible this first semester, while still maintaining full-time college student status.

In most cases, I'm all for taking as many courses at a time as possible and barreling through college quickly. The first semester of college after high school, though, is a time of tremendous transition. Much of your daughter's mental bandwidth is going to be taken up with learning to be away from home for months at a time, coping with roommate conflicts, making new friends, navigating unfamiliar public transportation, and learning how to manage academics as a full-time college student. Let's give her a little breathing space to be able to do that well.

This said, emphasize to your daughter that it's very, very important for her to (at all times) carefully maintain *at least* the minimum number of credits required for her to be a full-time college student. At many colleges, full time equals 12 credits, but it can vary. If your daughter falls below this minimum number of credits (as sometimes happens to students who drop too many courses or miss too many class sessions), she may find her financial aid suddenly cut dramatically. This could result in her receiving a large bill with the words "DUE NOW" stamped across the top, along with an unfriendly note from the business office: "You are prohibited from registering for additional semesters at the university until this bill is paid."

Encourage your son to always register for one more college course than he actually plans to take.

If he intends to take 17 credits, for instance, he should sign up for 20, even if this requires special permission from an advisor. Then, when classes start, he attends all the classes for the first week, watching carefully to identify which of these courses is the weakest. Maybe he can tell by looking at the syllabus that one of the courses requires five times as much work as others. Maybe one course is built around lectures that are unclear, vacillating, and disorganized. Maybe one of his professors has a habit of ridiculing and belittling students from the podium. Maybe it turns out that one of the courses is not really on the topic he was hoping for. These are reasons to pinpoint a course as weak.

After one week of attending all of these classes, he'll go online (or walk down to the registrar's office) and drop the weakest course on his schedule by the *free add-drop date*. Courses dropped by the free add-drop date won't cost him anything, and no reference to them will appear on his academic transcript.

> **MAYBE HE CAN TELL BY LOOKING AT THE SYLLABUS THAT ONE OF THE COURSES REQUIRES FIVE TIMES AS MUCH WORK AS OTHERS. MAYBE ONE COURSE IS BUILT AROUND LECTURES THAT ARE UNCLEAR, VACILLATING, AND DISORGANIZED. MAYBE ONE OF HIS PROFESSORS HAS A HABIT OF RIDICULING AND BELITTLING STUDENTS FROM THE PODIUM.**

If your son is going to do this, though, it's important that he mark the college's free add-drop date in his calendar the moment he registers for that extra class. If he accidentally forgets this important date and stays in the course beyond it, he'll have to finish the unwanted course or have a "W" (for "withdrawal") show up on his permanent academic transcript.

While your son is registering for his fall semester college courses, have him look at reviews of potential professors on Ratemyprofessors.com.

Sure, some of the comments on the site are snarky, negative, and mean. Ignore those, just as you do when reading obviously planted, mean reviews on Yelp or Amazon. Pay attention to the overall patterns in the reviews, and to reviewers who provide evenhanded and calm evaluations of a professor's strengths and weaknesses. Carefully choose professors with these thoughts in mind.

[7] *If your son received a federal work-study grant as a part of his financial aid package, have him call and ask his college financial aid office how soon he can apply for his work-study job.*

The college will have an array of work-study jobs available. If your son is among the first students asking what his work-study assignment will be for the upcoming academic year, he'll stand the best, highest chance of getting a job that dovetails nicely with his future career goals. If your son aspires to someday be a football coach, for instance, a work-study job in the college athletic department might be a fantastic fit for him. If your daughter's future is in law enforcement, a work-study job with campus security might be a good choice.

If your son finds himself choosing between two great work-study job options, have him take the one that can be done in the evenings if possible. This will help him keep his daytime hours free for focused academic work.

> **IF YOUR SON IS AMONG THE FIRST ASKING WHAT HIS WORK-STUDY ASSIGNMENT WILL BE, HE'LL STAND THE BEST CHANCE OF GETTING A JOB THAT DOVETAILS NICELY WITH HIS FUTURE CAREER GOALS.**

[8] *Every time you receive a bill from the college, check each individual line item on it carefully. Especially watch out for health insurance charges.*

As I mentioned in chapter 28, the college may try to charge your daughter for health insurance even though she's covered under your parental plan.

If this happens to you, challenge the charge immediately by calling the college's bursar's office. Be prepared to jump through numerous hoops to get it taken off of your bill. Then, make a note in your personal calendar to watch carefully and go through this challenge process again each fall until your youngest child has graduated from college.

[9] *Search for a list of CLEP and DSST exams, and see if there are any your daughter is now close to passing because she studied that subject during her 12th-grade year.*

Use the instructions in chapter 9 of this book to have her practice for and take as many CLEP and DSST exams as possible this summer. Every one that she takes and passes could save her thousands in future college costs, so if she balks at doing this, you might offer to pay her to do it.

One caveat to this: if your daughter has already accumulated so many of these credit-by-examination credits that her college or university won't give her credit for any more of them, she can stop taking these exams. Have your daughter contact her college registrar to determine exactly what the limit is and how close she is to exceeding it.

[10] *Log your daughter into her account on LinkedIn and help her update her profile there.*

Include in her LinkedIn profile any awards she won at the end of 12th grade, as well as any additional work experiences, job-shadowing experiences, and volunteer and service hours she's put in so far. Help your daughter link to more of her parents' friends, her friends' parents, and now her high school teachers on LinkedIn.

Even though your daughter is 18 years old, don't depend on her to do this for herself.

Primarily because of issues related to adolescent brain development, students aren't likely to take care of this themselves until they are 24 years old.

> **HELP YOUR DAUGHTER LINK TO MORE OF HER PARENTS' FRIENDS, HER FRIENDS' PARENTS, AND NOW HER HIGH SCHOOL TEACHERS ON LINKEDIN.**

[11] *Have your teen buy some nice new clothes for college, but get them on the cheap.*

Not surprisingly, students who make an effort to dress well for work and class typically do better academically and socially than students who maintain an "I just don't care" attitude about their appearance.

The summer before college starts, students should get some thoughtfully chosen, nice clothes to wear on campus. Don't pay full retail price for these clothes, though. It's possible to get great college student clothes for 75 percent off of retail by shopping at upscale consignment stores, many of which specialize in merchandise geared specifically to students under 22.

[12] *Encourage your daughter to use cut and paste to apply for 10 private scholarships this summer and every other summer all the way through college and graduate school.*

The competition for scholarships for your daughter just dropped dramatically, since most people don't realize that students can continue to apply for scholarships all the way through college and grad school.

If your daughter needs help creating an outstanding essay for these scholarships, she can check my free weekly email newsletter for information on how to access a live or recorded version of my *Make Them Say Wow* class.

Pay your daughter $50 for every scholarship application she fills out in a quality manner if that's what's necessary to motivate her.

[13] *Express enthusiasm as your son learns about upcoming college events and activities, meets future dormmates and friends, and connects with future roommates on social media.*

Your son will be able to follow his college on Twitter, read his campus newspaper online, check his college's admitted student website for things like orientation schedules, special freshman class events, and housing and dining options, plus start getting to know other students by joining the college's incoming freshman class Facebook page.

Many academic departments, clubs, dormitories, and campus organizations also have their own social media accounts. Some schools (for example, the University of Denver and Michigan State University) even have specialized apps that help incoming students connect with one another.

If your son is attending college out of state, it can be particularly helpful for him to connect with other students from his home state who will be attending the same college. Students at the University of Denver, for instance, use Denver's app to find fellow freshmen from the same state for meet-ups before the school year starts.

[14] *Set aside a relaxed, sibling-free evening at home for a heart-to-heart parent/student talk. Before the special evening arrives, prepare a couple of extra pages to add to the contract that you and your child signed after 8th grade.*

You've got a good kid; there's no question about that.

Still, this good kid is only 18, and that means that the prefrontal cortex of his or her brain is not yet fully developed (and won't be until he or she is 22–24 years old). This is the part of the brain responsible for emotional regulation, for evaluating risk, and for thinking through today's impulsive choices and connecting them to possible future outcomes. This underdeveloped prefrontal cortex can lead some college students to do things that derail every good thing their caring parents have worked so hard for. *Scary.*

So, what's a loving mom or dad to do? You can't control every aspect of your son's behavior and choices for the next six years until his brain is fully developed, but what

you can do is *influence him.* You can speak into his life in such a way that when he's about to reach his hand out toward risky behavior, he'll hear your voice in his head: "Watch out. Be careful. This is dangerous."

Parents, if it's important, you need to *say it out loud.* During this relaxed sibling-free evening at home, I'd like you to turn off the TV, put the phones on do not disturb, and say some very important things *out loud.*

For now, just read through the points below on your own, without your child present. At the end of this section I'll give you an online resource that you can download, modify, and refer to while having this conversation. At the end, you may want to get out a pen, have the student and all parents sign it, and then attach it to the contract you created back when your child finished 8th grade.

I want to emphasize: when you ask your son to sign this document, you *will not* be asking him to promise that he'll live by these principles. You'll simply be asking him to sign that he has *heard you say them.*

> **YOU CAN'T CONTROL EVERY ASPECT OF YOUR SON'S BEHAVIOR AND CHOICES FOR THE NEXT SIX YEARS UNTIL HIS BRAIN IS FULLY DEVELOPED, BUT WHAT YOU CAN DO IS** *INFLUENCE HIM.*

How do you open this conversation? You could say something like, "Mike, we want to go over this 8th-grade contract with you one more time, and then we want to talk to you about some things that every parent needs to cover with kids who are heading off to college. We know that you already get most of these things, but it's important that you hear us saying them to you."

Then, parent, share with your child your values and expectations on the following topics.

ALCOHOL AND DRUG USE

According to information from the National Institute on Alcohol Abuse and Alcoholism, underage college drinking exacts "an enormous toll on the intellectual and social lives of students."[38]

Staying away from alcohol and drugs throughout college can not only keep a student from potential career-destroying addiction, it can also help protect him or her from additional alcohol-related dangers, such as date rape; assault; sexual assault (either as victim or as perpetrator); of death by an alcohol-related car crash; of contracting a sexually transmitted disease; of unwanted pregnancy; of lasting and expensive legal problems; of death due to alcohol poisoning; of depression and anxiety; of academic failure; and of unnecessary heartbreak, sadness, and regret as adults.

If you hope your son or daughter will stay away from drug and alcohol use in college, and in doing so greatly reduce these risks, tell him or her that now.

KEEPING A SQUEAKY CLEAN ONLINE REPUTATION

Your child already understands that anything posted by or about him or her online is permanent and can never be erased. What he or she may *not* know is that more and more employers, scholarship committees, and grad school admissions committees are performing in-depth online searches before hiring candidates, awarding scholarship money, or accepting applicants. Online search tools are only going to become more sophisticated in the next 4–10 years, so any embarrassing things posted by or about your son or daughter are only going to become easier and easier for others to find and view. Your child should never post anything, anywhere, that she wouldn't be happy having broadcast in a national news conference.

EMOTIONALLY AND PHYSICALLY RISKY SEXUAL ACTIVITY

Some people view sex as being of little more importance than getting someone to scratch an annoying itch in the middle of their back. If you believe there's more to sex than that, tell your child that. Say it out loud. Tell him or her that you hope he or she will avoid emotionally and physically risky sexual activity, and get to have what most people *really* want deep down inside: long-term committed love that leads to the most intoxicating, most fulfilling sexual life in the long term.

---

38 "College Drinking," National Institute on Alcohol Abuse and Alcoholism, December 2015, http://pubs. niaaa.nih.gov/publications/CollegeFactSheet/CollegeFactSheet.pdf.

> **SOME PEOPLE VIEW SEX AS BEING OF LITTLE MORE IMPORTANCE THAN GETTING SOMEONE TO SCRATCH AN ANNOYING ITCH IN THE MIDDLE OF THEIR BACK. IF YOU BELIEVE THERE'S MORE TO SEX THAN THAT, TELL YOUR CHILD THAT. SAY IT OUT LOUD.**

DEBT, ESPECIALLY CREDIT CARD DEBT

Once your daughter steps onto her college campus, she's going to be inundated with enticing offers to sign up for credit cards. Credit card companies will be present on her campus and in her student mailbox, using every hook they can think of to get her to sign up. Free food, free T-shirts, free $50 gift cards, even the emotional ploy: "You're an adult now; time to start building your credit rating!"

It's not *credit rating* that matters in adult financial life, it's *net worth*—what you actually own once all your debt is subtracted. There is no better way for a student to show creditworthiness than to have a real job, pay bills on time, and be debt-free. Tell your daughter that you hope she'll enjoy her debit card and avoid credit cards like the traps they are.

> **IT'S NOT** *CREDIT RATING* **THAT MATTERS IN ADULT FINANCIAL LIFE, IT'S** *NET WORTH*— **WHAT YOU ACTUALLY OWN ONCE ALL YOUR DEBT IS SUBTRACTED.**

MENTAL HEALTH STRUGGLES

Tell your daughter plainly that if she ever finds herself battling a mental health problem, you want to help.

Some students get away from home and find themselves struggling with mental health problems such as depression, anxiety, a stress disorder, a sexually transmitted disease, an eating disorder, an abusive relationship, an unplanned pregnancy, the aftermath of sexual assault, or with drug or alcohol addiction.

Tell your child, "Honey, if anything like this happens to you, we want to help. We promise we won't flip out or freak out. Just let us know, and we'll get you the best help available. Remember, there's a counseling center on your college campus too—you can always go there to talk to someone as well."

NAVIGATING A SERIOUS CRISIS DURING COLLEGE

Tell your child, "If you experience an out-and-out crisis during college, we want you to try to finish the semester if you can, but after that take a break."

I (Jeannie) once had a med school application client whose single mother had been in hospice, dying of cancer, during my client's sophomore year of college. If I'd have been there at the time, I'd have said, "Don't try to do college right now! Just concentrate on getting through this crisis. Don't worry—taking a break from college won't wreck your future med school application!"

What her extended family told her, though, was, "I know this is hard, but you'd better not take a semester off of college for this. The gap might cause a problem with your med school applications." (This is *not true*.) The result was my client, lying in a hospital bed beside her dying mother, with one arm around her mom and her other arm cradling a chemistry textbook!

Tell your son that you wouldn't want him to do this to himself. If he comes down with a terrible illness or there is a devastating death in the family, you'd hope that he'd try to finish the semester if possible and then take a "leave of absence" break to recover. The gap will be easy to explain. Even a string of W's (withdrawals) on a transcript can be easy to explain (though painful to pay for) if that's absolutely necessary. The blow to a student's GPA if he tries to stay in school while not able to function, however, could be very hard to bounce back from later.

ATTENDING CHURCH OR OTHER RELIGIOUS SERVICES

If attending church or other religious services is important to your family, tell your daughter that you hope she'll find a great, supportive place of worship early on and attend services there regularly.

I (Jeannie) personally benefitted greatly from attending church every week while I was in college. There was something freeing and liberating for me about taking time every week to publicly acknowledge that I am not the center of the universe—but that the one who *is* the center of the universe loves me deeply and longs to partner with me in the good I hope to do in this world.

Parents, plainly state your beliefs, expectations, and hopes when it comes to your child attending church or other religious services. Doing so won't guarantee that your child will do as you've asked, but it *will* influence her.

THE IMPORTANCE OF THE DEGREE PLAN

Students whose parents have used the strategies in this book typically step onto the college campus their very first day knowing right off the bat what their college major is likely to be. During her first semester of college, your daughter should visit her college advisor and ask for a paper copy of her degree plan. This degree plan will be a list of every college credit she must earn in order to receive a bachelor's degree in her major field from that college.

Once she has this degree plan in hand, your daughter's college advisor and her college registrar's office can help her mark off every credit she's already earned from taking CLEP and DSST tests, from taking high school AP courses, and from taking dual enrollment college courses during high school. (For a reminder of all the best ways for your child to earn college credit in high school, see chapter 9.)

Many, many students who've been influenced by me through the years have had the college registrar look up at them during this meeting and say, "I know you just got here, but next semester you'll be registering as a college junior. You'll get preferential registration privileges that start two days earlier, so you'll be more likely to get all the classes you want. Be sure you take full advantage of that."

I want students to update this degree plan every semester, crossing off the courses they've finished and looking ahead to strategize how they can finish the rest of their college courses in the least possible number of semesters. Students who follow my advice on this don't waste time or money taking one single college course they don't need. They finish college in record time, and as a result are able to get going far earlier than others on thrilling internship opportunities, full-time professional work, and other exciting life experiences.

> **STUDENTS WHO FOLLOW MY ADVICE ON THIS DON'T WASTE TIME OR MONEY TAKING ONE SINGLE COLLEGE COURSE THEY DON'T NEED.**

THE IMPORTANCE OF JOB SHADOWING, VOLUNTEERING, AND INTERNING

Talk with your child very seriously about what you learned from me back in chapter 27: that great careers aren't built by simply sitting through required college lectures; they're built by developing career capital *outside the classroom.*

Students accomplish this by zeroing in on their career goal early on, *shadowing* multiple people who do that job, *volunteer-*

ing to work for free in that field, and—in college—finding and completing *paid internships.* It's in paid internships that students take their first steps toward being professionally employed in their career fields after college.

The career services office at your son's college or university will help him to find paid internships if he asks, but he'll have to find his job shadowing and volunteering opportunities on his own, by approaching people working in his future career field and asking to be a part of what they're doing.

And if your son reports back to you that he can't find any people doing the job he's planning to do after college? Maybe it's because that job *doesn't exist.* Maybe that's a red flag telling him that this is not a career he should spend $80,000 preparing for.

I said this earlier, but it bears repeating here:

> We want your son to approach his future career like a craftsman, developing his own abilities in his future career field from 10th grade all the way through his college years. When he does this, the college degree he eventually earns will simply add polish and credential to the greatness your son has been developing on his own for six years or more.

Your son may have already read my book *FLY: The 6 Things You Absolutely Must Do to Be Brilliant in College and Get a Job You Love Afterward.* If he did, he'll be nodding his head as you tell him this. Two of the six major sections in that book are about how to find and succeed at career-focused volunteering and interning.

> **AND IF YOUR SON REPORTS BACK TO YOU THAT HE CAN'T FIND ANY PEOPLE DOING THE JOB HE'S PLANNING TO DO AFTER COLLEGE? MAYBE IT'S BECAUSE THAT JOB** *DOESN'T EXIST.*

HOW OFTEN HE'D LIKE HIS PARENTS TO CALL HIM AT COLLEGE

You might tell your daughter, "A common pattern for college families is that they schedule a phone call where the parents call the student once a week, at the same time each week. How would Sundays at 1 p.m. work for you? Of course, you can call or text us anytime. We'll always be happy to hear from you!"

HOW OFTEN HE'D LIKE HIS PARENTS TO VISIT HIM AT COLLEGE

Experience, Inc., a career services firm, did a study of hundreds of college students and recent college grads. Of the students surveyed, 25 percent reported that their parents were so involved in their college life that it was either annoying or embarrassing.[39]

Make a firm decision that you will not be *that parent.* Resist the temptation to helicopter or control. Remember, your goal as a parent is to set your child up to launch, and then

step back. Even NASA engineers don't stand right on the launch pad when a rocket's blasting off.

> **REMEMBER, YOUR GOAL AS A PARENT IS TO SET YOUR CHILD UP TO LAUNCH, AND THEN** *STEP BACK.* **EVEN NASA ENGINEERS DON'T STAND RIGHT ON THE LAUNCH PAD WHEN A ROCKET'S BLASTING OFF.**

When you're talking to your son about visiting him during college, you might say, "When there are special performances or games you're playing in, then of course we'll want to come. But maybe one time per semester besides that? To take you out to dinner? Tell us what would feel good to you."

WHAT WE'LL EXPECT FROM YOU ON COLLEGE BREAKS

Some college students home on college breaks treat their parents' house like a Holiday Inn and their mother like a restaurant cook and chambermaid. Set clear boundaries now by explaining to your child that your expectations for college breaks are quite different.

Here are some things you might say:

"Alison, when you come home on break, we'll expect you to be kind and considerate to all the people in our home—just as all respon-

---

39   Neil Howe and William Strauss, "Helicopter Parents in the Workplace," Life Course Associates, November 2007, https://www.lifecourse.com/assets/files/article_pdfs/Helicopter_Parents_Workplace_112007.pdf.

sible adults are when visiting someone else's home."

"When you're staying with us during a college break and you go out for a day or an evening, we'll want you to let us know where you're going and when you plan to be back, so we'll have no reason to worry."

"When you're home on breaks, we'll expect you to consult us before having overnight guests. We'll ask you to keep your room tidy, and cheerfully pitch in with family chores such as meal prep, vacuuming, and doing dishes. Thanks for understanding. We appreciate it!"

WE LOVE YOU. NO MATTER WHAT HAPPENS, WE WILL LOVE YOU JUST THE SAME.

Gary Smalley and John Trent's book *The Blessing* makes a powerful argument that every human being has a deeply felt need to know that they are loved *unconditionally*, especially by their parents. "Without our parents' blessing," they say, "we may become angry and driven, or detached and empty."[40]

If you as a parent can take time to read *The Blessing* before your family sits down to discuss these topics, you may find that this moment is one of the most beautiful and meaningful in your entire parenting journey.

HAVE THE STUDENT SIGN THAT HE OR SHE HAS HEARD YOU.

Remember, parents, the discussion I've outlined is not designed to *control* your child's future behavior; it's designed to *influence* it. And according to studies too numerous for me to cite here, you have more influence with this child than you think.

REMEMBER, PARENTS, THE DISCUSSION I'VE OUTLINED IS NOT DESIGNED TO *CONTROL* **YOUR CHILD'S FUTURE BEHAVIOR; IT'S DESIGNED TO** *INFLUENCE* **IT.**

What follows is an online resource you can download, modify, and use as a guide as you have this discussion.

BONUS ONLINE CONTENT:
Download the special contract page "OUR HOPES FOR YOU: Final Thoughts as You Head Off to College" at JeannieBurlowski.com/LAUNCH.

If you do ask your child to sign this document, note the special text I've placed right above the signature lines: "Your life is your own. When you sign this document, you are not promising that you will *do* these things. What you're stating in writing is that *you have heard us say these things.*"

---

40 John Trent and Gary Smalley, *The Blessing: Giving the Gift of Unconditional Love and Acceptance*, Nashville, TN: Thomas Nelson, 2011.

[15] *Commit to yourself that unless she's having serious mental health issues, you will stand aside and let your daughter solve her own problems.*

When your daughter has a minor difficulty or a mild crisis or makes the inevitable poor decision during college, let her develop her own competencies. Respond with genuine empathy, and then immediately hand the problem back to her to solve. Here are some great parent responses I've learned from the child-raising experts at Loveandlogic.com:

"Oh, no. That stinks."

"That's interesting; tell me more about that."

"Wow. What are you gonna do?"

"So what's your plan now?"

"I wonder what resources there are on campus that you could tap into to get help with that?"[41]

[16] *If you know anyone who currently has student loan debt (whether that person is in college right now or has already left school), read and share the free bonus online resource I'm providing next.*

BONUS ONLINE CONTENT:
Download the article "PLOT YOUR ESCAPE: Precise Steps to Take If You Already Have Student Loan Debt" at JeannieBurlowski.com/LAUNCH.

This resource provides clear, step-by-step help for managing student debt *safely* and for getting rid of it *as quickly as possible.* This resource will help anyone, even former students who are on year *nine* of paying back onerous student loan debt.

This resource is especially important, though, for students who are currently in college. Without specific guidance, many of these students will leave college and, in their first six months out, make major financial decisions about buying cars and renting expensive apartments without having any idea what their eventual student loan payments are going to be. Students who do this can put themselves in dire, heartbreaking financial situations just six months out of college. The clear instruction in this free online resource may be able to head this off for someone you care about before it even becomes a problem.

---

41 Copyright 2016 Loveandlogic.com. Used with permission. Any unauthorized duplication is strictly prohibited.

LAUNCH

CHECKLIST

Early Summer After 12th Grade

1. Have your daughter create a printed thank-you letter with her picture on it and send it out.

2. Research how the public transportation works on and near your son's college campus, so he won't have to bring a car with him to college.

3. Even though your son won't have a car with him at college, keep him covered under your family auto policy.

4. Start getting packed for that family vacation you planned last spring.

5. Check to be sure that every bit of the college credit your daughter earned in high school has been officially transferred to her college.

6. Have your child register for college courses at the earliest possible opportunity using the four strategies I provide.

7. If your son received a federal work-study grant as a part of his financial aid package, have him call and ask his college financial aid office how soon he can apply for his work-study job.

8. Every time you receive a bill from the college, check each individual line item on it carefully. Especially watch out for health insurance charges.

9. Search for a list of CLEP and DSST exams, and see if there are any that your daughter is now close to passing because she studied that subject during her 12th-grade year.

10. Log your daughter into her account on LinkedIn and help her to update her profile there.

11. Have your child buy some nice clothes for college, but get them on the cheap.

12. Encourage your daughter to use cut and paste to apply for 10 private scholarships this summer and every other summer all the way through college and graduate school.

13. Express enthusiasm as your son learns about upcoming college events and activities, meets future dorm-mates and friends, and connects with future roommates on social media.

14. Set aside a relaxed, sibling-free evening at home for a heart-to-heart parent/student talk. Before the special evening arrives, prepare a couple of extra pages to add to the contract that you and your child signed after 8th grade.

15. Commit to yourself that unless your daughter is having serious mental health issues, you will stand aside and let her solve her own problems.

16. If you know *anyone* who currently has student loan debt (whether that person is in college right now or has already left school), read and share the free bonus online resource I provide at JeannieBurlowski.com/LAUNCH.

17. Check my book updates page at JeannieBurlowski.com/LAUNCH to see if I have made any recent updates to this chapter.

18. Always consult your financial planning professional before making any big financial decisions.

19. Make a note in your calendar to come back and read the next chapter of this book in early August after 12th grade.

Be the first to hear about updates to the material in this book by reading my free weekly email newsletter every week. Anyone can subscribe to it at any time at JeannieBurlowski.com.

31 | *Early August After 12th Grade*

When I'm out speaking to high school and college students, one of the things I teach them is the liberating, stress-relieving principle of *start fast and end slow.*

"When you're assigned a complicated paper or project," I tell them, "try to get a jump on it as soon as it's assigned. Head to the library and spend some time reading up on the subject, and then start right in on figuring out a topic. Even if the project isn't due for weeks. You'll instantly feel an exhilarating sense of being ahead of the game; you'll have more relaxed time over the next few weeks for your thoughts to percolate and go deep; and with any luck you'll finish the whole thing long before it's due."

Students who work according to this pattern end up slowing down, doing less, relaxing more, and thinking more deeply during the week and the night before a project is due. These students' projects tend to be finished, polished, and completed at deeper, more thoughtful levels than if they'd just slapped something together hastily the night before.

Parents, this is exactly the principle I've been using to guide you over the past four years or more.

We started *early*. We thought *ahead*. We completed strategic steps at the most advantageous possible times. Now we get the privilege of slowing down, breathing deeply, and savoring this last month before launching your child into college life.

There's relatively little left to do now, so please put *relaxing* and *slowing* at the very top of your parent to-do list.

HOW TO USE THIS CHAPTER

Start by just reading through this chapter. As you read, don't worry about committing to any of it. Decision time will come at the very end of this chapter, when I give you a clear, at-a-glance checklist of every task I'm suggesting you consider right now.

Remember, you won't have to use every strategy I suggest; just choose the ones you think will work for your family and either modify or discard the rest.

> **WE STARTED** *EARLY.* **WE THOUGHT** *AHEAD.* **WE COMPLETED STRATEGIC STEPS AT THE MOST ADVANTAGEOUS POSSIBLE TIMES. NOW WE GET THE PRIVILEGE OF SLOWING DOWN, BREATHING DEEPLY, AND SAVORING THIS LAST MONTH BEFORE LAUNCHING YOUR CHILD INTO COLLEGE LIFE.**

[1] As your daughter is packing for college, encourage her to take only the basics to dorm move-in day.

Sure, she'll eventually want a cozy, beautifully decorated dorm room. The problem is that many college students and their parents go shopping the summer before college starts and buy enough posters, throw pillows, kitchen appliances, lamps, and enormous round Papasan chairs to fill a three-bedroom apartment. When these students get to college and realize that their dorm room is only slightly larger than a postage stamp and their new roommate did the exact same thing, the results can be comical.

Students, save your money by planning to get by with bare necessities scrounged from home for the first few weeks of college, and

when you find yourself standing in your dorm room thinking, "Boy, I wish I had a two-foot-wide, six-foot-tall, dark wood IKEA cabinet to put right here," put that item on a list and buy it on your next school break.

Clutter can be de-energizing. It's the last thing a student wants to be dealing with when on a mission to figure out how to achieve and succeed in a new college environment.

One nonnegotiable item that your child *will* need is a sturdy, good quality, two-drawer filing cabinet with hanging folders and file folders. This is where she'll file the thousands of papers that will cross her desk during four years of college, and it's where she'll have one file for each class she takes, with her class syllabus and all associated papers all neatly organized inside.

A student experiences a great sense of personal power and confidence when she realizes that she can lay her hands on any piece of paper she needs in 20 seconds or less. The method of piling papers into a small mountain on the left side of the desk is not sustainable—it only works for so long. Get a filing cabinet.

> **MANY COLLEGE STUDENTS AND THEIR PARENTS BUY ENOUGH POSTERS, THROW PILLOWS, KITCHEN APPLIANCES, LAMPS, AND ENORMOUS ROUND PAPASAN CHAIRS TO FILL A THREE-BEDROOM APARTMENT.**

[2] As your son is packing for college, encourage him to declutter his bedroom.

Have your son go through every inch of his bedroom, sorting everything in it into four piles:

» This is something I really want with me at college right away.

» This is garbage.

» This can be donated; I'm done with it.

» This I really want to hang onto, even though I won't need to have it with me at college right away.

With the decluttering done, put the room back the way your son had it and keep it that way for a while if possible. It's stabilizing for a new college student to have his or her old room available to come home to on college breaks.

Once your son has securely and confidently flown the coop and is less likely to feel sentimental about coming home to his old model airplanes and Incredible Hulk bed sheets, you might consider neatly boxing up his belongings and storing them in your basement. Some parents who've done this have repainted the vacated room, moved in a new IKEA loft bed and desk, and earned thousands of dollars in income each school year by renting the room out to a student from a nearby college or grad school. (You can advertise on Craigslist, or tell a nearby university housing office that you have a room for rent.)

Renting out an empty room in your house can be a great way for your family to come up with some additional money to pay college bills. If you're trying to keep income low to maintain financial aid eligibility, though, wait to do this until January 1 of your youngest child's sophomore year of college.

> **RENTING OUT AN EMPTY ROOM IN YOUR HOUSE CAN BE A GREAT WAY FOR YOUR FAMILY TO COME UP WITH SOME ADDITIONAL MONEY TO PAY COLLEGE BILLS.**

[3] *Make a recurring note in your personal calendar that reminds you to fill out the FAFSA form every October 1 that you will have a child in college the following fall.*

Remember, I want you to fill out the FAFSA form *every year*, even if you think that your income and assets are too high for you to receive any help.

Why? First, you could still get need-based financial aid next year, even if you didn't get it this year. Remember, financial aid calculations are interwoven, complex, and dependent on a vast number of constantly shifting factors. Something could shift for your family that makes you more eligible next year. Second, your fortunes could at any time turn suddenly for the worse due to lost income, high medical bills, or some other stroke of bad luck. If that happens, you'll want your daughter in the financial aid pipeline where she can receive help. Third, if your child does at any point decide to take out a student loan, we want that loan to be one of the *Federal Direct Student Loans* that are only available to students who've properly filled out the FAFSA form the previous October.

Please put a recurring entry about this in your calendar now, and when you do so, remind yourself to revisit chapters 20 and 22 of this book in the weeks beforehand so you can avoid common costly FAFSA mistakes. You are truly doing something *great* for your son or daughter by doing this.

[4] *Make a recurring note in your personal calendar to take special care with your tax preparation each spring that you've had a child in college during the previous year.*

Your family may be able to significantly lower the amount of federal tax you'll pay during your children's college years with the help of the federal government's American Opportunity Tax Credit, lifetime learning credit, student loan interest deduction, or tuition and fees deduction.[42]

Your first step to qualifying for these education tax benefits will be to look over the Form 1098-T that your daughter will receive from her college each January 31 that she's spent any time in college the previous year. Form 1098-T will list specific details, such as how much grant and scholarship money your daughter received during the previous year, and how much money your family paid to the college for educational expenses. If you combine the information on Form 1098-T with the family educational expense records you've been carefully keeping in Evernote, you will have a very complete picture of how much your family has paid for educational expenses during the previous year.

This information will not only help you (or your tax preparer) to determine whether you qualify for certain tax benefits, it will also save your skin if you are ever asked to prove that the money you pulled from your daughter's 529 savings plan actually *did* go to pay for college-related expenses during a given year.

As a side note, if you or your child are ever asked to fill out a Form W-9S, do it. Form W-9S is used to obtain your child's name, address, and taxpayer identification number so that the Form 1098-T can be prepared and sent out to you.

To learn more about the tax benefits you may have coming as a parent of a college student, google "IRS publication 970," which provides the details. If you have questions about what you see in IRS publication 970, call 1-800-906-9887 to find volunteer income tax assistance near you, or consult a certified public accountant for specific help.

42　For more information, go to https://www.irs.gov/uac/american-opportunity-tax-credit.

TO LEARN MORE ABOUT THE TAX BENEFITS YOU MAY HAVE COMING AS A PARENT OF A COLLEGE STUDENT, GOOGLE "IRS PUBLICATION 970," WHICH PROVIDES THE DETAILS.

[5] *I have some special instructions for your son or daughter to read before leaving for college. Please read these instructions carefully yourself, and then print them out and give them to your child with my best wishes.*

These instructions explain to your child what to do his or her first semester in college to stay on an excellent path toward debt-free college graduation. You can download these special instructions and print them out for free at the link below.

BONUS ONLINE CONTENT:
Download the article
"YOUR GREAT FIRST SEMESTER:
What to Do First Thing at College
to Keep Yourself on a Path Toward
Debt-Free College Graduation" at
JeannieBurlowski.com/LAUNCH.

[6] *Plan a short cheerful good-bye for when you drop your child off at dormitory move-in day.*

That last good-bye at the dormitory front door can be fraught with parental emotion, but the last thing your child needs at that point is parental tears and long speeches. Keep it short and cheerful, with one big hug. "OK, bye! I love you. You're going to do great. See you in about a month!" And then turn and go. Turn back one time and smile and wave. You have done everything you can to launch this child into adulthood; now it's time to let her fly.

CHECKLIST

Early August After 12th Grade

☐ 1. As your daughter is packing for college, encourage her to take only the basics to dorm move-in day.

☐ 2. As your son is packing for college, encourage him to declutter his bedroom.

☐ 3. Make a recurring note in your personal calendar that reminds you to fill out the FAFSA form every October 1 that you will have a child in college the following fall.

☐ 4. Make a recurring note in your personal calendar to take special care with your tax preparation each spring that you've had a child in college during the previous year.

☐ 5. I have some special instructions for your child to read through before he or she leaves for college. Please download these instructions from my website, read them, and then print them out and give them to your child.

☐ 6. Plan a short cheerful good-bye for when you drop your child off at dorm move-in day.

☐ 7. Check my book updates page at JeannieBurlowski.com/LAUNCH to see if I have made any recent updates to this chapter.

☐ 8. Always consult your financial planning professional before making any big financial decisions.

☐ 9. Please accept my best wishes for the happiest, most successful life possible for you and your child. I hope to meet you in person sometime when I'm speaking at a conference or other event in a city near you.

Be the first to hear about updates to the material in this book by reading my free weekly email newsletter every week. Anyone can subscribe to it at any time at JeannieBurlowski.com.

SAMPLE CHAPTER FROM JEANNIE BURLOWSKI'S BOOK FOR STUDENTS— *FLY: The 6 Things You Absolutely Must Do to Be Brilliant in College and Get a Job You Love Afterward*

DEDICATION

To every ordinary high school, college, and grad student who longs to leave behind mediocrity and step into the extraordinary. This book is for you.

CHAPTER 1: STUDY LESS; ACHIEVE MORE

The university president's home was ivy-covered brick, with warm light glowing from multiple, large picture windows. Landscape lights illuminated the flowerbeds, the front of the house, and the trees. The home's immaculate front lawn had been fenced in with stout pillars of brick and long expanses of filigreed wrought iron, but when Ellie unlatched the gate, it easily swung wide to admit her.

Her high-heeled pumps made smart, clipped clicks on the flagstone walkway as she made her way toward the open front door. Light and laughter and piano music poured out onto the stately front porch, and for the first time Ellie thought to herself, "OK, maybe this isn't going to be that bad."

She had not been looking forward to this evening, frankly.

Even just an hour before, as she'd put on sparkly earrings while her roommate zipped her into black velvet, she'd thought about backing out.

"You know that this is going to be the worst night of your life," Sarah had teased her. "You're gonna spend a whole evening with people who haven't been out of the library in four years—except to go to class and run to the eye doctor to buy thicker glasses."

Ellie had laughed first and then groaned, largely because she'd already been thinking the exact same thing about the Phi Beta Kappa induction dinner. Really—who wanted to spend a whole evening with all the highest-achieving, highest-GPA students on an Ivy League campus? Ugh.

Ellie hadn't given up her entire college life to cram and study constantly, but she knew many students who had. Bleary-eyed and perpetually exhausted, they could be found at all hours of the night and all weekend long, holed up in the library or in claustrophobic dorm study carrels, agonizing over classwork they never seemed to master. Ellie hadn't studied this way. She'd tried the long, drawn-out cram sessions a couple of times early in her freshman year, but for her they'd been almost unbearably dull and tedious. Finally, one night, she'd dragged herself out of the library at midnight, set her backpack down on the sidewalk, and vowed that if it killed her, she was going to find an easier way to do college.

The following Saturday she'd put some time into figuring out faster, easier, and more efficient ways to get college studying and paper writing done. Camped out in a comfy chair in a large chain bookstore, she'd whipped through six different books on how to study in college. She'd quickly discarded every idea that seemed ridiculously impractical or time consuming, and zeroed in like a laser on every strategy that looked like it would relieve stress or save time. She'd come away from that afternoon with a life-changing book purchase and four insights that were the start of a revolution for her.

THE FOUR RADICAL STRATEGIES THAT CHANGE EVERYTHING

1. **Don't do all the reading.** Judiciously invest time only in the assigned reading that has the greatest payoff. Radical? Yes. Effective? Absolutely.

2. **Don't engage in long, mind-numbing, marathon study sessions.** Instead, study only in intense, highly focused 50-minute time blocks followed by 10-minute breaks. (Software engineers call this a "Pomodoro Technique.") According to several different books, students who use this method tend to accomplish far more than others do, in significantly less time.

3. **Be radically productive during the day, then rest and relax in the evening.** Multiple books had been adamant about this principle. "If you wait until evening to do your academic work," one author had said, "you'll have to study four hours to complete the same work you could have done in two hours earlier in the day." Ellie had found this to be absolutely true, and early on had started getting up early in the morning, alternating intense, highly productive academic work with breaks during her daylight hours, and then ending her hard-core academic work each night by 6:00 p.m.

And then, finally, the most important strategy. The one that had freed her from stress and sickening worry. The one principle that had *most* made it possible for her to place boundaries around her academic work and set herself free to spend time on far more fascinating things:

4. **Don't clog up your brain trying to keep track of tasks and due dates in your head.** Instead, use a calendar to plan when you're going to think about these responsibilities.

The first thing you absolutely must do to be brilliant in college and get a job you love afterward? *Use a calendar.*

You can find out how to purchase a full copy of **FLY: The 6 Things You Absolutely Must Do to Be Brilliant in College and Get a Job You Love Afterward** by reading the free weekly email newsletter available at JeannieBurlowski.com.

LAUNCH

HELP US WITH THE SECOND EDITION OF THIS BOOK

I'm currently gathering information for the next edition of this book. If you know of any additional great ideas on how to save money on college costs while setting students up for great jobs after college graduation, please let me know by emailing me at brilliantincollege@gmail.com. I can't use every idea submitted to me, but I can tell you that it's people like you who give me my best ideas for getting through college debt-free! Thank you!

I WANT TO HEAR YOUR STORY!

I'd love to hear your debt-free college story. Please post it on Twitter using the hashtag #RadicalCollegePrep and mentioning @JBurlowski, or email me at brilliantincollege@gmail.com.

ABOUT THE AUTHOR

Jeannie Burlowski is a full-time author, academic strategist, and speaker. Her writing provides parents a clear, step-by-step checklist so they can set their kids up to succeed brilliantly in college, graduate debt-free, and move directly into careers they excel at and love.

Jeannie's expertise in this field comes from over 23 years of helping students apply to highly competitive law, medical, business, and graduate schools. During those years, she became a curator (think: a person who collects and catalogs valuable artifacts for a museum) of every possible good idea for succeeding brilliantly in college, graduating debt-free, and moving directly into satisfying and well-paying career after college. (And sailing straight into law, medical, business, or grad school, if that is a goal.)

Her first book, *LAUNCH: How to Get Your Kids Through College Debt-Free and Into Jobs They Love Afterward*, clearly explains to parents what they need to do to achieve these goals, and its partner book for students, *FLY: The 6 Things You Absolutely Must Do to Be Brilliant in College and Get a Job You Love Afterward*, clearly lays out for high school and college students the steps they must take to succeed. Information on how to purchase *FLY* is found in Jeannie's free weekly email newsletter.

Jeannie lives just north of St. Paul, Minnesota, with her husband, Tim, one son, and one daughter. In her free time, Jeannie enjoys cooking, reading, traveling, and taking hot saunas and jumping into Lake Vermilion, where her family has had a lake cabin since the 1970s. She's currently working on her third book, a devotional entitled *Following Jesus for Just 12 Weeks: A Journey of Surprise at Who He Really Is and Who He Calls Us to Be as We Follow Him.* You can find Jeannie online at JeannieBurlowski.com, at Twitter.com/JBurlowski, and at GetIntoMedSchool.com.

LAUNCH

ACKNOWLEDGMENTS

Many thanks to:

Esther Fedorkevich of the Fedd Agency, one of the greatest literary agents ever, who read my book excerpt on a plane and signed me the very next day.

Mike Branch of Focus Financial in Minneapolis, who worked for years gathering information on paying for college and then patiently answered all my most technical financial questions.

M. J., my friend in the student loan servicing industry, who not only reviewed this manuscript and gave me invaluable feedback, but also supplied some of my scariest student loan debt stories.

Bob Shorb, 22-year veteran associate dean of admissions and financial aid at Skidmore College, who read my manuscript and gave me valuable feedback and some of my most encouraging rave reviews.

My editorial team: Stacy Ennis, Kim Foster, and Stephanie Hendrixon. Stacy, I love to tell people that when I searched for "best editor" on Google, your name came up immediately. Google wasn't wrong.

Lysa TerKeurst, Glynnis Whitwer, and all the staff at the *She Speaks* Conference. I was at your conference as a speaker the day it hit me: "I'm not just a speaker. I'm going to write a book too."

Cindy Mattson of DefiningPointConsulting.com, who first opened my eyes to the exciting possibilities that await when teens take three career assessments as early as age 15.

Dave Ramsey of DaveRamsey.com, for all he does to help families get out of debt so they can better help their kids get through college debt-free.

Michael Hyatt, who provides authors and speakers like me high-quality practical help every day at MichaelHyatt.com and at PlatformUniversity.com. I could not have done this without you, sir.

My husband, Tim, who supported me without complaint while I took massive amounts of time off to research and write this book; my children, Matt and Elise, who did without Mom on more sunny, blue-sky summer afternoons than I can count; and my mother, who prayed for me and for every reader of this book every single day for years on end.

My GetIntoMedSchool.com clients, both those whose student loan debt stories broke my heart, and those whose brilliant ideas for getting through college debt-free started me on the committed path to getting this message out to the world.

Thank you.

Made in the USA
Columbia, SC
11 May 2020